Men of Notes

by

Don Walker

DORRANCE PUBLISHING CO., INC.
PITTSBURGH, PENNSYLVANIA 15222

The contents of this work including, but not limited to, the accuracy of events, people, and places depicted; opinions expressed; permission to use previously published materials included; and any advice given or actions advocated are solely the responsibility of the author, who assumes all liability for said work and indemnifies the publisher against any claims stemming from publication of the work.

Dorrance Publishing Co., Inc.
701 Smithfield Street
Pittsburgh, PA 15222
Visit our website at *www.dorrancebookstore.com*

ISBN: 978-1-4349-2897-9
eISBN: 978-1-4349-2249-6

Dedication

In order to counter any possible accusations of male chauvinism arising from misinterpretation of this history's title, I wish, first of all, to dedicate this work to the women who have made it possible:

1. My mother, Blanche Stevenson Walker (nee Basford) who, after my father bought a player-piano, insisted that someone in the family learn to play it properly, without pumping.

2. Miss Mary Gillingham Brown, my first and only music teacher, who gave me a solid background of music theory equal to that provided by the best music colleges.

3. Mathilde Pincus, the world's most honored music copyist, whose devotion to clear accuracy is legendary and whose ever ready willingness to cooperate is heartwarming.

4. My loving wife, Audrey Irene Walker (née Langrill-Simpson), who has labored mightily all these years to protect me from concentration-breaking disturbance, while being a superlative mother, an inspired chef, and a lady with a robust sense of humor…and what is more, the contributor of the title of this reminiscent opus.

Don Walker

Foreword

In the course of a busy career in the American musical theater, working on the sort of shows whose goals are long, profitable runs on Broadway, this autobiographer has worked for a variety of men whose names should be familiar. He has also worked with ones who may not be as well known. The unifying condition is that they are all "Men of Notes": composers, lyricists, orchestra conductors, working musicians, orchestrators, music publishers, etc., who have played a significant role in the lifework of one Don Walker, #W-00961, Local #802, American Federation of Musicians.

For a number of years, I have had this idiot urge to write my professional memoirs, which would roughly parallel the development of the American musical theater in the twentieth century. Now, at the age of seventy-six, still playing a tough game of tennis, I find that I have the time to write this often postponed history. The question was: In what form shall I tell it?

At that point, my partner for over fifty hard years came to the rescue. To prove that I have absolutely no prejudice against the female sex by writing a book called *Men of Notes,* I hereby proclaim that a real, live woman—my love, Audrey—suggested this hairy-chested title, as she also hinted at the manner of narration. "Tell them about those wonderful and otherwise characters you had to work with," she advised. And so I have tried, keeping a weather eye on the obituaries.

For my task, I present these credentials: I have been actively involved in the creation of approximately one hundred ten musicals. In that activity, I have been mainly responsible for orchestrations, although at times I have been a composer, a lyricist, a collaborating author, a vocal arranger, and an orchestra conductor. In gaps between theater assignments, I have written scores for concert and symphony orchestras, radio and television shows, record albums, and dance bands. I have also been involved at times in the perpetration of certain television commercials, which employment I here shame-facedly confess to show you what a candid fellow I am, sworn to bring you the truth, the whole truth, and NOTHING BUT THE TRUTH (as I remember it).

In planning to write such a book as this one hopes to be, a series of diaries would be a great help. How I have tried to keep those invaluable records! And failed every time. On many a January 2nd, I would buy one of those handsome little leather-bound notebooks and before going to bed would religiously record the events of the past day for…every now and then…as much as three days…but then something in the crisis range happened, and since I was sitting up all night scoring, there was no end to the previous day! That's when poor, neglected diary got pushed to the rear of that pile of score pages…and remained there another night…and another…until its printed dates meant nothing. Finally the costly item was used for some arcane purpose, like listing phone numbers I never intended to call.

So don't look for FACTS in the following pages. I'll do the best I can but see no reason to omit a good yarn because I can't remember whether or not I met Mr. Dick Godalmighty Rodgers at 10:30 or 11:00 A.M. that 23rd or 24th day of April…or was it May?…in 1952 or thereabouts. All I can promise is to try, try, try, and if some FACTS do sneak into this monologue, believe that they have been researched beyond any shred of doubt by expert doubt-shredders. Beyond that unwarranted warranty, there is little to say except, "Abandon hope, all ye who burrow here, for hard-boiled, trustworthy, incontrovertible FACTS!"

You see, the fact (there I go again) of the matter is that when I am introduced to a man I have been told is very important, I assess him by what I see, hear (and smell?) *at that moment,* never having taken the time to research him previously. After all, everyone has something to hide, and wouldn't it be foolish for me to kill aborning what might be a pleasant new relationship by digging up embarrassing facts? (Can't get away from that word!)

So with the famous personalities and the lesser lights that will be the foci of this self-conscious account, all you will have to depend upon will be my skittish memory, which Audrey can tell you is occasionally surprising but often capricious, to say the least.

Don (Donald John) Walker
Fort Myers Beach, Florida
January 1, 1984

Note on Nomenclature

In the transfer of a musical thought from the mind of the originator to the consciousness of an audience, there are six (6) discernible stages. That of:

(1) The <u>Composer</u>: Who creates the basic theme(s) of a composition and writes down or records the invention.

(2) The <u>Arranger</u>: Who develops the basic theme(s) into the desired form. At this point the full harmonic structure is usually determined.

(3) The <u>Orchestrator</u>: Who adjusts the "arrangement" to fit the size and composition of whatever orchestral combination has been selected. The orchestrator makes a "score" in which the instrumental parts are placed one above the other with the bar lines running vertically down the page, all so aligned that at any given instant one can see (and hear!) exactly what is happening in the whole musical presentation.

(4) The <u>Copyist</u>: Who "extracts" the individual instrumental parts from the Orchestrator's score.

(5) The <u>Musicians</u>: Who play the parts on their instruments, which brings the Composer's musical idea to life.

(6) The <u>Audience</u>: Whose human ears pick up the frequencies coming to them through the medium of air and whose audio systems identify the signals as music.

These are the basic stages, subject to all kinds of combinations, contractions, and expansions. For instance, the operatic composer often performs the first three stages simultaneously; the orchestrator who isn't something of a composer and a good arranger isn't worth his salt; a copyist who doesn't understand orchestration and hasn't played an instrument in an ensemble is in trouble, as is his employer.

Through the 1920s and into the 30s, the terms "arranger" and "orchestrator" were practically synonymous. During the thirties, your chronicler fought to have the terms more specifically defined. By the forties, the meanings as set forth above in (2) and (3) were generally accepted in the theatrical world. During the forties, there was no confusion until Webster's Dictionary came out with a second meaning for <u>orchestrate</u>: "to arrange or combine so as to achieve a maximum effect." Then the flood gates opened and all kinds of people began to call themselves "orchestrators." So now I am trying to find another professional name to call myself, but it's late—very late.

1. Fletcher (Henderson)

There I was, a frustrated third-year-man in the Wharton School of the University of Pennsylvania, trapped in the residence of my parents in Lambertville, New Jersey, that fateful day after Christmas, 1927. A dreary week stretched before me: Two and a half years of absence from my home town had just about eliminated any local friendships that I could revive at short notice to help enliven the supposedly joyous week.

I picked up a stray piece of tinsel and threw it back on the ceiling-high spruce that was the symbol of the sentiments that had forced me to decline lucrative musical engagements in Philadelphia and come home for Christmas. How I missed honking my saxophone and clarinet for cheery, appreciative crowds of happy dancers! And then, as a bonus, receiving extra, holiday-scaled pay! Although I was in no desperate need of cash, to a student who was working his way through college, with a second semester looming, an additional cushion would have been most comforting.

All that had been rejected in a mad splurge of filial devotion. Christmas meant very much to my Britain-born parents, both members of large families, so I had, for once, done my duty: The only child had come home for the holidays.

I glanced at our aged crystal radio and its earphones, friends of former late nights when my parents were asleep. I knew there was no entertainment in that direction, only endless, hackneyed Xmas carols. Automatically, I sat down at the piano. It was a "player," one of my father's expensive follies.

Dad was "musical" and sang a very good bass in the Episcopal church choir. He yearned to vocalize at home, but he had no accompanist. Neither he nor my mother could play the piano, and they thought that it was money wasted to send a child under nine years old to a music teacher. So Dad thought he could solve his accompaniment problem by buying a secondhand Lester player-piano, planning to sing along with it. But the keys and routines on the punched paper rolls had been selected for pianistic purposes and were miles away from the tonalities and arrangements in his vocal parts. The scheme didn't work. Yet he pumped along, humming and hollering, exercising his voice, having a fairly good time as Mother stuffed cotton in her ears.

The old Lester had one excellent feature: It could be played as a normal upright piano, so at the age of nine I was sent to Miss Mary Gillingham Brown to learn how to use it properly.

On the top of the instrument, there were two piles of music. One was the timeworn remains of the studies I had sweated over until, at the age of thirteen, foolishly catching behind the plate wearing only a thin fielder's glove, a vicious foul tip had permanently reversed the customary action of the top joint of the fourth finger on my left hand. While the result did not impede fingering a woodwind, it eliminated any hopes I might have had of becoming a child virtuoso on the eighty-eight.

The other stack of music was my father's. It was mostly vocal selections, old semi-standards, and light classics from the "Merry Widow Waltz" to "The Sunshine of Your Smile." Then I came across, in surprising sequence, "The Waters of Minnetonka," "From the Land of the Sky Blue Water," and "Pale Hands I Loved (Beside the Shalimar)."

Hmmm, I thought, *that's a strange coincidence. Three tunes in a row all based on pseudo-Indian themes and very heavy on running water! What a medley they would make....*

Such quasi-classical arrangements, played by large dance-bands, were then in fashion. Paul Whiteman had led the way with his popular records of "Meditation from Thais" and "Song of India," among others. Such tunes, with their long, smooth, flowing melodies, were loved by gliding fox-trotters and were a welcome relief from a solid diet of jazz, blues, Charlestons, and Tin Pan Alley ditties that made up most of the repertoire of dance orchestras.

Suddenly I made a decision that changed the direction of my life, although at that moment, I had no idea of how consequential my action would be. I thought, *I know how I'm going to amuse myself this ghastly week: I'm going to try to write an orchestration for a full dance band, and I've got a title for it! I'll call it "AN INDIAN RHAPSODY"!*

I immediately went into action. I discovered a cache of unused, twelve-stave manuscript paper, left over from my harmony lessons. I found and sharpened two soft lead pencils and unearthed a long ruler and a nice, soft eraser, that most important piece of orchestrating equipment. I assembled the lot on my mother's desk, along with the three selections that were to form the bases of my East and West Indian masterpiece.

Ever since the age of nine, when I was required, as a piano student, to attend Miss Brown's Saturday "Kindersinfonie" and play various toy percussion instruments, reading from parts that had been especially written for them, I had wondered how all those individual pages of music could have been so organized, that when they were all played at once, a coherent ensemble was produced. "How does it all fit together?" I wanted to know. As I grew older, that puzzlement continued to plague me, until finally, at the age of fourteen, my brilliant teacher, Miss Mary Brown, exasperated by my persistent questioning, went to her extensive music library and drew out a book entitled:

THE ORCHESTRA
Volume I
Technique of the Instruments
By Ebenezer Prout.

"There," she said, handing it to me. "It's all in there. You may take the book home with you."

I began to read the text after dinner. I became so absorbed with what Ebenezer had to tell about the instruments, their combinations, and how to make an orchestral score that time flew by into the wee hours. Then when he showed me how that score could bring all the diverse sounds of the different components of the orchestra together into one harmonious symphony, I was lost; I had no awareness of the time until my mother came downstairs and began to make breakfast. I had stayed up all night and, entranced, read and studied the entire lengthy tome.

During the five years since that introduction, orchestration had become something of a hobby with me. I had bought and studied on my own the classics on the subject: Berlioz' treatise, Richard Strauss' revision of Berlioz, Rimsky-Korsakov's unfinished book, and Cecil Forsyth's chatty volume. These works, with their fragmentary examples, led me to pocket scores of great masterpieces of orchestration, which I had learned to read as one peruses the daily newspaper.

Yet after all that study, I had never scored an orchestration for a large group, not even for an average-sized dance band.

Instinctively originating a procedure that I was to employ all of my working life, I began to pace about the room, trying to "hear" in my mind the introduction to the deathless work I planned to create. When that came to me, I tried to analyse the thought in terms of musical notation. Then, and only then, when the musical thought was clear in my mind, did I sit down at the piano and physically check it out. (As I made more orchestrations, I gained confidence and learned to eliminate this later step most of the time.)

All was well: It was time to commit my evanescent thoughts to paper by allowing the conditioned reflexes of musical penmanship to take over.

Thus, by a process that became more refined and expeditious as I exercised it, I emerged from my self-imposed tunnel at the end of three days and nights with a one hundred sixty-four-bar score of my "INDIAN RHAPSODY," a roundelay that would salute Indians, Western or Eastern, especially if they lived near a large body of fresh water. The piece was scored for the following:

<u>Reeds</u>:	1st Alto Saxophone (Doubling Bb Clarinet)
	2nd Bb Tenor Sax. (" " ")
	3rd Eb Baritone Sax (" " ")
<u>Brass</u>:	1st Bb Trumpet (or Cornet)
	2nd " " (" ")
	Optional 3rd Bb Trumpet (or Cornet)
	1st Trombone
	Optional 2nd Trombone
<u>Rhythm</u>:	Piano
	Banjo or Guitar (Chord Symbols only)
	Bass (or Tuba)
	Drums

Having finished the score with three days left in my problem week, I set about copying the instrumental parts. If I ever hoped to have an orchestra play my ennui-born invention, I would need the instrumental parts, so I dug in to write them.

For an orchestrator, there is nothing more bringing down than to finish scoring an imaginative musical work in a fever of inspiration and then have to copy out the parts oneself. One moment you are a creative artist and the next, a mechanical drudge. In later years, I grew to understand what a treasure a good, cooperative copyist could be. But in the beginning, when I could not afford such a luxury, I considered copying the instrumental parts of my own inventions, as they say now, the pits.

So I sweated out my tedious but necessary job, and by the time I took the train from Lambertville to West Philadelphia on the day after New Year's, 1928, my briefcase bulged with the complete score and parts of AN INDIAN RHAPSODY, although I had no idea where it was going to be rhapsodized, if ever.

In Philly in those days, there was a popular second-floor ballroom on Broad Street, a few blocks south of City Hall, called "The Dance Box." Its advertised music was "Frank Winegar's Orchestra," which appeared to be as much of a fixture as a dance band can ever be. This was the outfit that later became known as "Milt Shaw's Detroiters," which had a fair amount of national success in the early thirties. I never met Frank Winegar or Milt Shaw, both of them always happening to be absent when I was present, so I cannot explain the later change of name.

This fine orchestra was unusual in that a large portion of its personnel were also students in various colleges about Philadelphia, working their way through school, as I was. A handful of them had enough school spirit to add powerful help to the Marching Band of the University of Pennsylvania.

I was then in my third year of playing clarinet in the Penn Band. During our first rehearsal of the New Year, lightning struck me in the middle of the Poet and Peasant Overture. I was on speaking terms with some of those fellows that played in "The Dance Box." Maybe I could get them to promote a trial reading of my unplayed "AN INDIAN RHAPSODY"! I could hardly finger the clarinet until the next rest period!

When it came, I approached Ruby Weinstein, who was Lead Trumpet, both in the Band and in the Dance Box. I said, "You don't really know me, Rube, but I'm in one of your classes."

He replied, "You think I don't know you? You're D. Walker, that damn genius in Finance II that knows it all."

"But I'm a musician, too."

"I've been blowing my horn opposite you for two and a half long years, and I'd say that last statement of yours is moot." (He was in Pre-Law.) Turning to a pleasant-looking fellow who played lead alto sax, he said, "Hey, Lyle, come over here and let us have your considered opinion. Walker here says he's a musician. What do you think?"

Lyle Bowen said, "If he isn't a musician, then he's fooling a lot of people, with the cut he's getting out of that Inter-fraternity ork he honks in."

"But I'm also an arranger," I put in.

"An arranger yet?" Ruby asked in surprise.

Lyle said, "I've been looking at him for ages, squeaking that licorice stick...and he was an arranger all the time!"

"Not all that time," I corrected. "I just made my first big arrangement, scored, and copied. I wondered if you characters at the Box would read it down...at a rehearsal, of course...so I can find out if it works."

They looked at each other.

"Why not?" asked Lyle. "We play all kinds of horrors at rehearsal, hunting for new material. Why can't we help a marching pal hear his first and maybe his last masterpiece?"

At the next break, we settled that I should bring my orchestration to the Dance Box late in the afternoon the next Thursday, which I did, not without a certain amount of trepidation.

After the Dance Box orchestra had finished working on what were obviously "trouble spots" in their repertoire, I was allowed to distribute the parts of my "INDIAN RHAPSODY." From the first downbeat, the living sound exactly duplicated the imagined sound that I had heard in my head when I wrote the notes. It was strange...I felt no unusual excitement, worry, or pride. I had heard it all before in my mind, and now the actual performance merely confirmed the accuracy of the musical symbols that I had written! Near the end there was a long build-up to a powerful, high finish with a sharp, clean "button."

On impulse, the band stood up and gave me an honest round of applause.

Ruby said, "If that's your very first arrangement, I can hardly wait for the second one! What do you think, Joe?"

All eyes shifted to Joe Glover, their pianist and arranger. He said, "It isn't bad, for a beginner."

I was told that Joe's grudging admission was extravagant, outlandish praise from him, a chronic understater.

A few of the players had spots they wanted to go over, accidentals to be checked out. Then, when everyone was satisfied, they played the "Rhapsody" again. The second time around, it sounded infinitely better than at first reading. I had learned a useful lesson: Never evaluate a new orchestration until the players are reasonably familiar with it.

Ruby and Lyle came to me and the former asked, "What are you going to do with this piece?"

I told them that I hadn't even thought about *doing* anything with it; I just wanted to find out if it "worked."

Lyle assured me, "It works and then some, mister. What we want to know is, what kind of a price tag are you going to hang on it?"

I said, "A half hour ago, it wasn't worth anything."

"But now it's valuable. It could fit beautifully into our repertoire. We want it. Just remember that our budget for new material is damn near zero."

I said, "I wanted to find out if I could write down the sounds I heard in my head and then have those same sounds come out of the instruments when what I wrote was played. You fellows have shown me that I can do it. That's enough payment for me. I've got my score, you keep the parts...no charge!"

"You're *giving* this beaut to us? What a gesture!"

Ruby added, "Wait till the rest of the boys hear this....You'll be aces high around here!"

"I have one request."

"Shoot."

"I'd like to come down here some night and see how your public reacts to the 'Rhapsody.' Would you play it for me then?"

"Of course...and if you write any more numbers that you want to check out, we'll find time for you."

During the rehearsal, there had been a scrawny-looking individual sitting on a chair near the band, busily taking notes on journalists' traditional yellow scratch paper. I wondered about him, asking Ruby, "Who's the scribbler?"

"Says he's from Detroit. A reporter for *In the Groove,* a new jazz weekly that's coming out soon...seems to know all the main hipsters...says he's collecting info on all the new bands here in the East."

The news hawk approached me. He introduced himself as "Wallie McNab, reporter for *In the Groove.* Did I hear you right, that you're giving this band that terrific arrangement for free?"

I said, a bit upset, "Please, Mr. McNab, don't tell in your paper that I gave away my first arrangement...this band did me a great service and I repaid them, that's all."

He reassured me, "Don't worry, kiddo, where you're concerned my pen is outta ink. Just go back to your cell and keep writing." He went back to his chair and note taking.

....

I was amazed by the speed at which the musical grapevine operated in Philadelphia that year of 1928. Within two weeks of the Dance Box rehearsal where "INDIAN RHAPSODY" had been unveiled, I had calls from Charlie Kerr at the Golden Dragon Restaurant and Billy Hayes at the Cathay Tea Garden to make special arrangements for their orchestras. At that time, large Chinese restaurants with good-sized orchestras were very popular for dancing at both lunch and dinner. I remember scoring (and copying) "Why Do I Love You?" for Hayes and "Ain't She Sweet" for Kerr as they both tried to outdo each other in their chop suey war.

Because of heavy scholastic demands and numerous bookings of the busy campus orchestra of which I was a member, in those early months of 1928 it became necessary for me to turn down a number of arranging offers, even when the going price for an average dance orchestration, *scored and copied* (!), was raised from the usual $20.00 to a tempting $25.00. By Easter vacation, I was sorely in need of a respite, if only for a few days, from the impossibly heavy work schedule I had thoughtlessly fashioned by becoming a music arranger.

I decided to drop everything and make Mother happy by going home for the long Easter weekend.

Back in Lambertville I found, by Saturday morning, that the only way I could stop worrying about put-off class assignments was to haul out the necessary material and start working. So I spent Saturday on "The Futility of Reciprocal Tariffs" for Economics III and Sunday on "The Profits of Bankrupcy" for Finance II. Wharton School's immediate demands attended to by late Sunday evening and my parents gone to bed, I sought a bit of relaxation from my old crystal set, putting on the timeworn earphones, turning on the juice. I didn't have to tune it; no one had touched it since I had used it ages ago. The dial was set to WOR.

As usual, at that hour of 11 P.M., the familiar music of the famous Fletcher Henderson Orchestra was being broadcast from Roseland Ballroom in New York City.

It was my favorite dance orchestra. I had listened to that powerful ensemble many times in the past, with their strong, natural rhythm, their respect for the composer's melody, even while rephrasing and inventing variations on it. An orchestra obviously made up of superior musicians who played together with the same gutsy good taste. I was familiar with many of their arrangements, made by Don Redman and Henderson himself.

They finished a number and paused. Then they began another. I could not believe my ears. Was I going crazy? It couldn't be! They were—yes, they were—playing my INDIAN RHAPSODY! Exactly as I had written it! But that was impossible! How could they have duplicated, by chance, all those notes and phrases that started in my brain? Yet there they were, sounding…every one of them, coming out of my earphones! Now and then, rarely, I thought I detected a variant note, not exactly wrong, but a little different, not enough to distort the whole. *Somebody's been monkeying a bit with my arrangement,* I thought, as it all went on, right to the end of the big coda that I had invented, almost exactly as it had popped out of my head! The loud applause was not only for Fletcher Henderson and his Orchestra, but for me, hooked up to an elderly radio set in Lambertville, New Jersey.

After my solitary triumph, the band began another number. A multitude of possible answers for Henderson's possession of my creation flooded my mind. I could not let this incredible concurrence go unmarked, unreported. At that moment, I was the only person in the world who knew about it.

I adjusted the earphones again. The band was still playing, other music than mine, naturally. I listened until they finished the set and another orchestra started to play.

In a state of involuntary motion, I put down the earphones and went to the telephone, reached Information, asked for and got the backstage phone number of Roseland Ballroom, 1658 Broadway, New York City. Then I called Fletcher Henderson, person to person, at that number and, miracle of miracles, got him to the phone! With my heart beating close to one hundred ten, I said, "Mr. Henderson, you don't know me, but I'm a student at the University of Pennsylvania in Philadelphia, who orchestrated a selection that you played in your last set, 'AN INDIAN RHAPSODY.'"

There was a brief silence, then he said, "Well, I'll be goldarned. I thought that fellow I bought it from wasn't the real arranger. There were a few wrong notes in it and he couldn't fix them, so we had to do it ourselves. But we loved the number so much I paid him anyway."

"Who sold it to you?"

"A runty little guy…I think his name was Wallie…Wallie McNab! Said he was a reporter…from a new magazine in Detroit."

WALLIE McNAB! So he wasn't a reporter at all! He was a professional arrangement thief! When I told the crew at the Dance Box the story, Ruby said, "He always went up on the stand between sets and sat on one of the chairs making notes. We all thought he was making reporter's notes…not *music* notes! He was copying the parts of your arrangement, one by one! What a creepy crook!"

I hurriedly continued my phone call, saying, "Mr. Henderson, I'm not hoping to get any money out of you for that arrangement. It's my fault that it got away from me. But now that you are playing a sample of my work, would you be willing to try over some other arrangements of mine, at a rehearsal, of course?"

"Certainly. We would be glad to go over more of your work. Our next scheduled rehearsal is here, at Roseland after hours, that is, at 2 A.M., a week from Tuesday morning."

"Thank you so much! I'll be there, with more material."

"Thank *you*! For clearing up our little mystery. Goodnight."

He hung up. Suddenly I was back in Lambertville, New Jersey, with a definite appointment at an ungodly hour in New York City only nine days hence, to rehearse…what? At that moment I didn't have the faintest idea. I knew that in my room at school I had the scores of about fourteen popular songs that I had arranged for my Chinese connections. I knew I could pick out the two best and recopy them, adjusting in the process to more closely fit the Henderson band. But where was the knockout, the killer-diller, that would excite those experienced, sophisticated musicians and make them want to play my work? I knew that I didn't have that winner, as yet. Meanwhile, until that longed-for electricity crackled, I would prepare the two numbers I had.

On Monday, back at my boarding house, I went through my growing pile of musical scores and picked out "Ain't She Sweet?" a humorous cute-hot arrangement, and Berlin's "Russian Lullaby," a moody waltz treated as a wild, jazzy Charleston, to be candidates for my Roseland adventure. But for the all-important, brand-new sensation, my synapses remained on vacation.

By Friday, "Sweet" and "Russian" were revised and copied, but I was no further advanced on the big knocker-outer. I had rejected dozens of hazardous possibilities. There was Saturday, Sunday, and part of Monday left in which to score and copy…WHAT?

That Friday afternoon, I was in the phonograph record shop of Houston Hall, waiting for an empty booth in which to play a few new releases, hoping to hear some fresh musical idea that would stimulate my sluggish noggin. Those booths were never soundproof; the one nearest me was leaking the famous Bill Challis arrangement of "I'm Looking Over a Four-Leaf Clover," played by the legendary Goldkette band. The listener in the booth seemed to be fascinated by the "pyramid breaks" in the orchestration. In the jazz musician's argot of the period, a "break" generally occurs when after the downbeat of the seventh bar of an eight-bar phrase the entire rhythm section of a band stops short, not playing again until the upbeat at the end of the eighth bar, the empty gap being filled by a "hot" solo or other interesting effect. In the case of "Four-Leaf Clover," the space was filled with a brass "pyramid," wherein the horns "stung" and held the notes in a rising chord of the dominant augmented seventh. The fan in the booth seemed to be hypnotized by the effect. He kept moving the stylus back and playing a "pyramid" over and over again. I began to feel sorry for the eventual purchaser of a worn-out disk.

I gave up waiting for the booth and trod back to my room in a trance, barely dodging a Woodland Avenue trolley. At Thirty-Eighth I got a sudden flash. *Wouldn't be exciting,* I surmised, *if instead of limiting "pyramids" to "break" bars, continuing, overlapping pyramids could be developed as an* <u>accompaniment</u> *to a unison melody in the saxophones…Oh, no,* I changed my mind, *that would be too restrictive. I'd never find a tune whose harmonic structure would make the trick possible.*

Throughout the rest of the afternoon, during dinner and right up to a certain moment when our orchestra was playing a dance engagement, my mind was constantly toying with the problem of the "constant pyramids." Although my conscious mind had discarded the idea as hopeless, my subconscious wouldn't let it go.

My alto sax teammate (I played tenor) said, "You're playing all the right notes, Don, but I have a funny feeling that most of you is elsewhere."

At a dancer's request, we played the Gershwins' great song, 'S'WONDERFUL, and as we hit the chorus I suddenly realized that I had found the perfect vehicle to carry the constantly changing, ever suspended brass pyramid that I had imagined. I relaxed and enjoyed playing the party, secure in the knowledge that by the time the weekend was over, I would have the explosive orchestration, with a new, exciting concept, that I needed to win the respect of Henderson and his great dance band.

On Monday night, after a hard day with my classes, I took the 9:45 to New York City, reaching Penn Station about 11:50. I wanted to get to Roseland in time to hear the famous Fletcher Henderson orchestra play the last hour. I rode the nickel subway to 50th and 7th Avenue, then walked a block north, dazzled by all the lights, to the Roseland Ballroom at 1658 Broadway. At the ticket booth, I was amazed and gratified that Fletcher Henderson had remembered to tell the ticket seller that I would be coming and to let me in free. What a kind, thoughtful man!

Within, I found a good observation spot and treated myself to a thrilling display of virtuosity as Fletcher's band showed off. That night the personnel was:

Trumpets:	Rex Stewart
	Bobby Stark
	Russell Smith
Trombones:	Charie Green
	Jimmy Harrison
Reeds:	Buster Bailey
	Don Pasquall (replacing the great Don Redman)
	Coleman Hawkins
Rhythm:	Fletcher Henderson (piano)
	Charlie Dixon (Banjo)
	June Cole (Tuba)
	Kaiser Marshall (Drums)

...a list of some of the greatest black musicians ever.

I was lucky to be at Roseland that night. The relief band, filling in so that music could be continuous, was Billy Lustig and his Scranton Sirens. In that aggregation was the young trombonist Jack Teagarden, destined to have a revolutionary influence on all players of the sliphorn, by extending the formerly conservative limits of that instrument's technique and range. It was clear that Fletcher and his men admired and respected Teagarden, going so far as to invite him to "sit in" with them. On one number he contributed to the hilarity of the occasion by discarding the "bell" section of his trombone and holding an empty water glass over the exposed joint of the slide section, then taking an unbelievable chorus on what was left of his instrument.

Time flew by and soon the crowd was reluctantly filing out of the hall as Fletcher's men prepared for rehearsal...of my arrangements? Not so fast, boy. They've got one of Fletcher's own to smooth out first...you have at least half an hour of stomach shivers to somehow survive before you're on, so conserve energy, kiddo.

When Fletcher's magnificent arrangement was finally played to his satisfaction, it was then about 3 A.M. He called me to his piano.

"What do you have for us?" he asked.

"Only three numbers," I answered.

"Three! We better get going. Pass one out."

I handed out the parts of "Ain't She Sweet?"

"Nice easy tempo," I suggested.

"Gotcha," he replied,

"Cutie-pie stuff."

He beat off.

The band played the arrangement almost perfectly at sight. Where were those ignorant criticizers who claimed black musicians couldn't read, that they had to be taught a note at a time, by ear? These men were well-schooled musicians, equal or better readers than comparable white instrumentalists. They possessed the rare ability of immediately sensing the style of an arrangement and adjusting themselves to it; as soon as they played the introduction to "Ain't She Sweet?" they grasped my humorous, satirical intent and fell in with it. After the last note, Fletcher said, smiling, "Hey! That's fun!" And to the players, "Clean it up, boys."

As the musicians went to work on the individual passages, I knew that Fletcher had approved the number that I considered the weakest. From then on, I didn't need to worry about acceptance.

The band had a lark with my alla breve, jazzed-up version of "Russian Lullaby," although I doubt that Irving Berlin would have been amused or anyone lulled to slumber by it. I had provided for several hot "ad lib" instrumental solos, but not knowing the intimate details of Henderson's personnel, I didn't always have the "lead" on the proper chair. After some quick adjustments and passing around of parts, the problems were solved and the band played with great verve and freedom my berserk treatment of what had been, once upon a time, a gentle waltz.

I said to Fletcher, "Two down and one to go."

He replied, "I don't know how you're going to top the first two."

"I'm beginning to worry about that myself," I gloated, passing out 'S'Wonderful, praying that my revolutionary counterpoint would work.

As I look today at the dog-eared, 1928 score of my arrangement of 'S'Wonderful (I save all kinds of ridiculous clutter), I realize that the introduction, first chorus, and verse were only good, solid statements of the basic material, nothing unusual. It was only in the second chorus, where the brass built constantly modulating pyramids against the unison saxophone melody, that the arrangement proclaimed anything fresh. The variation took Henderson's brass by surprise, and by the time four bars had passed, they were in a discordant tangle, every man for himself.

"Stop! Stop!" cried Fletcher, waving his arms.

The band came to a ragged halt.

Sternly he looked at me. "What the devil is this mish-mash supposed to be?" he demanded.

I rushed to him with my score open at the proper place. "Here it is," I blurted. "The brass have to sting and diminish each individual note, one after the other, fortepiano."

Reading my score, he immediately saw the entire picture and was intrigued by it. "Say!" he exclaimed, "there *is* something new here…and I like it!" He told the reeds, "Take five, fellows, while I woodshed this with the brass."

He took the horns very slowly at first; as they became accustomed to the constant pyramids and their individual parts in the structure, Fletcher gradually increased the tempo until they were up to playing speed. It was hard to stop them when they got the hang of it; they were like children with a new toy. When the saxophones were added, the ensemble sounded in reality as it had in my imagination.

As I was putting my scores into my briefcase, preparatory to leaving, Fletcher approached me, smiling. My hopes rose.

He said, "There is just one problem about all three of your arrangements that I must take up with you."

My hopes fell.

"It's about my banjo player, Charlie Dixon. He considers himself a *legitimate* musician, who prides himself on being able to read notes. As a matter of fact, he can't read symbols and that's all he's got in your arrangements."

I thought, *Good God, I can't let this whole business fall through because of a goofy, old-fashioned banjo player who can't read modern symbols and has to have* notes, *of all things, to read.* Hurriedly I said, "Let's assume I replace his parts with notes instead of symbols. Do you want my three numbers?"

Fletcher smiled and said, "Of course, can't you tell from the way we enjoyed playing them? We want all three."

My hopes rose again. I said, "I promise to take care of Charlie Dixon. Let's settle on price."

"I regularly pay for a new orchestration, scored and copied, the sum of twenty-five dollars. I admit that 'S'Wonderful, with that sensational new effect, is worth more." (Later Richard Himber based a whole style on the idea.) "But if we take all three of your numbers, which we desire, will you accept seventy-five dollars, in full?"

I had been successful far beyond my most extravagant hopes. I quickly said, "It's a deal!"

We shook hands.

As Fletcher was counting out the money, he asked, "So what are you going to do about Charlie Dixon?"

I said, "I have classes at school in Philadelphia this morning. I must catch the 5 A.M. train. All I can do is promise to mail back those three banjo parts as soon as I possibly can. You will have to trust me."

He looked me over, holding the greenbacks in his hand. He said, "You know, I could hold back on some of this money until you came up with those banjo parts."

I held my breath.

And then he smiled that warm, friendly smile and said, "But you look trustworthy to me. Here, take the whole seventy-five." He handed me the full payment, saying, "There's an extra fiver in there for your expenses. Thank you for coming at such an awkward hour."

I said, relieved and buoyant, "It's been a 'S'Wonderful hour."

We exchanged our private telephone numbers and addresses. I shook hands with the finest man I had yet encountered in the music business and with most of his men. Back I went to the subway, Penn Station, and the 5 A.M. local to Philly. I had planned to sleep all the way back on those rocklike cushions, but with eighty simoleons in my pocket and leaping exultation in my head, how could I ever go bye-bye?

....

Charlie Dixon got his banjo parts on schedule, but it wasn't easy, writing those four-note, widespread, unfamiliar tenor banjo chords instead of easy symbols. That spring of 1928, my precious time was devoured by heavy scholastic assignments, the demands of danceband engagements, and arranging for my Chinese restaurant orchestras. That year, mainly to please my parents and my instructors, I was pushing for Beta Gamma Sigma, that analogue of Phi Beta Kappa in the business colleges. I was too busy in Philadelphia to think about New

York and Fletcher Henderson until one day in May, my landlady told me he was on the phone.

"I'm in a bit of a jam," he said. "I need an arrangement of 'Old Man River' from 'Showboat' for recording next week, about 3:30 in length. In the show it's a serious bass solo, but we think it could be a driving, up-tempo specialty if arranged properly. Want to try it?"

"I think I could do it," I said. "I'd like to try, but I'm terribly busy. I would have to use a copyist."

"Okay, we'll work out a reasonable price. The rehearsal is at the usual time, 2 A.M. next Tuesday. But it isn't at Roseland...it's at Connie's Inn on Lenox Avenue. We're not working there now, just renting the space for rehearsal."

"I'll be there, Fletcher, but you could do a small thing to help me."

"What's that?"

"Just sit down and write out a single lead line of the first eight bars of 'Old Man River' in the style you want."

"Can do."

I got the scrap of manuscript the next day, pinned to a copy of "Old Man River." There was another song copy in the envelope, "I've Found What I Wanted In You." The note pinned to it said, "If you can possibly squeeze this in, score it for recording."

The following Monday evening, I took the 11 P.M. to New York with the two arrangements in my briefcase. Arriving at 1:20 A.M., I again took the subway, this time to 125th Street. People kept getting off with none getting on. By the time we got to 125th, there was hardly anyone on the train. Emerging from deep underground, I found a grimy, deserted crossroads under a heavily overcast, threatening sky. I started to walk up Lenox Avenue, leisurely at first, but slowly accelerating as tension grew. The solid walls of masonry on the sides of the street seemed to keep pressing in upon me. In addition to apprehensive me, there were only about four people on the street, all large, all black, all motionless, all watching me, so I thought. I pulled my hat brim down as low as possible and kept my hands in my pockets to conceal the ghastly gleam of my telltale white skin. I was just plain scared.

Approaching Connie's Inn, I had to pass one of those ebony statues, and it took all my self-control to keep from running. But safely by what was probably a harmless drunk, I found, to my thankful relief, that thoughtful Fletcher had posted the janitor of the shuttered club at its marquee, to usher me into the big room where the band was rehearsing.

Most of the band members were the same as at Roseland, and they greeted me warmly, which was reassuring after my spooky hike. They were just finishing working on an arrangement of Fletcher's and he gave them a fifteen-minute break, calling me over to the piano, where I delivered my two scores.

He read through "Old Man River" rapidly and said, "It's almost exactly what I wanted; it's as if you have been reading my mind."

I said, "I find that's an ability to be cultivated when working for a leader who has definite ideas."

"Hee-hee-hee. You're a smart one. Tell me, what are you studying at the University? Psychology?"

"No, Accounting and Business Management."

"Lord, help us! I thought you'd be studying music or some kind of arts course."

"No. My folks want me to become a C.P.A."

"Donald," he said, "you're just like me! My father wanted me to become a chemical engineer. To make him happy, I studied four long years at Atlanta University. But when I was graduated, nobody seemed to want a young, black chemical engineer, so in order to keep eating, I started to play at dances on the piano, which up to that time had been for fun. It soon became a business. You see what happened. Here I am, rehearsing a dance orchestra at three o'clock in the morning."

I said, "I've got another whole year to go before I have to make the big decision: accounting or music."

"After reading your scores, I'd bet with confidence on which way you will go. You will follow your instincts…your heart. It won't be in those ledgers and balance sheets…it will be in music…like mine?"

I looked at that son of a Professor of Education, that intelligent, good-looking, left-handed gentleman…yes, that is what he was: a true gentleman if there ever was one…and then and there I lost forever any racial prejudice I might have had. Why, he could have been my brother…and *was* my brother in music…giving me elder brotherly advice. All my life I have remembered with affection the few, brief encounters I had with Fletcher Hamilton Henderson, Jr. The influence of his unique personality has always guided me in my relationships with members of his race.

....

Recording Note: Apparently the recording date, for which I prepared "Old Man River" and "I've Found What I Wanted In You," never took place as first scheduled. But my two arrangements must have stayed in Fletcher's "book." He contacted me in 1931 to inform me that he had recorded "I've Found What I Wanted In You" for Columbia Records. I was able to buy the record, Columbia 2414-D, and I still have it.

On Tuesday, October 3, 1933, in New York City, there was a recording of "Ol' Man River" made for Decca by either Fletcher Henderson's Orchestra or (his brother) Horace Henderson's Orchestra. It is known that the two orchestras often shared personnel and Fletcher's "book." It is probable that my orchestration was used as a basis with a certain amount of "head" variations. I have never been able to find this recording, which is on Decca 18172B and Decca DL 5383 and a number of foreign Parlophon pressings in Europe.

D.W.

2. Fred (Waring)

Early in September of 1928, on a Sunday afternoon the day before senior classes would commence at the University of Pennsylvania, I was sitting with my roommate, Billy Saunders, in our comfortable quarters in Mrs. Shepard's boarding house near 39th and Spruce. We had come to Philadelphia a few days early in order to get settled before studies swamped us, slightly overshooting the mark. We were ready for school but now face to face with the ghastly prospect of an evening as empty as only a Sunday night could be in the blue law capitol of the United States, circa 1928.

Billy pointed to the sealed letters on his desk. He said, "I've written to my girlfriend and my parents. I had nothing to tell them but wrote anyway. Now I've finished the only novel I have with me." He tossed *The Sun Also Rises* on the desk.

"I've read it, too," I said unhappily.

"We had a couple of Sundays like this last year. What did we do?"

"We went out to Wayne."

"That's it! Wayne! Out to see that gorgeous tennis-playing dazzler and avoid her doctor father. Wow! Was she a peacherino! It was worth the trip just to sit there and goggle, even when nothing else happened!"

"I imagine that now she looks even more beautiful...."

...In the summer of 1927, I had worked in a dancehall on the North Jersey coast, playing my saxophone and clarinet. For recreation I had joined a seaside tennis club, where I met a Dr. Dillon and his splendacious daughter, Rose. They were tennis devotees, and we became playing acquaintances. Finding that the doctor's home and practice was in Wayne, PA, only a commuter ride from the Penn campus, I made sure that I obtained the Dillons' home phone number before the summer ended. During the following school year (1927–28), I kept the enticing contact alive by occasionally taking several student friends to Wayne with me on Sunday evenings, there to endure decorous social encounters, a sort of junior salon, with Rose and whatever girlfriends she could muster, well chaperoned by the presence of a parent or two in a nearby room. If a boy wished to continue and amplify his relationship with any of the birds, and had reason to believe that the object of his desire was flashing him "go" signals, then it was up to him to covertly arrange an assignation elsewhere and never, by any chance, involve any member of the Dillon family....

Coming back to the matter at hand, I said to Billy, "It's awfully late to try to make a date for tonight, but I'll give a buzz. One never knows...."

To my surprise, Rose not only remembered me but was not looking forward to a needlework evening.

I said, "You'll only need to dig up one girlfriend. I haven't had time to contact other studies. I'm bringing my roomie, Billy Saunders, and that's all. You know him from last year."

"I certainly do. Isn't he the boy who asked my father what he should do about an ingrown toenail and Daddy told him that he couldn't give him any advice because it was after doctors' hours?"

"I'll see he doesn't make a faux pas like that again. We'll be out there about eight-thirty."

The fourth member of our little coterie turned out to be one Terry (Theresa) O'Brian, a small compact colleen with bright auburn hair, fierce blue eyes, and an immovable opinion on all controversial subjects—except, maybe, the preservation of sharks.

It was well that Rose had recruited Terry, for there was not much we could do, in that well-patrolled, evangelical household on a Sunday, but talk. And talk, to Terry, was a synonym for argue. Alleviating her excessive ardor was her looks as she held forth on immaterial matters, but she was so small, so cute, so intense!

Considering the company and the season, it was only normal for the conversation to get around to football. It was then we discovered that we had been harboring an archenemy within our supposedly friendly circle. We discovered that Terry's father was an alumnus of that provincial academy called Penn STATE and Terry an ultra-loyal daughter, contemptuous of any team, band, or student faithful to urban, sophisticated Penn. Not helping at all was the regrettable fact that the Penn STATE behemoths frequently beat the hell out of Penn's more cerebral gladiators, and here we had a dedicated partisan of those rustic upstarts, ever ready to grind the salt of well-remembered, ignominious defeat into our still quivering wounds.

Rose, hoping to divert the conversation to less painful channels, said, "Apropos of Penn State, I see by today's paper that Warings' Pennsylvanians are opening at the Stanley tomorrow for two weeks."

Billy moaned, "Warings' Pennsylvanians again and again?"

Terry gushed, "I'm just crraaazy about that wonderful orchestra from State! I love that drummer with the frog voice! And when they put on those funny hats and sing 'Collejit,' I'm in stitches!"

Disgusted, I said, "That isn't an orchestra. It's a comedy act."

"But they're all dreamy singers. When the lights dim down and they group together and croon in perfect harmony...."

"Then they're a glee club with laughs; still not an orchestra."

"Oh, I hate you. Just because they're from State, you won't admit they're the bee's knees."

"And just because they hail from State College and all the hick towns around it like Phillipsburg, Tyrone, Lemont, and Lord Knows Where, you think they're perfect."

I was beginning to aggravate her.

She jumped up, waving her fist, to deliver what she thought was the cruncher: "But they make records!" she proclaimed. "Only the very best orchestras are allowed to make records!"

Rose intervened, "You had better sit down and take it easy, Terry, or Mother will be in here separating the gladiators."

As Terry cooled off a bit and seated herself, I said quietly, "Have you ever listened to those records? They are miserable. In the first place, they use a big marching-band tuba for a bass. That's very old-fashioned. All the smart, up-to-date orchestras are using a string bass for recording."

"And how did you get wise to that, Mister Know-it-all?"

"By listening carefully to records."

Billy horned in, "He's an authority, Terry. Working his way through college playing saxophone and arranging for big bands like Fletcher Henderson."

"Never heard of him," disparaged Terry. Warings' Pennsylvanians are *my* orchestra. I'm for them all the way."

"But they're so far behind the times," I protested. "What they need is fresh arranging blood. Someone to write out hot choruses that will make that moth-eaten brass section come to life."

She took a long breath and, pointing an emphasizing finger at me, said, "Well, Mister Smartski, listen to this: Since you know so *well* what is *wrong* with Warings' Pennsylvanians and know so *well* what to do to fix it, I hereby *DARE* you to go to Fred Waring and *tell* him your precious information, or forever hold your peace. *There,* I said it. I not only *DARE* you, I *DOUBLE-DARE* you!"

We were all shocked by her vehemence, including she who did the shocking.

After a moment, Rose said quietly, "I can't believe what I think I heard you say, Terry. Do you know the consequences if Don takes your dare and satisfies the challenge?"

"I don't think he'll be lucky enough to get to Waring," said Terry. "And if he does he won't have the nerve to tell him that his band needs a new arranger. I feel pretty safe...." She took a long look at me. "Or do I?"

The evening soon broke up. There weren't many trains back to Philly on Sunday night, and if one was missed it was a long hike.

As we were leaving, Rose said to me, "Please don't take Terry too seriously. She's a good gal at heart."

"You're referring to that dare?"

"I certainly am."

"There is one fact that your Irish spitfire didn't know when she declared that I 'didn't have the nerve' to tell Fred Waring that he needs a new arranger."

"And what is that, Mister Bones?"

"The indisputable fact that both my parents were born in England. By heritage I'm stubborn British."

....

I stood on the southeast corner of 19th and Market in Philadelphia, keeping my eye on the half-open stage door of the Stanley Theatre, which was further south, down the block and across the street on the western side. Earlier, I had circumnavigated the huge motion-picture-with-stage presentation and had passed that stage door, noting its tough-looking guardian who, from my corner observation post, I had seen send unauthorized visitors packing.

By this time I was on palsy terms with the seedy character who ran the newsstand adjacent to what I was beginning to think of as "my corner." He, who had seen, done, and disliked almost everything, said to me, "Why don't you buy a paper, Bud? It's now twelve-twenty, and at twelve-thirty Joe Doorman over there crosses the street to that greasy spoon for coffee and cakes, leaving the door unmanned for a bit. So you've got ten minutes to wait. Might as well spend the time reading."

I gave him a quarter for a tip, but he handed me back twenty cents and a paper, saying, "We don't take bribes around here." I noted that the *Inquirer* was an early, superseded edition.

I edged down the east side of 19th and stalled about, reading the paper. Sure enough, at exactly twelve-thirty the doorman abandoned his post, crossed the street, and entered the beanery.

I wasted no time and was inside the unmanned barrier in a flash. Before me was a long, dimly lit corridor. Far away I could hear instrumental music. Warings' Pennsylvanians were on stage, the picture was off, the live show on. I tiptoed down the corridor and came to a half-open door with a big silver star on it. I assumed that it must be Fred Waring's dressing room, with that big a star. I pushed the door farther open and entered. I sat down in an empty chair and looked around. It was what one might expect in a star's dressing room in a working theatre: the makeup seat before the bulb-bordered mirrors, the curtained-off changing area, the clothes racks, and making that dressing room different, several piles of sheet music and a full bag of golf clubs.

Suddenly, without warning, there was loud finale sort of music followed by heavy applause. Then there was "acknowledgment" music and more applause, tailing off. The act was over. Then I heard many feet rushing down the corridor, and after that the door opened wide and the famous Fred Waring had returned.

He was a pleasant-looking man in his middle twenties, of medium height, well built, rather handsome, with a beautiful head of wavy, light brown hair. When he saw me sitting there, he stopped short in surprise, frowned, and said, "Who are you?"

I stood up and hurriedly blurted, "My name is Don Walker. I'm a senior in the University of Pennsylvania. I'm working my way through college playing in dance orchestras. I am also an arranger, having sold arrangements to Fletcher Henderson in New York and also to several professional dance bands here in Philly."

As I took a long breath, he asked, "How did you get in here?"

"There was no one on the stage door. I just walked in and your door was open, Mr. Waring. Here I am."

"Well, I'm hornswoggled. You could have walked away with my clothes, my wallet, everything. But you didn't...."

"I'm not a thief, looking for loot. I came hoping to see you."

He had seated himself at his dressing table, switching on more bordering lights, preparing to take off his makeup. "And why is it so important to see me?" he asked.

"Well," I said lamely, "it was…all on account of a dare."

"A dare?" He laughed. "That's kid stuff."

"I know, but she's red-headed Irish and I'm obstinate English. It was like oil and water. She dared me. There were witnesses."

"Ah…so it's girl trouble that's behind all this. Tell me more, come clean."

"This Irish girl's father is a Penn State alumnus. She thinks anything from State is the cat's pajamas. We got to talking about your records. She thought they were perfect, I said that they could be improved. The argument got hot. She said that since I knew so much about music and instruments and records, why didn't I tell it to your face instead of talking behind your back. When I said that was impossible, she *dared* me to tell you and when I told her, 'Don't be ridiculous,' she *double-dared* me. So I just had to try."

"And you're trying. But you haven't completely satisfied her challenge. You are supposed to tell me how to improve our records. I'm waiting. I know that delivering me all that weighty mountain of information could take a lot of time, so give me a 'for instance.'"

"I think the tuba is a fine bass for a marching band or even in a stage show, where it looks so impressive, but on records of popular songs, especially behind vocals, you should use a string bass. The tuba could be added in big moments, in codas."

He had finished removing his makeup, and now he swiveled around and faced me. He was even better looking with the grease paint off. He said, "You could be right. Recording engineers have made the same suggestion to me. Tell me, is there any place here in Philadelphia where I could hear some of your arrangements?"

"Only four blocks away! At the Golden Dragon Inn, where Charlie Kerr's orchestra plays for dancing at lunch and dinner."

"Chinese food?"

I nodded.

He said, "I love it if it's good."

"I've heard that it's excellent…best in town."

"Now listen: Tomorrow, be here at this time, when I come off the first show. We'll walk to this Golden Dragon and while we have lunch, I'll listen to some of your arrangements. Have the orchestra primed to play them."

"Charlie Kerr is a good friend; he'll be glad to show off his orchestra for you."

"And have him make a reservation for us. Not way up front but in the rear with a wall behind me."

I had learned that although Fred Waring sought the spotlight onstage, he did his utmost to avoid it offstage.

....

The next day, I didn't have to wait at the corner of 19th and Market until the Stanley stage doorman slipped across the street for coffee. When I arrived, he was pinned to his post. Although he had obviously been told to admit one "Don Walker," the admission was certainly not accompanied by good grace.

After the show, Fred was most affable, the band having had an appreciative audience. As he removed his makeup, changed, and walked with me down Chestnut Street, he put me through an interrogation in depth. By the time we got to our rear table in the Golden Dragon, my private life, aims, and accomplishments had been thoroughly examined.

Charlie Kerr, who had been well briefed by me, was with us as soon as we were settled, excited to meet Fred Waring and play for him. He said, "If you had only let me book you a table up front, you could hear better."

Fred said, "This table is fine. I can hear better where we are, away from the noise of shuffling feet." He had fabulous hearing, "an ear like a bucket," as musicians term it.

Charlie, as rehearsed, continued. "Altogether we have eight of Don's arrangements in our books, all made last spring. We generally spot them here and there in our repertoire, like pearls. They are our feature numbers. But today we'll assemble them in two sets of four each so you can hear them all in the shortest possible time and then not have to rush to get back to your next show. Let me say that your presence here is a great honor for me and the boys in the band. Hope you like your lunch. Try the Hoo-Goo-Guy-Pan."

Fred, who was usually on a health kick that hustled vegetables, asked, "Is it good?"

Charlie proudly said, "Scrumdumtious!" and went back to work.

The orchestra, on its mettle, played beautifully. People danced, enjoyed, and applauded. Diners even paused in their greediness to approve. It was obvious that the waiters and management knew that something special was going on. The food and service, for once, were absolute perfection.

Fred listened but made no comment. At one point in a swinging number, there was a rousing hot trumpet solo and he asked me, "Is that trumpet player adlibbing that chorus or is it written out?"

I told him the truth. "It's all on paper, he's reading exactly what I wrote, except here and there he may change the phrasing a bit. I always try to leave a soloist a little room for self-expression."

He didn't say anything, just went back to his food, which he seemed to be enjoying.

Fred insisted on paying the check. We retraced our steps to the Stanley. He was strangely silent.

At the stage door, we paused and he said, "I hope you're not cutting too many classes today. Have you time to step inside for a moment?"

Had I time?! He hadn't said a word about the quality or effectiveness of my arrangements. And I wanted to know, oh, Lord! how I wanted to know what he thought about them! Of course I stepped inside, past the glowering doorman.

He walked down the dim hall to his dressing room. He unlocked the door, went in, and signaled me to follow and sit down. There was a pile of sheet music on his dressing table about four inches high. He rummaged through it and pulled out four songs, which he examined carefully, finally returning two of them to the pile. Then he handed me the two remaining numbers, saying, "Here...we will record these two songs at the Victor studio in Camden a week from next Sunday. Have these two songs ready. Look up Petey Buck, he's the arranger with the band. He'll give you all the dope on the orchestra, the instruments, the doubles, and so forth. Work out with him where the vocals will be, who'll sing them and in what keys. Maybe you'd better discuss the routines of these numbers with him, but understand, you're in charge...all the way."

I was stunned. So much responsibility, so suddenly! I was no longer a growing, ambitious youth; I was a man! With a man's work to do and little time in which to do it. I looked at Fred...he was no longer Mr. Waring...and said, "The arrangements will be ready at nine in the morning a week from next Sunday."

As I went out of the door with the big silver star, Fred said, "That ought to take care of a double-dare, shouldn't it?"

All the way down the corridor, I could hear him busting a gut, laughing.

....

I sought out Peter (Petey) Buck, Waring's regular arranger, who had been with the band from its State College beginnings. He was a thin, permanently exhausted, pleasant young man who was delighted to find that Fred Waring had enlisted another arranger to help prepare for the looming record date. He said, "Thank the Lord and all the little angels that I'm getting assistance! Fred always tries to get in four numbers on a three-hour record session, and on top of that, I'm writing a new, long, closing medley for the stage show. I couldn't see how I was going to squeeze out all those notes in time. Now, with you pitching, it's almost possible."

He gave me the orchestra combination. It was by far the largest and most diverse group of instruments I had ever tried to handle. An embarrassment of riches! I was thrilled and worried. I showed Peter the two songs that I had been given.

"Ah-ha!" he declared. "This 'Tell Me You Love Me' looks like a perfect song for Tom...that is, Tom Waring, Fred's brother. You should listen to a record of the band with Tom singing the vocal. I'll find you a good example. Get his good, commercial light tenor sound in your ear."

He studied the song and suggested the key of "D," along with other helpful hints.

Back I went to my drawing board, determined to get my assignments ready as quickly as possible so that the band members could become familiar with their parts before that nearing Sunday, only twelve days away, when each orchestration would have to be recorded in the maximum time limit of three-quarters of an hour.

Finding out that my arrangements were ready early, Fred, the worrywart, decided to have a reading on the empty stage of Stanley Theatre after the end of the last picture showing, at 2 A.M. on the Saturday morning the day before the recording date.

Neither of Buck's two assignments were ready, so my work was taken at once. "Tell Me You Love Me" went smoothly, and Tom Waring's solo was in the right key. Everyone was pleased but me. I was shocked by the rapid tempo taken by Fred, so fast that Tom could hardly get in all the words of the release. But then I realized, "He's the boss. He must know what kind of style sells his records, with that big tuba pushing the beat all the time. At least he didn't throw me out for suggesting a string bass for recording."

The other number I had been assigned was unusual. It was a story-ballad called "A Love Tale of Alsace-Lorraine." I don't know how or why I got the idea to have the vocal parts of the recording sung by a male quartet, but Buck liked the idea and told me which members of the orchestra should make up the foursome, encouraging me to proceed.

So early on I wrote out the vocal parts for the proposed quartet and gave them to its members so that they could rehearse privately in advance, but due to my ignorance of the physical problems of recording in the late twenties, I made a big boo-boo, which quickly came to light when the whole band started to play "Alsace-Lorraine."

There was an impressive introduction using the full orchestra. Then came the motif, announced by the male quartet with the backing of the rhythm section. All that happened as planned, but the quartet sounded very strange and weak, with its sounds coming from four individuals widely scattered about the stage. I hadn't considered that male quartets like to get their heads together and harmonize. I had them all over the place, forgetting that they were not only singers, but instrumentalists. Today, with our sophisticated recording equipment, there would have been no problem, but this was 1928.

Fred stopped the band and turned to where I was sitting in the front row of the theatre, checking my score against the live sounds. "This isn't going to work," he announced.

I hurried up on stage, carrying my opened score, saying, "I can fix it! I can fix it!"

Arriving at his podium, I spread the score and began to show him how, in the number's introduction, I could shift to other players the important instrumental notes I had given to the members of the quartet, so that the foursome could be assembled close together near the microphone.

"I don't need to look at that scribble!" Fred growled, gathering up the score and heaving it back to me. "I can hear what you're planning to do, so see that it's done by Sunday morning!"

I slunk back to my former observation post in the house, near where Petey Buck was sitting. I whispered to him, "Why didn't he want to see how I was going to maze the fix?"

He whispered back, "He's embarrassed. He can't read your score."

"Can't read my score?...Come on...."

"He can't read music. And what's more, he doesn't want to *learn* to read it. He's afraid learning to read music might formalize him and cause him to lose his touch with singers."

There was no doubt that Fred Waring was gifted with a sort of wonderful magic in the training and conducting of vocal groups. Leading them with his hands, arms, face, and occasionally voice, shunning a baton a la Leopold Stokowski, a Fred Waring trained and led chorus sang with a joint clarity and emotion that was the despair of all other choral conductors and the joy of those odd listeners who prefer to understand the lyrics. His treatment of phrase endings, those delicately fading nnn's and mmm's, proclaimed a rare touch of genius.

If Fred thought that learning to read a score would impair his miraculous gift…well…we all have our quirks and I suppose that one was his. To the shade of Fred Waring, I genuflect.

....

The Sunday morning session at the Victor studio in Camden was my introduction to top-level, professional recording. To me it seemed a hysterical mess. To everyone else, the ruckus appeared to be the customary routine when the attempt is made to record four three-minute-plus sides in three hours, theoretically allotting three quarters of an hour to each number.

Buck's two assignments were ready, the ink barely dry. Since they had none of the benefit of prior rehearsal, Fred tackled them first. The theoretical allotment of time per number was violated immediately. There was a harrowing engineering delay devoted to "getting a balance." There were wrong notes in the copying of Petey's scores, one of his numbers ran overtime and a cut had to be made. There were other hair-pulling problems. Through it all, Fred was a tower of stability, holding the shaky jelly of temperamental performers together, getting the job done.

Today, with the ease and flexibility of electronic recording, it is difficult to remember the agony of those early days of mechanical transcription of sound. An obvious musical mistake meant that the whole process had to stop and wait while the spoiled wax master disk was replaced by a fresh one and recording started again from bar one. Often the mistake remained in the finished product.

Buck's two arrangements ate up almost two hours, leaving only about an hour to record my two. Thanks to that "after midnight" rehearsal and the fixes I made, "Tell Me" and "Alsace-Lorraine" breezed along with no perverse problems. The musicians were packing their cases by the time those three precious hours were up.

The Waring aggregation left town that afternoon, and I didn't see them again until the following May. The powers at Victor liked the unusual treatment of "A Love Tale of Alsace-Lorraine" and soon had it in the record stores, where it became a popular item. From time to time, in that school year of 1928–29, Fred Waring had his business manager, Bus Seeds, send me songs that he wanted arranged for recording. Occasionally I would consult with Fred by phone, but most of the time I was on my own. I had become Fred's favorite recording arranger, all because of a dizzy dame's dare!

In the matter of that "dizzy dame," I had no illusions about the sort of proof I would need to convince her that I had faced her challenge and emerged victoriously. So I waited until I had (1) the issued commercial record of "A Love Song of Alsace-Lor-raine" and (2) a photostat of Warings' Pennsylvanians' check for $100.00 in payment for the first two arrangements I had made for them. So armed, I set up another Sunday evening social at the Dillons' where, in claiming my forfeit from Terry, I could parade my magnanimity before Rose, currently the object of my dream-fantasies.

When I presented my documentary evidence to Terry and then held back, specifying the forfeit she owed me, she had some shaky moments. Finally, showing off, I relieved her tension by demanding that during the coming May, when the Pennsylvanians were scheduled to perform again at the Stanley, she and Rose would be my guests at a show and after that would allow me to take them backstage to meet Fred, Tom, and the rest of the band. That was the anticlimactic, once-feared, received-with-relief forfeit.

I had admitted to myself that I was deeply indebted to Terry for her dare, which led me to consider making an attempt to meet Fred Waring. But the major urge that had pushed me to sneak into that unguarded stagedoor was the fact that she had challenged me in the presence of Rose, the one I wanted to impress. It was Rose, ROSE, *ROSE!* who spurred me to gumshoe into that dressing room, an action that I would never have performed if I had been in my normally timid mind.

....

That school year of '28-'29 was an extremely difficult one for me. In the previous June, the campus dance band that had been my main financial support was completely wrecked by the graduation of four of its six members. I was now down to about one "pickup" playing date per week. Although I was doing well with my arranging, that work was rather sporadic and I didn't feel as secure as I had when sure of at least three profitable engagements a week, playing my sax and clarinet at convivial dances. Orchestrating music is lonely work, and I missed the fun and excitement of "swingin' the gate" with boon companions in music.

At the start of my final semester, a scholastic problem arose to harass and complicate my life. In the Accounting Department of the Wharton School, I was something of a favorite. My instructors and professors knew that I was working my way through college and as long as I kept up my averages, they would ignore my tired tux and rumpled dress shirt when I staggered into those early Saturday morning classes. In those days the faculty of the department in which you were majoring assigned to you the subject of your graduation thesis. There was no appeal from the topic and no diploma if a satisfactory thesis on the designated subject had not been submitted by the given deadline.

My major was Accounting and the thesis-subject assigned to me was "Accounting Systems for Life Insurance Agencies," which seemed, at first, appropriate and easy. But when I made the first move that any aspiring thesis writer should make—the gathering of a bibliography on the designated subject—I discovered, to my horror, that my supposedly benign mentors had concealed a HUGE JOKER in my apparently simple assignment. The nasty fact was that there was *no* bibliography on the subject. If anyone had ever tried to write a book, or even a pamphlet, bringing order out of the chaos that then existed in accounting systems, if any, of life insurance agencies, they had either torn up or burned their meager conclusions.

Since there was *nothing* on the subject, it was clear that my mentors wanted me to try to create *something*.

I had a professor who was intimately connected with the life insurance establishment, having recently served a term as State Commissioner of Insurance. I suspected that he was behind my vexation, hoping that one of his students could come up with a brilliant answer to a problem he very well knew existed.

In my heart I thanked my teacher for giving me such an extraordinary opportunity. In my head I bewailed the innumerable hours that the planning and composition of my thesis would require. It was going to be costly, in terms of playing jobs and arranging work refused. For once the fear of going in the red began to gnaw on my nerves.

At last, on a Friday in early May, 1929, I turned in my thesis a few hours before the deadline and breathed a sigh of relief, looking forward to a weekend of relaxed catching-up with my other, purposely shelved studies. I heard the phone ring downstairs and then Mrs. Shepard called me.

"It's long distance!" she called.

I hurried to the phone. It was Bus Seeds, Waring's man of all tricks, calling from New York City. I was surprised because I knew that Warings' Pennsylvanians were in Hollywood, playing and acting in one of the first musical films, *Syncopation.*

Bus, obviously agitated, said, "Don, you've got to help us. The picture is finished and they tell me the rough cut looks good. But RKO is screaming for a phonograph record to use in promotion. They say they need it yesterday! The band's scheduled to open in New York next week. They're on the Chief with Fred right now!

"They'll be here Sunday, and I've reserved a sizable sound studio where we can record numbers from the film. The arrangements used in the picture won't work for commercial use, and Fred hopes you can help us."

"How about Petey Buck?"

"He's quite sick and couldn't possibly face a panic like this one."

"Exactly what will I have to do?"

"Two sides for Sunday P.M. and two more later in the week if you can make it."

"I'll stick with you for Sunday afternoon, but I don't know about those two later in the week. Do you have the scores from the picture with you?"

"Yes, but Fred wants new, real recording arrangements."

"Of course, but those scores can be a big help. Here's my situation: I have a playing date tonight that I simply can't cancel. I'll catch an early train and be in New York about eight-thirty tomorrow morning. Where do I go?"

"The Warwick Hotel. I'll have a room for you."

"And you better have an adjoining room for a couple of copyists who are willing to work all night."

"Where do I find them?"

"Try Harms and Co. on 45th Street. They specialize on musical comedy work. Their copyists are used to all night sessions for a healthy fee. Have them report about 3 P.M."

"Will do. See you tomorrow A.M." He hung up.

So there I was in a mell of a hess. (Sic) On the dance job that night, my alto saxophone pal (the same one) whispered, "When we are paid tonight, we will each receive the same amount. Do you think that is fair?"

I whispered back, "No, that is not fair. My tenor sax is larger and cost more than your crummy alto. By rights, I should be paid more than you."

"But you only brought a body. The brain is out of town."

....

When the alarm clock went off, I had logged about three hours' sleep but was able to add two more on the cozy early train to New York. By the time I got to the Warwick, I was in good shape and ready to go. Seeds had reserved me a nice room with a flattop desk and a connecting door to a room for the copyists. Percy Buck's film scores of "Jericho" and "I'll Always Be In Love With You" were on my desk. I decided to tackle the former, a rousing, driving song by Leo Robin and Dick Myers.

I was working for the first time with absolutely no recourse to a piano; to my surprise, I found that I could score quicker and better than when I was jumping up and down, from desk to keyboard, using the piano as a crutch. Buck's film score was a great help with its definition of the song's harmonic structure, although it was full of effects that were obviously intended to point up visual incidents and therefore of no use to me.

Bus took good care of me. When I started to get hungry near noon, room service arrived with sandwiches and coffee, without the necessity of a phone call. The scoring progressed between sips and bites. By 3 P.M., when the copyists promptly arrived, I had plenty of score to keep them busy. Disgruntled as usual because they were not handed a complete score, they set to work as from time to time I fed them continuing pages.

Afternoon tea arrived, then dinner was served and consumed with one hand while the other wrote notes. Bus was a master of crises logistics, keeping the troops comfortable and fed.

It was about ten-thirty P.M. when I wrote the final note of "Jericho" and added the little scrawl, dying away, that I always use to signal the end of an orchestration. I stood up and Bus, suddenly startled, thinking that I might be skipping, said, "Hey! Get back in your seat! Do I have to get a whip?"

"I've just finished 'Jericho'!" I announced triumphantly.

"But you've got another number to write! Pick up that pencil!"

"Aw, Bus, ease up on me...I had only three hours' sleep last night. I'm burnt out...need a break...."

"What you need is a good stiff drink. That'll pep you up." He picked up the phone, got Room Service, and ordered ice and mix.

I said, "Listen, Bus, I don't drink. I tasted some rotgut once and hated it."

"Don't worry. I've got some real good stuff in my room down the hall. I'll get it." He came back with a bottle of Johnny Walker. He said, "This is right out of your grandfather's vat." He mixed me a highball. "Here," he said, "this'll keep you going for hours."

I tasted it. With the mix it wasn't so bad and got better as I cautiously imbibed at first and then swilled down the remainder. Almost at once I began to receive musical brainwaves suggesting how to orchestrate "I'll Always Be In Love With You."

In amazement I laughed. "I've got all kinds of good ideas! Got to get back to that desk!" I rushed to my workplace and waited expectantly for a stroke of genius.

The trouble was that I had too many good ideas pushing and shoving each other around in my mind. Try as I did, I could not concentrate and come to a decision on what to write. I sharpened pencils, numbered and titled blank score pages, studied Buck's work, thought and thought, but set down nothing. At last I felt that I had a good approach and started to score. The problem was that there seemed to be ten horizontal lines on a staff instead of the usual five. It was while I was trying to straighten out that handicap everything went black and then I woke up with Bus shaking me.

"Come to life!" he said. "You've got the waltz to do!"

"Waltz...waltz...what waltz?"

"The waltz from the picture, rum-dum."

"Oh, that." Sense was returning, but not for long. "I'll never get that schmaltz done 'less I get some kip," I mumbled as my forehead nestled on the scorepage and the fog descended. He shook me a few times to no avail. He gave up. When I awoke, my watch said 4:50. The dawn was just beginning to show color. I felt wonderful and after ablutions started to write the waltz arrangement.

My modest encounter with Johnny Walker had taught me a lesson that has governed me all my life, i.e., that it is impossible for me to summon the concentration necessary for good orchestration if I have partaken of any kind or quantity of alcoholic beverage during the preceding six hours or so. It is advantageous to know one's physical limitations.

On that early May morning in 1929, the scoring of "I'll Always Be In Love With You" fairly flew. When I had sufficient score pages to start the copyists, I awoke them and ordered food for them and myself. During the wee hours of the previous night, they had finished "Jericho" and as soon as they had eaten, I started them on the waltz.

We were all working away when Bus Seeds dropped in about 10 A.M. He was pleased with the industrious atmosphere. I brought him up to date on our progress.

He exclaimed, "What an operation! You really turn out a product!" He complimented the copyists. When we were back in my room, he said, "Yesterday I was worried that you strangers might not be able to work together at such short notice and make my eight P.M. deadline, but now I'm confident."

"Wait a minute!" I yelped. "What's this eight o'clock deadline? You told me that you're having an *afternoon* session! We've been killing ourselves to make a two or three P.M. call!"

"The boys' train doesn't get in till noon. They have to eat and get settled in their hotels. An afternoon session would be too tight, so I booked one in the evening."

"And you knew all this while you were leading me on?"

"In this beeswax every once in a while you have to use a little treachery. How did I know you were going to be so damned efficient...and those two," he pointed his thumb toward the copyists' room, "don't let them know it's an evening date or they'll be going home for Sunday dinner."

I promised to keep his strategic secret and went back to work. By 3 P.M. I had completed the score and by 5 P.M. the copyists were finished, so I had to concede that Bus Seeds' "treachery" was justified.

That night the quality of the Pennsylvanians recording was greatly improved by the luxury of making two sides instead of trying for four. "Jericho" quickly became a hit record (Victor 21870-A), which substantially raised my stock in the Waring organization and at Victor. For once Fred's tuba pal sounded right at home, blatting away in the martial "Jericho," but in the romantic waltz it was still the case of the elephant in the boutique. I wondered if Fred would ever shift to a proper double bass for ballads.

....

After the Pennsylvanians had played out their two-week engagement in New York, they came once again to the Stanley in Philadelphia. There I successfully managed Terry's "forfeit." Fred and the boys complimented me on my taste in femininity. Bus Seeds was backstage and drew me aside while Fred was bantering with the girls.

Bus asked me, "Is it true that you will be graduated this June?"

"That's right."

"Do you have any plans? Know what you're going to do?"

"No...the future's a big blank."

"Fred wants to have a serious talk with you."

"Will you be there?"

"Of course, I'm his business manager."

"That's what worries me."

"Damn it, you're still holding that session call against me. You know you would *never* have made an afternoon session. I saved your neck."

"Okay," I said, giving in. "Where do we meet?"

"In his suite at the Bellevue, tomorrow morning at ten."

"I'll be there."

Because of my averages, I had been granted unlimited cuts in my senior year at Penn. So I was right on time to see Fred, who came into the living room in his golfing plus fours.

He explained that he had just finished nine holes at Bala and would have gone eighteen if he hadn't had this meeting with me.

He said, "Bus tells me that you have no specific objectives after you are graduated."

"Lots of ideas but nothing definite."

Hummm...I'm going to tell you something in strict confidence. Petey Buck, who has been my close friend since we were kids, has T.B. The doctors tell him that he could be cured with the proper regimen, but that it is impossible to achieve it on the road with an orchestra. As he is living now, he can only get worse."

I could only murmur inadequate words of shock and sympathy.

"Now something else is happening in our outfit. Tell him, Bus."

"Fred Culley, our first violinist and assistant conductor, is leaving us because he has a fantastic opportunity. In his home town of Toronto, Ontario, Canada, they are now just finishing the Royal York Hotel, which will be the biggest hotel in the British Empire. Culley has some powerful political pull because he has been offered the job of musical director in the new hotel. That means one big band for the main dining room and a flock of small units for private parties. It's too good a chance for him to miss, so he will be leaving us soon to get organized."

Fred Waring took over, saying, "It's my idea that Petey Buck should go north with Fred Culley, who is going to need an arranger to help him build a new, important orchestra. Then Petey won't have to travel or breathe the muck down here. Toronto is famous for its fine hospitals and clinics, Petey could have regular, top-grade medical help."

Bus said, "That would leave us here with no arranger."

Fred said, "I need an arranger with me all the time, to help plan new numbers and orchestrate them…"

…I could sense what was coming. At this point I feel that I should report that all through my life I have been blessed with (or cursed by) a visage which, under certain circumstances, can become, involuntarily, an enigma, a poker face, a deceptive deadpan. This look, enhanced in its inexpressiveness by spectacles with heavy rims, has led lecturers to believe that I am hanging on to their every word while my thoughts are on my topspin backhand; has caused composers, demonstrating a new score, think that I hate their music when I am only searching for the best way to orchestrate the excellent tunes; has prompted prospective employers to believe that I am not happy with their offered terms when I am, in fact, paralyzed by their unexpected largess. I must have turned on this cryptic aspect during the following:

"…and you have proven yourself by your fine recording arrangements."

Bus chimed in, "You know the band…"

Fred carried on, "…making you the obvious replacement for Petey…"

B.: "…who has been with us from the beginning, receiving all those Christmas-present increases in salary…"

F.: "…who has high expenses with a wife, traveling with him on the road…"

B.: "…but you couldn't expect to be paid his salary, built up over a number of years…"

F.: "…but your chips'll be better than what you've been making on piecework."

I had on my mystery mask, my noncommittal nonchalance.

Bus carried the ball on the first proposition. He asked, "How does a hundred a week hit you?"

I just sat there, afraid to move.

Fred caught the pass. "I think we could go to a hundred and ten. Yes? No?"

I was numb.

Bus said painfully, "One-twenty is our absolute top."

After a moment of silence that seemed like a week, Fred said, "I think if we squeezed hard enough, we could just possibly go to one twenty-five, but that's the downright limit."

"Oh, thank you!" I caroled, breaking my silence. "That's an attractive offer…it would be quite satisfactory…but…."

"But?…but?…But what?"

"My mother and father expect me to become a C.P.A. That's their fondest hope. Please understand: I *want* to go with you, the salary is satisfactory, but first I will have to tell them what I am doing and get their blessing. It wouldn't be right for me to just go off on the road with you, ignoring them."

Later I found out that Fred was exceedingly high on filial devotion, I must have touched him on a tender spot. I left our meeting with the understanding that Waring's offer was still open, pending my meeting with my parents.

I floated back to school. One twenty-five a week! That was a fortune for a student just graduating from college in 1929! At my boarding house, a message from the Accounting Department of the Wharton School awaited me. I was to report as soon as possible to Professor Lockwood, the lecturer I suspected was implicated in the selection of that most difficult subject for my thesis.

I phoned and got an appointment for the next morning, leaving me twenty-four hours to worry. Was my thesis rejected? Were my unlimited cuts withdrawn? Had they by some slip averaged in my two month's ghastly marks in Conversational French, a course I didn't need, which a kindly instructor had allowed me to drop in order not to spoil my otherwise excellent record? I had a restless night.

When I entered Professor Lockwood's office the next morning, he got up from his desk, walked around it, and shook my hand, saying, "Congratulations!"

"What for, sir?" I asked.

"It will be announced today," he said. "Out of six hundred twenty eligible students in your class in the Wharton School, only seven have been picked for Beta Gamma Sigma and you are one of the seven. Isn't that wonderful?"

I said, "It will make my mother and father very happy."

"And it gives you so much prestige! A boy who worked his way through college, yet had the discipline to establish such an outstanding record!"

I mentally thanked that thoughtful, benevolent French instructor as I asked, "Is this good news the reason you summoned me?"

"It's just a tasty side dish," he chuckled, going behind his desk. "Pull up a chair and enjoy the main course."

I sat down, facing him.

He picked up a letter and explained. "This is from a friend of mine who is a Vice-President of the Penn Mutual Life Insurance Company, an organization with which I have close ties. He thanks me for sending him a copy of your thesis, 'Accounting Systems for Life Insurance Agencies.'

"His company has been conducting research preparatory to setting up a series of such systems to be recommended to their independent agencies, whose present systems are in uncoordinated disorder. He believes that your thesis will be a great help to them. Best of all, the company is very interested in you, the author. Upon graduation they are willing to offer you, sight unseen, thirty-five dollars per week, an unheard-of starting salary, to continue your work under their supervision. Isn't that wonderful?"

I had to say something, so I echoed. "Thirty-five whole dollars a week! That's sensational!"

Lockwood exulted, "I've had a few other students picked up by big companies because of theses, but the best any of them got was twenty-five a week at the beginning. Starting at thirty-five you'll be president of the company in thirty years!"

He was a fine man and brilliant in his field. The startling success of one of his students would boost his reputation as a teacher.

Once again I fell back on parental concurrence as a means of procrastination. I was getting quite good at it. I explained that my parents expected me to become a C.P.A. Shifting to life insurance had to be approved. Promising to report to my sponsor as soon as I had an answer, I trudged back to my room, turning over and over in my mind my ENORMOUS PROBLEM.

My puzzle did not arise from the necessity of making a choice between two divergent careers. That important decision had been decided instantly, instinctively, without serious thought. I remembered Fletcher's prediction, that when the time of choosing arrived "you will follow your heart. It won't be in those ledgers and balance sheets…it will be devoted to music…like mine!"

The ENORMOUS PROBLEM was how to tell Professor Lockwood and my parents that I had rejected a promising position in a famous corporation for a shaky job with a touring orchestra that, quite possibly, might be nearing the end of its popularity.

After a couple of days, I took the easy way out, writing to Lockwood, thanking him for his interest and help, informing him that I had decided to take a bid that was far better, financially, than that of Penn Mutual. Then I wrote to my parents, who had no knowledge of the insurance company proposal, informing them that I had been offered a job paying $125 a week. I thought that information would help dry a flood of tears.

....

I had just mailed my letters, rejecting Penn Mutual's fine offer, when the telephone rang summoning me to a meeting in Fred Waring's suite in the Bellevue-Stratford. Bus Seeds let me in. Already there were signs of departure for Washington, D.C., in the stacked, half-packed luggage. I thought, *In two weeks I'll be on the road with the Pennsylvanians.* It was exciting to anticipate.

Room Service arrived with the great man's breakfast and as soon as it was laid out, he appeared. While Fred ate, Bus and I chatted with him about Rose, Terry, my coming graduation, and Victor's satisfaction with the record of "Jericho." After Fred had his last sip of Postum, he got down to business.

He said, "A lot has happened here this week, and some of it affects you directly. On Wednesday Petey Buck and his wife ,Dina, took a train to Toronto amid tearful goodbyes and so forth. They were planning to get organized there so he could start scoring for the orchestra Fred Culley is going to front in the new Royal York Hotel. Ben Bernie and his band have been hired to open the place, but after two weeks Culley has to take over with a green orchestra."

Bus said, "And yesterday, Thursday, who do you think showed up here? Petey and Dina Buck!"

F.: "So help me, Petey's wife is a Russian citizen!"

B.: "She's never been naturalized, and right now there is something nasty going on between Russia and Canada!"

F.: "They got to the border, and the Canadian Immigration officers wouldn't let her across it!"

B. : "So what could they do? They came back to Father Waring!"

I said, fearing the answer, "So what are *you* going to do?"

Fred admitted, "We haven't much choice. Petey is sick and weak. He needs money and a job. We have to take him back."

"Where does that leave me?" I asked. "Can you use two arrangers on the road?"

"No, and even if we could, the budget won't stretch that far!"

"Damn it," I remonstrated. "I've burned my bridges to go with you, turning down a promising job with a famous insurance company here in Philadelphia."

Fred said, "We want you in our organization, Don. We wish to help you reach your full potential. I picked you out myself and have always had faith in you and your ability. You have proven that my estimate was not wrong. But right now the only solution to this mess that we can think of is for you to go to Toronto with Fred Culley."

I was stunned. It was such a radical shift of circumstances.

Meanwhile, Fred went on, selling the idea. "What a challenge! Creating a brand-new orchestra for a great hotel in a foreign country! You will be able to experiment, try any crazy idea that comes into your head!"

"Won't Culley have anything to say?"

"He's a fair, cooperative fellow, most friendly...and excellent musician himself. What an opportunity for you!"

I felt the need for specifics. "How about nuggets?" I asked.

"It will be the same deal," promised Bus. "Just what Culley had agreed to pay Petey, one twenty-five every Saturday."

"In Canadian money?"

"Well...yes...but the exchange is nearly even and you'll be getting a free room in the hotel."

That made me feel better, but there were still some unsettled items. I asked, "How soon will I have to be in Toronto?"

Fred told me, "As soon as possible. Culley is leaving tomorrow night after our last show. You should have a talk with him before he goes."

"Who pays my transportation to Canada?"

Bus said, "We're sharing it with Culley."

I explained, "If I'm going to be leaving early, I'll have to cancel some playing jobs I've booked for next week. I was counting on that cash to clean up some campus tabs I owe. I don't want to run out on any debts."

"How much are you in the red?"

"About eighty frogskins."

"We'll advance that. Pay back when and as convenient. Is that all?"

"Sorry...not all...."

Bus groaned.

"If I have to leave early next week, I won't be here on graduation day. The University has some strict rules concerning the conferral of diplomas to those persons eligible for degrees. The candidates must attend the ceremonies, sit in their designated seats, join the queue in the proper order, and receive their diplomas in person."

Fred said, "What a crazy rule! Suppose you were sick in bed."

"There is an out. Under certain circumstances, maybe like mine, one is allowed to hire a substitute, who performs exactly as the graduate would, collects the diploma, and mails it as instructed. That way, the University can be certain that their elaborate rituals will be well attended."

"And how much will that cost?"

"The going rate is five dollars plus cap and gown rental, plus mailing costs. There are Philadelphians who make a business of being surrogate graduates every year."

"They must get awfully sick of those speeches. Bus, do you have a sawbuck?"

Bus found a tenner and gave it to me, saying, "I hope you don't have any more little surprises, or we might be filing for bankruptcy."

"I could help you there," I quipped. "My class spent a whole semester last fall studying how to profit by insolvency."

On the following Tuesday, I managed to get out of Philadelphia on the overnight sleeper, trusting that my hired stand-in would collect my diploma and mail it to my parents. Awakened at the border at six in the morning, I found the Canadian Customs and Immigration officers just as intransigent as they had been with Petey Buck and his wife. It seemed as if they didn't want *anybody* to enter the Dominion. Not being alert the previous night while filling out a printed declaration, I had thoughtlessly put down "musician" as my occupation. There they were sure they had me, since one of my bags looked suspiciously like a saxophone case. But when I unlocked and opened it, displaying two racquets and other tennis gear, they grudgingly allowed me to cross the line.

I lived and worked in Toronto for about eighteen months, surviving the stock market crash and a record-breaking frigid winter, changing my status as an orchestrator from amateur to professional. The Pennsylvanians were on the road all of that time; the expected summons from Fred Waring never came. During my "Canadian period," there were two happenings that were of lasting consequence to me.

First, it was in Toronto that I met, wooed, and finally won my dearest lifelong partner, Audrey Langrill-Simpson.

Second, not nearly as important but helpful, the Canadian Pacific Railroad System, owner of the Royal York Hotel, put in a transcontinental radio "wire," broadcasting Fred Culley's orchestra "live" every Saturday night to all of the United States and Canada, frequently giving me credit for an arrangement. Instead of being buried in the sticks, I was getting nationwide publicity!

The dreadful American stock market collapse of October 24, 1929, did not wreck Canadian business immediately, but all through the frigid, record-breaking winter of '29-'30, the occupancy of the hundreds of rooms in the new Royal York gradually decreased. Booked conventions were cancelled, tourist trade disappeared. By spring it was obvious that sooner or later Culley's expensive orchestra…and its arranger…would have to take a cut or else. Before the ax fell, I began looking for another job, preferably in New York City, the center of the commercial music business.

I wrote to Fred Waring, who was on the road. He replied that he always thought of me as a potential member of the Pennsylvanians, but sorry, Petey Buck was still with him, health a continuing problem. "Keep in touch," he wrote, "so I know where you are in case Victor suddenly decides to have us make some new recordings, a rare request these days."

I had another promising opportunity: Philip Cohan, who had been my alto saxophone teammate all through college until he was graduated a year before me, had profited by a typical Hollywood stroke of luck. Coupled with hard work, he had become the administrative head of the music department of Paramount Pictures Astoria (Long Island) Studios. They had no staff music arranger and could use one. He was sure he could put me on the payroll, after which my tenure would be up to me.

So on October 24, 1930, one year after the big stock market bust, four days before my twenty-second birthday, three days after the Royal York job kerflopped, I took off in my Canadian Ford roadster, full of hope and confidence, leaving behind Audrey, my love, in the first of many unhappy separations.

Arriving in New York City, I looked up Phil Cohan. He was living in a roomy cooperative apartment on Riverside Drive, near 72nd Street, with three sharing mates. Two of them certainly qualify to be named "Men of Notes."

One was E.Y. (Yip) Harburg, the great lyricist who put the inspired words to Burton Lane's music for "Finian's Rainbow." At the time he was working with Jay Gorney on "Brother Can You Spare a Dime?" the theme song of the thirties.

The other was that Russian composer of serious music, Vladimir Dukelski, who had fled from the Communists at about the same time as Stravinski. Although he had written symphonies, (and had them performed!), for obvious financial reasons he was trying to write for Broadway musicals under the name of Vernon Duke. His success in the less elegant field of music is evidenced by the many "standards" he produced under that un-Russian name. Such as "April In Paris," "I Like the Likes of You," "What is There to Say," and "I Can't Get Started with You," etc.

Duke had two overwhelming passions: extra-large women and overage cheese. He hunted obscure cheese shops with a connoisseur's enthusiasm. The apartment reeked with his glorious finds.

There was no bed for me in the communal apartment, but I was welcome to sleep on the large window seat that looked out on the Hudson River. The seat was solid oak, but there was a quantity of pillows that tried to make up for the missing mattress.

As soon as I was acclimated, I went along one day with Phil when he went to work at the Long Island Studios of Paramount Pictures. There I met the famous English conductor, Frank Tours and, working there as a vocal coach, Johnny Green. I also saw a distant glimpse of Ginger Rogers, walking down a corridor. I was in the big time!

The next afternoon, back at the ranch, Phil arrived early. He had shocking news: As of immediately, Paramount was closing down all Eastern operations, leaving only a couple of watchmen on salary at the Astoria studios. Phil was out of work and so were all his friends: Yip, Vernon, Ted, and most of all, me, laid off before I even punched a time clock.

I had saved a healthy stake in Canada, so I was far from destitute. I found a nice room in Tudor City, the new development at the eastern end of 42nd Street, far from the Limburger-pervaded atmosphere of the westside apartment.

I started contacting the professional managers of music publishing houses, men who had benefited from my cooperation while I had been programming the network performances of the Royal York orchestra. To my surprise, they remembered me and were most helpful, an influential group of boosters. Yet when it came to giving me cash-producing work, all they had to offer were the so-called "stock" arrangements, the all-purpose orchestrations of their most popular songs.

I soon found out that "stocks" were not my field. In my whole orchestrating life, I have adhered to a stringent, self-imposed rule that

I must "hear in my head" every note that I write. But how can one "hear" music that is being written for an indefinite number of musicians playing unspecified combinations of instruments? Arranging "stocks" put me in constant conflict with my adopted method of work. Although some I scored were tried out, accepted, and published, my compensation never paid for the mental agony I suffered.

The holidays approached. I received a card from Fred. It was nice to know that I was still remembered, but you can't eat "Good Tidings." I went to Lambertville and spent Christmas with my folks, then took off for Toronto in my Canadian Ford. I had discovered that I could net much more for it if I sold it in the country where I bought it. Of course, the main reason for the trip was to see, hear, and touch Audrey again and, with her, come to a most important decision.

That drive, in the dead of winter, took two full days, a distance that now we travel between an early breakfast and a late dinner. It was worth the effort; we agreed that neither of us wanted to live any longer without the other. With her parents accepting the inevitable, we set the wedding date to be March 14, 1931, at their home in Toronto. Then I sold my Ford and took the train back to New York and my spotty assignments.

In retrospect, I am constantly astounded by the blind audacity of my Canadian bride and myself, leaping into matrimony with no visible means of support, other than her ingenuity and my musical chirography. We were up to all sorts of immaculate deceit; for instance, she had a number of aunts and uncles living in Canada who wanted to give us wedding presents. Since we didn't wish a tussle with U.S. Customs officers on the train our wedding night, we suggested that they give us cash with instructions for spending it in the U.S. for specific gifts. We lived very nicely for about two months on that rake-off. The only trouble with the dodge was revealed in later years when our Canadian relatives came to visit us, requiring hurried purchases of the proper gifts that always seemed to have been kept in mint condition.

We rented a furnished apartment in Forest Hills, near tennis courts, and I made a serious but unhappy attempt to lick the detested stock arranging business. I tried but could not break into the growing field of special orchestration for commercial radio programs. I did a lot of studying of strings, the only orchestral instruments I had never played.

Near the end of July, 1931, about when our cash was dangerously low and it had been confirmed that Audrey was pregnant, I received a letter from Bus Seeds informing me that Petey Buck was being retired.

As Fred preferred to have a non-playing arranger with him at all times, he was offering me Buck's job and salary.

It was in the nick of time, an example of his shepherd-like concern for every member—and wife, if any—of what he considered his personal flock. I was more than willing to be included in that special fraternity.

There was a tearful parting, the first in our marriage, on the elevated platform of the Long Island Railroad at Forest Hills. Donald to Penn Station and a train to Cleveland, Audrey the next day to Canada. She was beginning to have some physical disturbances, obviously connected with her pregnancy, and wished to go to her stepfather, an eminent Toronto physician, for the check-up.

I hadn't seen the Pennsylvanians for over two years, and there had been important changes. A Frenchman, Leo Arnaud, who played trombone, saxophone, and cello, had been added. My former bête noire, the tuba virtuoso, was playing the waltzes and ballads on a string bass, properly reserving the tuba for heroic moments. (Even in absentia, I seemed to have some influence.)

The most surprising change was a tiny one, the subtle shift of an apostrophe, changing a possessive case from plural to singular. Now all the signs read: "Waring's Pennsylvanians," not "Warings' Pennsylvanians" as before. Tom was no longer at the piano, that spot being managed by a cheerful, competent musician named Charles Henderson. I never asked why. It is not my nature to pry into personal motivations. Tom had disappeared—that was all I knew. He was a nice person, a gentle person; it follows that he was very easy to hurt. I have always harbored the hope that his departure was his own decision and not forced upon him.

From Cleveland I traveled with Waring's Pennsylvanians through the Midwest and as far south as New Orleans. They entertained and also played for dancing in hotel dining rooms and nightclubs. About a dozen of the men had their wives with them. I grew familiar with the cliques and clubs, the clans and coteries that inevitably form under traveling conditions. I gained more experience in orchestrating without the help of a piano.

In New Orleans, the Pennsylvanians went through a fundamental change. To what had been a close all-male fraternity was added a girl's singing trio. Musically they enriched and diversified the sound of the vocal ensemble. Physically their presence created the sort of locker room problems that arise today when female reporters besiege what used to be the sanctuaries of our macho sports heroes.

Fred Waring's early recognition of "women's rights" didn't sit well with the "Waring Wives." Oddly enough, the female who caused the greatest wagging of tongues was not one of our three new canaries but the non-performing "duenna," who was supposed to be chaperoning the sixteen-year-old member of our trio!

As I was packing to leave New Orleans, Bus Seeds came to my hotel room to pay me my weekly salary. Handing me the loot, he said conversationally, "In about three weeks, I'll be dishing out your bread and butter in the Roxy Theatre, N.Y.C."

"Great!" I crowed. "How long will our engagement be?"

"Unlimited. It will last till they're tired of us. Besides performing our specialties, we're going to be the house band, accompanying singers and dancers, working up a new show every time the picture changes...."

"Terrific!" I exclaimed. "Sounds as if a lot of fresh orchestration will be needed."

"That's for sure...and Fred wants you to take charge of it. Three weeks from now, you'll be bossing a whole crew of arrangers and copyists, getting ready for our big opening on New Year's Eve."

I saw my hope of holly-trimmed relaxation fading away, while fading in there came a solitary desk in a lonely room, covered with sheets and sheets of virgin score paper that had to be covered with notes while from without came the hubbub of happy people celebrating the holiday. I have never discovered why the orchestrator has to work at such times, but it is normal.

Leaving New Orleans, I took the Crescent Limited, a train that still runs. Arriving in New York the next day, after finding a hotel near the Roxy, I thought it sensible to visit the music department of that theatre and alert whoever was in charge to the onslaught that was soon to occur. Thus I met the Roxy's music librarian, a warm, cooperative gentleman named Edwin Zimmerman; everyone called him "Zimmie." He had been a famous string bass player in his time and upon his retirement, his place in the Philharmonic had been taken by his son, a master on the same instrument.

Zimmie was a thorough professional, a veteran of a thousand musical crises. Working with him was like taking a postgraduate course in tact, discipline, and anticipation. On leaving him, I felt relieved and lucky for finding, in all that enormous city, a friend I could count on when there was too much music to orchestrate and not enough time to do it.

At the time of the Waring experiment, the Roxy was still vibrating from the shock of the defection of S. L. Rothafel, its founder, producer, and guru. Only recently he had deserted his own ship, sold it to 20th Century Fox, and skipped a block eastward to mastermind the new Radio City Music Hall, taking most of his Roxyettes with him, to be reborn as Rockettes. Our new producer was the old choreographer, Russell Markert, a clever, competent, but very nervous leader who, among other concerns, had the problem of bringing his decimated dancing corps up to their formerly proud standard.

In theory, the film part of the entertainment, the feature, the news reel and the short, were supposed to run approximately one hour and forty-five minutes, five times a day, starting at eleven A.M. The live show was designed to run about forty-five minutes, alternately with films, four times a day.

The Pennsylvanians were no strangers to this type of schedule, having played many engagements in the so-called "presentation" houses. What made a big difference in the Roxy was the fact that they not only entertained in their own spot but had to accompany the other live performers…and Fred, our musical director who didn't read music, had to conduct strange routines with only his hands, arms, and face, shunning a baton, from the bottom of that enormous pit. His performance at the first rehearsal of a new act would have to have been seen to be believed. He would have the pianist play the piece once through without stops, then take it himself with the orchestra, flawlessly. He had a fabulous memory of both pitch and rhythm.

The routine of the live show at the Roxy varied considerably, but its main outline was (1) to a big fanfare the pit was raised and the Pennsylvanians went into one of their typical presentation numbers. Rather soon we ran out of these set arrangements and had to invent new ones, or at least bring old ones up-to-date. (2) The pit descended and we accompanied what would have been, in a vaudeville house, an opening turn: jugglers or acrobats or knife-throwers or animals, etc. These acts almost always carried their own dog-eared orchestrations, which we had to expand to fit our large orchestra. This was a mean, unrewarding job. (3) Then the Roxyettes would have their innings, dancing to a newly choreographed number that contained all the old, surefire clichés. This always required a fresh, clever orchestration. (4) Then there would be a vocal effort, either by a reigning star or group, or even the Waring choir, all requiring augmented or additional orchestration. (5) A long finale, based on a production idea, using all the performing cast. The pit was raised partway, adding the Pennsylvanians…and Fred…to the big picture. The finale required a completely new orchestration and was my most difficult and tiring task.

In the remote regions of the Roxy, on the third floor with a connecting door to the music library, there was a fairly large room that had been used by Rothafel for screening and evaluating new films. The windows were painted black. There were two large, comfortable black couches and a few straight wooden chairs, all painted black. On one wall there was a big white screen, but the facing projection equipment had been removed. With wooden horses and long plywood boards, I had two tables set up that would accommodate four arrangers. There was no piano; I deliberately omitted it so that one searching orchestrator couldn't cripple the others by playing reiterated fragments of his assignment. In a dire necessity, there was a battered box, far away, in a seldom-used rehearsal room, where a stymied arranger could try to work out his problems.

Zimmie set up similar working tables that would accommodate four copyists in his adjoining music library, saying happily, "This is going to be like old times."

The New Year's show was a sellout-knockout, but the trusting souls who remained for the picture started to leave in search of entertainment by the end of the second reel.

That pattern continued. It was disheartening to prepare a stage show that audiences acclaimed but then walked out on the film. That year of 1932, 20th Century Fox disgorged a record number of turkeys and sent them all, bust after flivver, to the Roxy. During the whole five-month engagement of the Pennsylvanians at the Roxy, only one picture ran for more than a week, barely staggering to a fortnight. Producing a new show every seven days put constant pressure on all concerned. There wasn't a civil tongue in the organization by the time Fred Waring and his outfit decamped.

....

In the middle of January, 1932, I received an unexpected offer from the Mask & Wig Club, associated with the University of Pennsylvania, to orchestrate and conduct their yearly all-male show, scheduled to go in rehearsal in February, opening at the Garrick Theatre in Philly in early March.

While I was in college, my relationship with Mask & Wig could be described as curious. In my junior year, when even then I was arranging for the best dance orchestras in town, in a foolish fit of misdirected devotion to my Alma Mater, I offered to score that year's M. & W. show for the dubious unpaid glory of the deed. My gift was summarily rejected. When the show was in rehearsal, surprise! surprise! I received a call for help from the professional arranger who had been contracted by M. & W. to score the show. I ended up orchestrating about one-third of the production and getting paid for my labor, all unbeknownst to those who snubbed me.

The rebuff that backfired had little to do with my disenchantment with M. & W., as then constituted. I believed that a college show with a student cast should be 100 percent a student effort, which includes conception, writing, composing, staging, and accompanying with a student orchestra conducted by a student.

Those principles were commendable, but were they strong enough to make me turn down Mask & Wig's offer? And how about my good, new job? How could I leave it when it had just begun? With a baby due in March? I decided to take the whole problem to Fred Waring.

He said, "I think that offer is a wonderful break for you. For an orchestrator to have to stand up and conduct his own score…in front of an audience…that's an education in itself. We will have to adjust matters so that you can do this Mask & Wig show."

I said, "You must be satisfied with the way our arranging team is operating."

"It's great! I had no idea we had so much writing talent in the organization. You haven't had to go outside once for help! But who will take your place?"

"No one. We'll split up the work a different way. Leo Arnaud will be given the big numbers to orchestrate, but Charlie (Henderson) will do all the assigning. You may have to hire a second piano player so that Frank Hower can have more time to score; he isn't very quick. Then I think we can get Don Bryan to do the fixing and adjusting that is necessary on the arrangements the acts bring in."

"You've got it pretty well worked out. But are you sure you can handle Mask & Wig? Haven't I heard through the clothesline that you're expecting a blessed expense any moment?"

"Not that quickly…only sometime in early March."

"Isn't that going to interfere with your work?"

"I've got the problem all figured out. You may not believe this, but it's true. My uncle Leon Basford lives next door to the hospital…Honest!…The nearest house to Mercer Hospital in Trenton, New Jersey. That's where Audrey's going to have the baby! Uncle Leon is loaning me a room where I can work on an orchestration while

Audrey's waiting. My cousin Ronny can run messages back and forth if necessary. I won't have to fall back a single page of score!"

Fred threw up his hands and said, "All this time I've been harboring a Machiavelli! Now he's going to bring another like him into this frightened world!"

....

The leave of absence granted me by Fred Waring stretched from the middle of February to the final week of March, giving me three weeks to orchestrate the show, a week to conduct it in Philadelphia, and another week for a modest road trip to Reading, York, Harrisburg, Pennsylvania, and Wilmington, Delaware.

When I arrived in Philly with my writing equipment, all ready to start orchestrating, I found that the score of the show was far from complete. So, discarding my proudly proclaimed principle concerning student participation in the face of a dire necessity, I pitched in to complete the songs, aided and abetted by my newspaper reporter friend, Bixley Reichner, and that piano player extraordinary, Joseph Follmann. We came up with all six missing numbers, one of which was "A Five Year Plan for Two," which gained a certain amount of notoriety. That title suggests that the permutations of the Soviet economy were of general interest to Americans as far back as 1932.

The name of the show was "Ruffneck," a typical collegiate lampoon of contemporary mores exposed against a background of Elizabethan times and characters.

The baby cooperated and arrived, a perfect tiny girl, on March 8, 1932, as I was scribbling notes next door, two days before I had to be in Philly for an orchestra rehearsal.

Fred Waring was right: The experience of conducting my own orchestrations was invaluable, in practical matters worth a couple of years in Juilliard. It was the start of my infatuation with the musical theatre, which has guided my entire working life. The episode also contributed to a frightening nightmare that plagued me for a number of years.

In Harrisburg, conducting a score in which I had written every single note, that I knew so well that I had conducted ten performances without a mistake, a score that I was so sure of I didn't even bring my conductor's music into the pit, suddenly, after a blackout in the second act, I *blanked* out! For a split second, *I did not know what came next!*

I gave an automatic downbeat and the band went along with the change music, unaware that there had been any crisis. Only Don Walker knew…and how he knew! As time went on, I did a lot of conducting, in recording, radio, and television, but never in the theatre, for that meant repeating the same music over and over again, the repetition that nearly brought me down that dreadful, covert, scary night in Harrisburg. It has been many years since the nightmare spawned by that episode has wakened me, but even now the memory of it hurries my pulse.

....

"Ruffneck" successfully terminated (Mask & Wig signed me to score and conduct their 1933 show, whatever it might be), I returned to Waring's Pennsylvanians at the Roxy, to the relief of a hard-pressed arranging staff, worn down by the necessity of scoring a new show every week. I have some vivid memories of the dear old Roxy. There was:

The Night the Mike Died: When our girls' trio rehearsed in a studio with our male chorus, there was an interesting vocal blend. The girls were far outnumbered by the men, but they added an interesting patina to the ensemble. Knowing that when they were exposed to the great tone-devouring cavern of the Roxy their sound would approximate that of bewildered mice, I finagled with the guardians of the motion picture equipment to give the girls their very own microphone, whose electrically boosted signals would emanate from the house speakers. This was very early in the use of electronic amplification in the theatre; it may have been the first time mixing live and amplified sounds had been tried. Since the whole idea was experimental, the connective equipment was rather makeshift, but at rehearsal it had worked nicely.

I don't know whether it was some joker who had pulled the plugs apart or the unallowed, for rise of the pit that did the damage, but when the antiphonal section of the Waring choir's specialty was reached, where the men and women alternately exchange declarative statements, the result sounded like an angry army of Volga boatmen being answered by a few cheeping sparrows. Fred looked rather ridiculous, calling mightily for triple-fortes and receiving only undernourished peeps. The disconnection was found before the second show, but the damage was done.

Then there was: The Princess Wah-Hoo-Ah. At some time in the past, the Roxy had presented a show glorifying the American Indian.

In their vast warehouse, they still had a set of spectacular feather headdresses for the Roxyettes and costumes to go with them. Russell Markert, at his witty end for a production idea to go with a Western picture, wanted to use those headdresses, somehow, anyhow. He remembered well the rocky pyramid with the priestess of the tribe seated at the top of it, singing her incantation as the curtain rose, while the Roxyettes kneeling, feathery heads bent forward, covered the rest of the stage in a breathtaking tableau. Since the accompanying film was the usual banality about a little white girl being raised by a bloodthirsty Indian tribe, Russell's brainstorm seemed appropriate.

So the word went out, and such was the velocity of casting news in the Big Stem that the very next day we had twenty-two genuine Indian priestesses, all from Brooklyn, with accompanists, all from the Mills Building, lined up to audition.

We had barely begun our boring task when Priestess #23 stalked in and took over. She claimed she was a full-blooded Sioux, standing six feet tall with a nose like an eagle.

Russell whispered, "She's perfect! All she has to do is sit on top of that pyramid and everybody in the house will know what our show is about!"

I, the cautious one, asked, "But can she sing?"

She saw us whispering and walked to the middle of the stage, announcing, "I am Princess Wha-Hoo-Ah. I have just returned from a triumphant engagement in Paris. I have many things to do today. My accompanist, Jacques," she indicated a short, dumpy, nondescript individual oozing down the aisle, "will give you my repertoire and my keys. Au revoir." She walked out.

Markert told the stage manager to dismiss the twenty-two hopefuls. He said to me, "Get together with her man and find out what she wants to sing."

As the party broke up with a lot of angry women, I approached Jacques. He was a five-foot-two beauty with a moist handshake. I said, "I'm Don Walker, the orchestrator. I have to know what the Princess will sing and set her keys."

He had a cute lisp, saying, "And my name is James…James Hotlingsworth. In Paris all my dear friends call me 'The American Debussy.' The Princess has decided to sing three selections in German from her favorite Schubert song-cycle. The numbers will all have to be orchestrated because we have only piano accompaniments."

I was shocked at the prospect of having to make three…count 'em…*three* extra orchestrations in what looked like a heavier than usual weekly arranging schedule. I immediately took the information to Markert.

Russell was indignant. "What does she think she'll be doing up on that rock? Entertaining the Ladies' Aid Society of Squeedunk? This is the Roxy! She'll sing one appropriate song, *in English!* Got any ideas?"

"Well, there's always 'Indian Love Call.'"

"That's it! One chorus of 'Indian Love Call' and zip!"

I got out of the controversy that ensued. Luckily, the Princess had signed her contract without benefit of agent and hadn't studied the fine print, agreeing to abide by staging directions of the producer and scream as she did, there was nothing she could do about it. I was ordered to prepare one chorus of "Indian Love Call" in her key.

During the week, there was much conjecture backstage regarding the exact sexual relationship between the Princess and her accompanist. An analogy to spiders could not be ignored. She seemed to be twice his size and ferocious; he was diminutive and pacific. One wag could not stop there, pointing out that after the small male arachnid had fertilized the large female's eggs, she had him for supper. There were all kinds of imaginative suppositions.

Then came the Friday morning dress rehearsal. The sound system boys, having scored a victory by successfully amplifying our girls' trio, had continued their adventurous experiments by implanting a microphone in the apex of the pyramid in the opening Indian set. Later they swore that the Princess Wha-Hoo-Ah had been notified of the location of the mike, which notification she had disregarded in the same manner as she had ignored any instructions. As a result, she kept trying to direct her "Indian Love Call" to all parts of the auditorium, back and forth, side to side. That's no way to treat a microphone, for the message came out "when I'm CALLING *YOU*—OO-OO-oo-oo-oo," with alternating crescendos and diminuendos, blasting one second and fading out the next. The engineer on the control board couldn't keep up with her. The Roxyettes were in stitches under their feathered headdresses, the orchestra in contortions, even Fred was wiping tears from his eyes.

Markert stood up, waving his arms. "Stop the music!" he cried.

There was silence, all except the Princess, who kept calling, "Yoo-hoo-Hoo-HOO-*HOO*-HOO-Hoo-hoo-hoo."

"Get that goddamn microphone out of that rockpile!" yelled Russell. "Not now," he added, as a couple of sound men hurried out. "Just turn it off now," he continued, "but get it the hell out of there by show time!"

With the offending mike silenced, the dress rehearsal continued. When our grandiose Princess at last sang it was a shock; out came a weak, amateurish soprano, nothing like the peremptory clarion that was her speaking voice.

At the end of dress rehearsal, there were the usual hurried calculations to find out exactly how much playing time there was in the new show. The projection was fifty-three minutes, eight minutes overtime! Drastic cuts would have to be made, or by the end of the fourth show the final picture would be thirty-two minutes late! Stagehands would be into costly overtime!

An easy cut that would save three minutes was the elimination of "Indian Love Call," jumping into the Roxyettes' routine immediately after the opening tableau, cutting the song of the Princess Wha-Hoo-Ah!

She was told the news just as the first showing of the picture was ending. She was offered her full salary just for sitting on top of the rockheap. But she had the pride of the Sioux to uphold! Throwing down her cloak and headdress, she stalked out, never to adorn the Roxy again. A cooperative stagehand, with a beak as bold as Wah-Hoo-Ah's, grabbed her discarded cloak, jammed on her feathers, and took her place on the pyramid just as the curtain rose.

Our mute substitute was content to sit quietly for a while, but then he began to feel that anyone holding such a commanding position should contribute something...anything...to the proceedings. Suddenly, in a rare lyrical passage while the Indian tom-toms were silent, our leader and teacher heard a sepulchral, disembodied voice chanting, "Hello, Fred...Hello, Fred," etc., and he had no idea where the muttered salutation was coming from. By this time, all instruments requiring wind were out of action, their players in the hysterics of suppressed laughter, leaving only the strings and percussion to carry the ball. Russell Markert subsequently tried hard to find out exactly what happened, but the stagehands, the Roxyettes and the musicians all closed ranks and clammed up, driving Russell out of what was left of his mind.

....

I'll never forget, because it happened to me:
The Case of the Astral Arranger. Near the end of April, after I had returned from the Mask & Wig show, Markert decided to base a production on "rain" songs. There was plenty of material. At the time

Anne Ronell, the organist, had a hit called "Rain on the Roof." There was Jack Lawrence's "The Wind and the Rain in Her Hair." Other appropriate songs we used were "April Showers," "I'm Always Chasing Rainbows," "Stormy Weather," and "Let a Smile Be Your Umbrella." Even with an expanded staff of arrangers, that show was the most demanding of our stay at the Roxy. As usual, I took on the longest and toughest orchestration, the interminable "Singin' in the Rain," the big finale.

Although the "Rainshow" was Markert's idea, he seemed to have extraordinary difficulty in staging it, holding back the release of numbers to be orchestrated until the music department was in despair. Naturally the Finale was the last routine to be set: I wasn't allowed to see it until late on Wednesday afternoon. Even then I wasn't allowed to work on it until I had seen a revised edition after the last Wednesday night show.

Having been running around, getting nowhere all day Wednesday, I longed for bed that early Thursday morning. Instead, I had to go to work, for the copyists who were to extract the Finale were due to arrive at 9 A.M., and I had to have enough pages by that time to keep them busy.

All my professional life, under great pressure, I have been able to produce a large quantity of orchestration in a limited amount of time by using Thomas A. Edison's system of catnaps. When I can go no further, if I stretch out, I can go to sleep almost at once, stay that way for twenty to thirty minutes, and awake refreshed with the problem that put me to sleep solved! This sequence can repeat about every eight hours, for an approximate total of forty-eight hours, after which I will not be available for some time. Such a session was facing me as I tackled the "Rain Finale."

All during Thursday, Markert kept sending me small but irritating changes in the Finale. Luckily, in my scoring, I had not reached the bars where those changes were to occur, so I and my copyists were not required to fix work that we had just recently completed. My eight-hour routine continued, Zimmie bringing me food and drink, my only exercise being the occasional dash to and from the MEN'S.

At 3 A.M. Friday morning, Zimmie, three copyists, and yours truly were all that remained working in the Roxy's Music Department. I had then been at my desk for nearly forty-eight hours, keeping going by my Edisonian catnaps. I had finished the score of the Finale up to the last sixteen bars and big coda. I had just dashed down a sketchy pencil sketch of those finishing bars, but try as I might, I could not bring myself to concentrate well enough to write out those bars in full score. I was out of gas, the tank was dry, I desperately needed one of those half-hour naps to replenish my rained-out brain. So, with my working light burning brightly, I lay down on one of those big black couches for that precious kip that would make me operational again.

If I oversleep, Zimmie'll wake me, I remember thinking.

When I awoke in that black room, I didn't know where, why, or who I was. It was so dark I couldn't locate the white screen. I had to prop my eyelids open with my fingers to make sure my optics were operating. I felt for and turned on my desk light. It was blinding! I looked over my working table. There were no score pages on it!

From afar I heard faint music, a strain of it sounded familiar. I opened the corridor door and ran down the dim passage toward what I had been told was Roxy's private observation post. The music kept getting louder! It was the arrangement I had been working on before I took a nap, the Rain Finale! Note for note!

I reached the door to the snoopie spot and flung it open, stepped inside as per posted instructions, and closed the door, then pushed the viewing slide open. There they were, the whole company and the full orchestra, just six bars away from where I had fallen asleep! What would happen?

On they came, bar by bar, beat by beat on a musical juggernaut that knew no stopping, right up to the last note I had written...AND BEYOND! Playing the notes I had in my head but couldn't make my work-worn fingers write? Pounding out the last strain of the final chorus and then the applause getting, trumpet screaming coda, just as I had planned it!

Russell Markert, in the house, blew his whistle and called, "That's great! Now you've got almost two hours to relax and polish any spots you're shaky on. Half-hour at eleven-thirty!"

I never found out how the "Rain Finale" was finished on time. Zimmie was very secretive. Did he get one of the other arrangers out of bed to finish my score? Did he, or one of the copyists, score it from my pencil sketch? Or was it possible that I woke up after my usual naptime, scored those last bars, and then lay down again, blacking out my memory of finishing the damn score in that black, black room?

Or was the ghost of Roxy involved?

....

P.S. From that crisis onward, I carried an alarm clock in my working briefcase. Not an electric one but the kind you wind by hand. Sometimes there are power blackouts.

....

When I returned to the Roxy after "Ruffneck," the climate was far different than it had been when I left. Then every Pennsylvanian had seemed fired with a passion to show Broadway that our outfit could make the Roxy successful by our own ability and determination. When I came back, DEFEAT was written on every face: The endless succession of miserable films had broken the spirit. Between shows most of our musicians were out sniffing about the Main Stem, searching for alternate employment, carrying the news that the ax was expected to fall at the Roxy any minute. The atmosphere in the huge house was not conducive to relaxation.

We weren't handed the pink slip until early May, revealing the incompetence of the management, which should have divested itself of the expensive Pennsylvanians weeks earlier. Our final show was nothing special, and we slunk away with a sigh, when our trumpets should have been blaring a triumphal exit.

It was the utter depth of the depression. There were no places of amusement that could afford the large, costly act called Waring's Pennsylvanians. Fred escaped to England and remained there a considerable time, playing every major golf course and even some of the minor ones. Veteran members of the band retired to their homes in Jackson Heights and trimmed grass in their backyards. Younger unmarrieds partied in Manhattan. I retreated to my parents' home in Lambertville, New Jersey, where Audrey and I could enjoy our new baby, Ann, with a grandmother handy to babysit. There wasn't much cash about for an out-of-work orchestrator, but I improved my forehand drive.

In the middle of the summer, I received a call from Bus Seeds to come to New York and organize, orchestrate, and conduct a recording session that would produce some Waring's Pennsylvanians' records without Fred. It was surprising how many members of the club had found other work and were not available. We patched together a group, filling in with top-level recording musicians who were probably musically better than pure Pennsylvanians, although not nearly as handsome.

With my managerial duties, I didn't quite have the time to orchestrate the entire date, so I gave one number of the four to Leo Arnaud, our versatile Frenchman. He produced an excellent score that included a fantastic first trombone part, one I would never have dared to write. Since Leo was going to play it himself, I confidentially O.K.'d the arrangement.

Leo and punctuality being two differing concepts, on the morning of the date, after I had met Bus Seeds for early breakfast, we decided to make sure he was getting himself ready for his important part in the 10 A.M., three-hour session. His phone rang and rang, but there was no response. We became worried. His ancient apartment house was only a couple of blocks away, so we decided to tackle the emergency in person.

At Leo's building, we went up to his room and hammered on the door. Nothing! The door had an old-fashioned lock with a big keyhole. Looking through it, there was Leo, fully dressed, sound asleep in a chair, directly facing the peeper. Within the room the phone was ringing, ringing, ringing!

Bus looked at his watch. "My God!" he groaned. "What are we going to do? It's nine o'clock already!"

"Go downstairs and get a key. We've got to get in this room! Somehow, anyhow!"

Bus was soon back. He said, "That attendant's impossible. What's worse, Leo has all the regular keys and they're inside! I asked for the master, but that damned clerk won't let me have it. He's strange, I can't even bribe him!"

I had had a flash while Bus was away; now I put it into action, going to the room of George Culley, our second trumpet player, who had his digs in the same apartment house. George was just leaving for breakfast, carrying his trumpet with him.

"George!" I panted. "Do you know the French reveille?" (George was a Canadian, Fred Culley's brother.)

"As a matter of fact, I do," he said. "I had to learn it in school."

"Well, you better limber up your lip; we're going to need some powerful notes."

At the locked door, George got out his trumpet and following my directions, placed the bell over that great big keyhole, and blasted a bugle call that would rouse a dead Frenchy. After about twelve noisy bars, an improvised tenor part was added to the vociferous tantara. Leo was awake and blowing! It was an interesting three-part fugue, with the telephone supplying a cantus firmus. I cut them off in a hurry, got Leo to open the door, and twenty-three skidooed before stunned tenants could revive and start screaming.

After that melodramatic prelude, the professional recording date seemed almost peaceful. There were no crises; everyone played well, Leo in particular. The hovering spirit of the absent Fred Waring should have been gratified.

....

After his exhausting five-month grind at the Roxy, I could well understand Fred Waring's need for a long recuperative vacation, but his protracted stay abroad seemed to extend far beyond that remedial need. It was probable that the question of his lengthy sojourn had a very simple answer: There was no work for Fred and his organization at that point in the American depression, which was exploring new lows in '32.

In that hard-up summer, Audrey and I came to an important decision. I had learned during the "Ruffneck" engagement that when I orchestrated for a theatrical production, the notes came easier and were more effective than when I wrote for radio. In some curious way, the combination of sight, sound, and story stimulated my creative ideas when sound alone did not. I had to admit that I was not pure musician, interested in only what the orchestra played, but a *theatre person,* deeply involved in the whole show, anxious to write notes that would enhance the performance.

If my future was to be in the theatre, there was only one place where I, at the age of 24, with a wife and a child, could learn my trade while making a living. That place was, of course, New York City where, in those days, almost all musicals were created.

So we decided to gamble our modest remaining funds and tackle the metropolis once again. This was to be my *fourth* assault on the ramparts of Levity Lane, counting (1) Tudor City, (2) Forest Hills, (3) Hotel Wellington, and (4) The Last Ditch.

Number four, above, was Jackson Heights in Queens, where an enclave of the married members of the Pennsylvanians had taken root during the long Roxy engagement. We went where decent, furnished apartments could be rented, where Audrey could contact members of the "Waring Wives" when she yearned for female companionship, where we would be near our dear friends, Don and Lois Bryan.

Don Bryan was a famous trumpet player, in later years Don Voorhees' Number One assistant. In the past our paths had crossed several times, in odd places. I had first heard him play in 1927, in the Ben Bernie Orchestra, almost every night when I was hoofing it from the job I was playing in Bradley Beach, New Jersey, down the boardwalk to my sleeping quarters in Allenhurst. I would stand in awed attention outside the open window of the Berkley-Carteret Hotel in Asbury Park, listening as Don Bryan traded hot licks with tenor sax Jack Pettis. Two years later, when Bernie opened the Royal York in Toronto, I sat in an alcove of the Roof Garden, listening to the band, finally meeting Don B. the night before Bernie left. When I joined Fred Waring in Cleveland in '31, there was Don Bryan, blowing the lights out from the First Trumpet chair! It was one of those naturals; we were close friends by the time the band got to the Roxy. When our wives met, they immediately clicked! Audrey and I found a furnished apartment in Jackson Heights, only a short go-cart stroll away from the Bryans.

In the late fall of '32, Bus Seeds finally put together the bookings for an extended tour of the Pennsylvanians. It included "presentation" theatres, hotels, and night clubs. The personnel was reduced to the barely essential men, but those lucky enough to hold jobs had to be very versatile.

At last Fred returned from abroad and went into rehearsal with a band that was almost fifty percent new. Most of the old reliables, like Poli McKlintock, had hung on during that long period of drought, being sure that Fred would eventually sally forth again. The deserters of the ship were the brilliant young musicians, later additions to the orchestra, who out of dire necessity had found other life-sustaining jobs; they had to be replaced.

I stuck with Fred Waring while certain numbers, scored for the Roxy, were reduced to fit the much smaller personnel of the new traveling orchestra. There were also some recent song hits to be added to their repertoire. It was then that I was told by Bus Seeds that the budget could no longer afford a traveling, non-playing arranger, news that I had anticipated weeks before.

"You're not upset?" asked Bus, in surprise, after I hadn't cracked up when he gave me the shaft.

"Not at all," I assured him. "Last October One I signed a lease for a year in Jackson Heights. Now I don't have to worry about breaking it."

"Oh," said Bus. "You want to stay in New York."

"Of course, and if you need a new orchestration, there's always the Postal Service...just as we used it while I was in college."

So Fred and his reconstructed Pennsylvanians took off on a long, long tour. Occasionally I would be commissioned by mail to make a new orchestration for Fred, assignments that in time became embarrassing as I became increasingly involved in radio shows, with their steady weekly musical requirements.

After about a year and a half...or was it two years?...

I received word that Fred's tour was ending and he was bringing his Pennsylvanians into New York to make a pilot radio program for Old Gold cigarettes and would I "hold myself in readiness to attend rehearsals and orchestrate whatever new material that is deemed necessary?"

It wasn't easy, but I arranged for substitutes to handle my regular radio programs for a week while I helped Fred prepare for his big new chance in an unfamiliar medium, advertising what was for him a strange product, since he didn't smoke himself and hated the habit in others.

I attended rehearsals and made myself ready and equipped to do whatever adjusting and fixing in the parts that Fred wished. He never asked me to orchestrate an entirely new number. In fact, he seemed to be afraid to allow any new music into the program, determined to depend entirely on old, tried, and true material that had been conceived for visual entertainment, with sound only a byproduct.

By the end of the week, Fred was obliged, by union rules, to give the musicians a day off from his endless rehearsing and miniscule changing of ancient orchestrations. The mandatory respite gave me time to assess the discontent that had been growing within me, all through that unhappy week. It also gave me the opportunity to do something about my dissatisfaction. I sat down and wrote a letter to Fred Waring.

As is my custom with serious decisions, when I had finished the letter I gave it to Audrey to judge.

"Whew!" she exclaimed. "That's awfully strong. Do you really mean it?"

"I certainly do," I replied. "You should have seen my first draft...the one I tore up."

"I don't know about this," she warned. "It's rough. Tell you what you should do: Isn't Don Bryan off today with the rest of the band?"

"Of course. Fred added him for safety. and he's on the same schedule as the rest of the band."

"Well, before you mail this bombshell, have Don read it."

By this time, heady with the thrill of composition, I was itching to get the letter, special delivery, into the box, but I deferred, trusting as usual to Audrey's instincts. I went around the block and found Don Bryan washing his car.

He dried his hands and started to read the letter. He began to smile, then laughed, then hooted. He said, "Oh, God, how I have wanted to say some of these things to him...."

"You like it?" I asked. "Think I should send it?"

He stopped laughing. "Of course not," he said, shaking his head. "Waring is a very important man in our business. He could ruin you if he wanted to...and I feel that he just might want to after reading this shocker. Quit if you have to but burn this" (He shook the letter) "before the wind catches it. It's too dangerous to have around!"

So I took his advice, went home, and wrote a *third* letter. Although the rough draft of it has vanished along with its predecessors, I remember it fairly well. It went like this:

Dear Fred,

Ever since that crazy day when I snuck into your dressing room in the Stanley, not to be thrown out as I deserved, but in the morrow handed two recording numbers to orchestrate; ever since then I have always thought of myself as a Waring's Pennsylvanian. Your trust and confidence in an unproven kid arranger was extraordinary and has directed my life. I will be everlastingly thankful to you for the interest and advice you have given me, as well as the profitable musical assignments that have helped sustain me and mine in these desperate times.

I am sure that you understand that during your recent protracted road trip, the income from the work you have sent me has not been even close to sufficient to maintain me and my family in the Metropolitan area; by necessity I have had to find additional sources of revenue. I now have several steady accounts in the commercial radio field that guarantee subsistence.

Since you have been away, I have orchestrated, conducted, and co-composed another Mask and Wig show: "Out of the Blues," in the spring of 1933. You must remember that you encouraged me and gave me "leave of absence" to do "Ruffneck" while we were at the Roxy. From the valuable experience of handling those two Mask & Wig shows, I have come to the conclusion that although radio work is keeping me solvent at the present time, the Broadway theatre is my true goal, the musical environment where whatever talents I may possess could reach their greatest fulfillment.

If I can become an orchestrator of Broadway musicals, such a career will inevitably lead me away from Waring's Pennsylvanians.

This past week, I took leave of absence from all my regular radio programs in order to be available to you during your preparation for your big chance in a new medium, one in which I have had a great deal of experience during the last two years. I have sat through all your rehearsals, ready and uncomplaining, in order to make adjustments for radio purposes in your "presentation" repertoire. At all times, I was prepared to score whole new orchestrations if you wished. To my frustration, all that I was asked to do was to "smooth out and make musical" certain rough cuts and segues in some of the oldest orchestrations in your books, jobs that could be done by any one of several members of the organization that you have brought in from the road.

Is it any wonder that I felt useless, sitting there, doing nothing worthwhile, listening to arrangements that were made for the stage, knowing that they won't work very well on radio?

So, Dear Fred, I beg to be released from my non-helpful role in your new, exciting venture. May you and the Pennsylvanians be a big hit! Please remember, if you call, I will always be ready to clear the decks and do my best for you.

I will never forget that you gave me my first big break, as you have to many other young people. I will shout that fact whenever I have the opportunity to do so.

With regret,
DON

I never received an acknowledgement of that fateful letter. Neither did I ever converse or correspond with Fred again. To paraphrase Howard Dietz, we got along very well without the other.

Risking the sin of tiresome reiteration, I once more confess my indebtedness to Fred Waring for setting me on a path to a far more interesting career than most people have the luck to pursue.

3. <u>Al</u> (Albert Goodman)

Going back to the end of 1932, after Fred Waring and his Pennsylvanians had left on the tour that lasted almost two years, the Don Walkers settled down in Jackson Heights, Queens. I was determined to make a success of my *fourth* attack on New York City and the opportunities it offered to an orchestrator of music. I knew that I could expect, via the mail, the occasional assignment from Fred, but never enough work to keep us financially afloat. I was ready to score anything, including the detested "stocks," if the recompense was adequate.

To my relief came an offer from that Mask & Wig club of Philadelphia to repeat my stint of '32 with their '33 production. Naturally I was delighted to accept their offer since it affirmed their satisfaction with my previous "Ruffneck" job while giving me one more paid experience of standing up and conducting a musical comedy orchestra playing my own orchestrations. The proposed fee was very satisfactory, but the production did not go into rehearsal until late February and there was a nasty problem of subsistence till then. To heighten the tension, Audrey reported that she thought she was pregnant again.

The scene shifts to Don Bryan's apartment, where we were having a neighborly chat. He was in a position similar to mine: He had passed up that long road trip with Waring and was trying to "make it" in New York. On this occasion, he was feeling great.

"Yesterday," he announced, "I got a good job! Al Goodman's taking over 'Your Hit Parade,' and I'll be playing third trumpet!"

"Third?" I asked in surprise. "How come you're not playing first?"

"Because Charlie Margolis is on first and Manny Kline's on second."

"Wow! That's some kind of section! The top Gabriels! But isn't Al Goodman a show conductor?"

"He is…the best. But now he's branching out into radio."

"Ordinarily, I'd not call leading 'Your Hit Parade' branching out. I'd say it was branching back, with its 'Happy Days Are Here Again.'"

"Al wants everything different from the last schmaltzer. He sold George Washington Hill a real swingin' band. Up-to-date…Modern."

I can't believe it. How can an old tomcat like G. W. Hill change his spots?"

"He must have rabies or something…SAY!"

"Now what?"

"Al needs an arranger! Not one of those square show guys he usually works with, but somebody new…present-day…YOU!" He calmed down. "What are you doing Monday?"

I said, "The same as every other day…nothing much."

"You're coming with me to see Al Goodman. Bring a couple of your best Waring records."

"They're too icky."

"Not 'Jericho' and that new one we made last summer."

"'New Sun in the Sky'?"

"That's it!"

....

Early the next week, I met Al Goodman. He was of average height, strong and stocky. I could visualize him forcing an unruly chorus to follow his baton. In the twenties, I had been told, his engagement as musical director almost guaranteed the success of a show. In spite of his aura of absolute authority, the twinkle in his eye betrayed the fact that there was a warm human being present. We got along together at once.

He asked me a few questions and listened carefully to my records. He selected two numbers from a pile of piano copies and handed them to me, along with a mimeographed sheet listing the orchestra combination.

"Make these between three and three-and-a-half minutes each," he instructed. "Give me good solid arrangements with plenty of melody. Don't get too fancy. The boss likes to be able to whistle the tune along with the radio speaker. We rehearse Saturday morning at ten, Studio 8H in the RCA building."

"How about the copying?" I asked.

"You're responsible for it. Include it in your bill."

That's all there was to the negotiations. It was just like Waring after that Chinese lunch. I wondered, *Why are these conductors so confident that I'll turn up at the right moment with the right baby? There must be something about me that inspires confidence…or is it that deadpan covering up the fact that I'm scared stiff?*

So I went home and got to work, first on Irving Berlin's ballad "How Deep Is The Ocean?" I had decided to make that arrangement as broad and full and cantabile as possible. As soon as I had that score finished, I called in my good, slightly mad copyist, Romo Falk, and turned the number over to him, warning that "You should get this copied as soon as possible because there's another, more difficult score in the works, both arrangements to be ready at 10 A.M. this coming Saturday."

Then I got started on "Get Happy," that exciting tune by Harold Arlen. As I played it over and over in my mind, I kept phrasing it in an odd, staccato way, using a biting, rhythmical attack that I had heard jazz improvisers employ while faking variations on other standard tunes. I had never seen that particular anticipation written out before. After some thought and foot-beating, I figured out how to get it down on paper. The more I played it over in my head, the more I liked it. I began to imagine successive developments of the syncopated phrase, even the climatic ending! I said to myself, *The devil with George Off-the-cob Hill! If he can't whistle this, it's his problem, not mine.*

I wrote that arrangement at frantic speed, ideas coming so quickly that my fingers could hardly keep up. When I handed the score to Romo on Thursday night, he took a quick look and said, "You're out of your swingin' mind."

I said, "Look, Romo, I appreciate your concern, but if this scorcher doesn't work, I just have to go back to square one, that's all. But I *know* it's going to work, I can hear it working <u>in</u> *my head!*" He went back to his copying bunker.

On Saturday morning, the instrumental parts of my two arrangements were ready. When Romo handed me "Get Happy," he didn't say a word, just rolled his eyes up into his forehead and crossed himself. He whispered, "Have you looked over this band yet?"

I really hadn't, having just arrived, but now I checked. "Who's the drummer adjusting his cymbals?" I asked Romo.

"Only Chauncey Morehouse."

"And the character tuning his guitar?"

"Eddie Condon."

"Gee! And the rest of the rhythm section?"

"The poor man's Artie and the rich one's Arthur: Bernstein on bass and Schutt on piano."

I was in awe, saying, "I can't believe my eyes. Benny Goodman and Jimmie Dorsey side-by-side on alto saxes...."

"And clarinets, with Larry Binyon on tenor and flute!"

"Who's filling out the sax section on baritone?"

"Whiteman's loss and our gain, the great Strickfadden."

"The ultimate trumpets I know: Charlie, Manny, and Don."

Romo said, "It must be the finest dance band that could be assembled in the whole wide world."

"But what if they don't like what I wrote? They could tear apart everything I've scored!"

"Don't worry about that. They are all top professionals. They'll play anything you invented, and I copied as if it were pure gold. Just hope Al likes it...and most of all, *George Washington Hill!*"

Romo crossed himself again as Al tapped his stick on his music stand, saying to the orchestra, "We'll take the signature song to warm up."

They played "Happy Days Are Here Again" seriously, no one satirizing it, a very disciplined group.

Then Al had the parts of "How Deep Is The Ocean?" passed out. As far as I was concerned, those great musicians read it perfectly at sight, but after hearing it Al had some dynamic emphases he wished to introduce. The men had their pencils out and marked their parts.

"Isn't he going to rehearse those accents?" I asked Romo.

"Why waste time?" he replied. "Al will get exactly what he wants on the show with that bunch of musikers."

Al called me to his stand and said to me, "That arrangement's exactly what I wanted. Full and rich, plenty of color and lots of melody, *but not too fancy!* You're in, kid, you're in!"

It was thrilling to hear that acceptance, but I knew I had "Get Happy" coming up, in which I certainly had not treated the melody with reverence. What would happen then...would I be in, or instantly out?

From the first downbeat of "Get Happy," each member of that great orchestra seemed to realize that he was being challenged and was welcoming the combat. They tore into that orchestration with all the verve of a high school bugle corps. Excited by the unfamiliar rhythmical notation of phrases heretofore limited to ad libitum solos, they buried their noses in their instrumental parts. As the organized madness approached its finish, reaching the final chromatic triplet variation, the players suddenly stood up as one, the moment was too impassioned for sitting. The number ended with a bang, at its peak of intensity. There were various yells of approval, topped by Tommy Dorsey, who threw his trombone up in the air (and caught it), cheering.

It was scary, seeing these hardened performers so moved. I wanted to hide, afraid of the consequences of the furor I had caused. I could see Al waving me to come to the podium.

While almost everyone in the band was noodling, practicing passages with which they had some trouble, Al said to me, "Kid, that's one of the greatest jazz arrangements I've ever heard, but I don't know if Mr. Hill is going to stand for it."

I argued, "Look at the score, Al. There isn't a note changed in the melody of 'Get Happy' until the wild triplet variations in the last sixteen bars, and even that finish is based on the original melody. Mr. G. W. can whistle the tune against any part of the orchestration." I showed him where the melody was clearly laid out in the score. I explained, "Only the rhythmic attack has been changed to give that hurrying impulse."

"Maybe we can get away with it," temporized Al. "I've never seen this bunch of hard cases so whipped up; if I don't let them play your brainchild, they'll never forgive me."

The following Saturday at the orchestra rehearsal, the account executive from the advertising agency told me that "Get Happy" had made the regular Saturday night party at George Washington Hill's country estate a big success.

So that was one way to get a steady job that lasted through two seasons, the first of three engagements I would have with the Lucky Strike Hit Parade.

4. George M. (Cohan)

In the spring of 1933, I was once again offered the post of orchestrator/conductor of the annual production of the Mask & Wig Club of Philadelphia, the traditional all-male show with a cast made up of students in the University of Pennsylvania. Although my financial status had vastly improved since working for Al Goodman, I did not wish to turn down the opportunity to gain more practical experience in the creative stages of the musical theatre, no matter how sophomoric the vehicle.

Just as Fred Waring encouraged me, making it possible for me to be musical director of 1932's "Ruffneck," so Al Goodman gave me leave of absence to function in the same capacity for 1933's "Out of the Blues." Al was a theatre man himself and understood my aspirations.

When I returned to New York after the short road trip of "Blues," "Your Hit Parade" was just closing up shop for the summer. However, Al was facing a much greater challenge. He was to be the musical director of a summer radio series—starring George M. Cohan, who would be appearing on radio for the first time, presenting every song he had published, singing some himself, casting professional vocalists for others, and being his own commentator.

Well beforehand I conferred with Al regarding the usefulness of the printed general-purpose orchestrations of Cohan's many hits and the manuscript pit arrangements he had saved from his shows. We agreed that it would be foolhardy to try to use that material, for none of it had been scored with the physical circumstances of radio broadcasting in mind. Yet the old scores had to be studied for any inherent distinctive features, characteristics that were as much a part of a piece as the melody, without which George M. would be uncomfortable.

It all added up to many, many pages of score. Much of Cohan's music is in rapid 2/4 time, as fast as 132 beats per minute. That pace devours written music, making page turning a problem and leaving wind instrumentalists gasping. It also makes an orchestration feel endless, eating up all those pages of manuscript in so little time.

That summer I had personal problems. I was a bachelor, Audrey having retired to my parents' home in Lambertville to await our second child, scheduled for an early September delivery. In the hectic preparations period for George M.'s radio debut, it seemed that it was necessary for me to consult Al every day, sometimes more than once a day. Between running into New York from Jackson Heights, trying to get myself three meals a day and sleeping four hours a night, I found that I was falling behind with my orchestration.

In my quandary, Mrs. Goodman saved my neck (and my stomach). Although I didn't know it at the time, a few months before the Cohan project the Goodmans had lost a son to a lingering, incurable illness. Seeing the predicament I was in, she kindly invited me to move in with them until the Cohan crisis was over. There was an unused room available, she said.

I have always hoped that my presence during those two hectic months helped her as much as she helped me. She treated me as a son, I gained ten pounds on that rich Hasidic food, sitting on my tuchis, scoring, scoring.

Al would often use me as liaison between himself, living on Riverside Drive and Cohan, in his house on the eastern side of Fifth Avenue in the lower seventies. A great deal of my coordinating was done with John McLaughlin, George M.'s piano accompanist, drinking partner and jokesmith. We would set George's keys and musical routines by mutual agreement in that narrow, second-story front room overlooking Fifth Avenue, where Cohan's transposing piano was located, that rare oddity whose twin I was not to see for sixteen more years.

At that time (1933), George M. Cohan was starring in the leading role of the Theatre Guild's solid hit, Eugene O'Neill's "Ah, Wilderness!" and here was this sixty-six-year-old man taking on the planning, production, and performance of five one-hour radio programs to be aired on Sunday nights, robbing him of his only possible day of rest. What energy! He was hardly human!

As a little footnote to his extraordinary endurance, I must report that six days a week George *walked* through Central Park and down

Seventh Avenue to the Guild Theatre, just to stay in shape! Although Prohibition did not officially end until December 5 of 1933, one can be sure there was an obliging pub along the trek, where George and Johnny could obtain Old Grand-Dad spiked with Abbott's Bitters, which would help keep the stumps moving.

My most cherished memory of George M. was born on a day in June, 1933. Al Goodman had sent me to see him to check on a routine that seemed suspiciously incorrect. I was admitted to his Fifth Avenue home about eleven o'clock in the morning. We went immediately to that second-story front room, where the transposing piano was located. For once, John McLaughlin was absent, and I was alone with George. We were trying to straighten out the kinks in the routine of a song when we heard, from afar, a "roll-off" (the traditional percussive introduction to a march played by a parading band) and the first strains of "National Emblem."

We listened for a moment, long enough for the Doppler effect to tell us that a band was advancing in our direction. George walked to the big front windows that looked out on leafy Fifth Avenue and across the street to Central Park.

"After all," I said, "we can expect this kind of an interruption today. It's June fourteenth, Flag Day."

"Correction, my bright young friend," said George. "Don't you know that the fourteenth of June is a bastard holiday that can be used by any State in the Union to honor anything that particular State wishes to praise? I don't care how many States choose to celebrate The Flag on this day. Here, in the State of George Michael Cohan, the fourteenth of June is *Army Day!*" He turned to watch the approaching band, which was followed by a long, street-wide column of smart-looking troops.

As the soldiers passed, George M. spoke as if to them, forgetting my presence. "There you march," he declaimed, "each one of you the pride of your parents, the cream of our youth. When you are called on to stand between us and the enemy, who wishes to rob us of our precious freedom, you will not flinch! So now you march…right, left, right, left, strong, determined and ready! Staunch supporters of our way of life!" He applauded the column, raising his voice: "Give it to 'em, boys, give it to 'em! Stand fast! No retreat! Charge! Charge! Char…!"

Suddenly aware of me, he stopped cheering in mid-charge. Somewhat sheepishly, he said, "With all that going on out there, it's hard to concentrate, eh, kid?"

I agreed, thinking, *So this is the <u>real</u> George M. Cohan! All that I have considered chauvinism, phony patriotism, that born-on-the-Fourth-of-July flag-waving, even the dog-eared clichés, are in actuality honest expressions of conviction! Unbelievable as it may seem, the man is sincere! Rock-bottom, undeviatingly genuine!*

I continued my work with George M., regarding with newfound respect a man who had complete belief in himself and his own opinions, no matter how plebeian they might be.

....

The summer of '33 dragged on and with it my in-depth exploration of George M. Cohan's catalogue of published songs. By the time I had finished orchestrating the second of his five radio programs, I had become exceedingly bored with the crude harmonic content of his compositions. I could not quibble with his lyrics and melodies: They were untouchable, many of them having reached the status of established folk songs.

It was his harmonic structure that irritated me, for he had only the one, that one being the simplest harmony possible, the most unrefined, the supremely obvious. I grew desperate, fearing that under such influence I was writing dull, unimaginative scores.

At that point, I took account of stock. Rejecting other opportunities, I had chosen music, specifically orchestration, as my occupation, which had been the sole support of my growing family and myself for over four years. Now I was faced with my most important assignment, working in close collaboration with a famous star of the theatre, and I feared that I was going sour on the job. What could I do to get interested?

For some forgotten reason, my mind skidded back to the Roxy and the day that the librarian-head copyist, Edwin Zimmerman, disgusted with a messy pencil score I had handed him, decided to teach me a lesson. He reached up to a high shelf and brought down a large, dusty score and spread it open on a table. "There," he said, "isn't that beautiful?"

It was a complete partitura of the opera "Martha," and what it was doing in the Roxy I have no idea. Written in ink, by a fine Italian hand, it was as pretty as a musical score could be, which isn't exactly heaping on praise.

I said to Zimmie, "No wonder this score is so neat. It's a copy. Von Flotow, the composer, was a German and the lyrics here are in Italian."

Zimmie knew his stuff. He replied, "As a matter of fact, the original libretto was in French! But what difference do *words* make? It's the notes...the *music* notes that count. This Score is crystal clear; there is absolutely no guessing on the question, 'What are the correct notes?' Look at *your* score: This one you just handed me...half the notes are problems, are they this or are they that? Are they on spaces or lines? If you had thought a little bit longer before you started to write, you wouldn't have had to score in pencil and make so many erasings and corrections. You could write in ink like a real professional."

Zimmie's final remark stung me. I thought that I was already a pro. At that point I vowed to learn to score in ink, but that pledge was soon overrun by the usual imbroglio on the day before the change of show. After that crisis was over, I had forgotten about my promise to myself, but now here I was with a personal crunch that required drastic treatment.

So I went to an enormous stationery mart and picked out two fine-pointed, gold-plated fountain pens, a bottle of Higgin's Engrossing Ink, a packet of heavy tissues for pen-wipers, a packet of ink erasers (this was before the days of electric erasers), a dozen Gem razor blades (for scratching out notes), and a package of heavy-duty blotters...all the paraphernalia I would need to score in ink...wondering all the time whether or not my substantial investment in equipment was going to be used...what if I couldn't summon the discipline to orchestrate in ink?

The shift in physical technique worked. By thinking longer before I rushed to write, I found that I was avoiding awkward passages, making smoother transitions, giving musicians more time to change instruments, adjust or remove mutes, move to microphones, or return to their original seats. (This was 1933.)

I also discovered that I was writing faster with a pen and that my fingers, hand, and arm did not tire as quickly or as painfully as they did when pressing a pencil.

It was only natural that the first people to notice the change in my penmanship were my copyists, who were delighted upon getting much easier-to-read scores. The shift was not as obvious to the playing musicians, only the most astute realizing that there had been a subtle change for the better in the passage of inner voices in all my scores. That was a profit from scoring in ink that I had never expected.

....

Adding to the dither surrounding the final episode of George M.'s five-part magnum opus was a personal problem…as personal as a problem can get: Our second child decided that it was time for him to make his debut. Once again I borrowed a room in my Uncle Leon's handy house next door to Trenton's Mercer Hospital and kept scoring music until the delivery was over. Looking at David, our second child, I wondered how such a long, scrawny baby with jaundice could ever develop into a healthy citizen, but he did, beautifully.

Kissing my happy, relieved Audrey, I hurried back to New York to sit with the sound engineer as he turned his dials on George M.'s last program. By that time, George had actually run out of hit songs and filled in with an excerpt from his melodrama, "The Tavern," which only needed a few ominous musical cues instead of a big orchestration. With one ensemble chorus of "I'm a Yankee Doodle Dandy," which I had scored for the first program, the seemingly endless job was over.

In the radio world, George M.'s series of programs was deemed a great success and everyone connected with it profited. I found that in that milieu, I was in demand. Now I had the pleasant task of sorting out my opportunities. Keeping in mind my desire to write for the musical theatre, I decided to take only those radio jobs that were financially necessitous, now that I had a wife and *two* children to support.

In the spring of 1937, George M. Cohan wrote a march and gave it, with its royalties, to one of his many charities, this one located in St. Louis, Missouri. Its first performance was to be at a large concert in that city.

He contacted me and begged me to orchestrate the piece and see to the copying of the instrumental parts. Since it was for a charity, he asked me to be charitable. Since I was being asked by George M. Cohan, whom I wanted to please, I agreed.

There was a small budget for the job, enough to pay the copyists. My payment was the handwritten letter (in pencil!) that he sent me, which I have carefully preserved. The contents appear below:

New York, N.Y.7
April 15, 1937, 4:30 PM
Donald J. Walker
% Chappell and Co. Inc.
R.K.O. B'ld'g, Room 208
Rockefeller Center;
New York, N.Y.   *Thursday.*

Dear Don Walker—

Enclosed find check for bill for scoring and copying the march.
Of course I know very well that is about one-third of what it should be, and I want to thank you ever so much for your kindness and interest in the matter.
I sent the stuff to St. Louis by airplane yesterday.
Hope to see you soon again and have another nice chat and maybe see another parade.
Thanks again, Don, and best to you always.

Geog. M. Cohan

There was something about the man that made one love him, in spite of the well-advertised combativeness.

5. <u>Rommy</u> (Sigmund Romberg)

I knew a modest amount about Sigmund Romberg before I met him in person. It was common knowledge that he was born a Hungarian Jew of a well-to-do family, immigrated to New York City, became a citizen of the United States, and led salon orchestras in some of the better metropolitan restaurants, in particular the famous Bustanoby's, in the years between the turn of the century and the First World War.

During that war, he became a workhorse composer for the brothers Shubert, finally leaving them to compose a surprising number of sensationally successful operettas in the twenties.

I had learned about Romberg mainly from Bobby (Robert Emmett) Dolan, a friendly pianist I had met while we were working on the same radio program. Concurrently, Bobby was arranging the vocal score of an operetta that Romberg was writing, to be produced in Paris, with the rather unimaginative title "Rose de France." Bobby, who grew up in Montreal, Canada, spoke French like a native and had been engaged by Romberg to not only make the vocal arrangements of "Rose de France" but to go to Paris with him when the show went into production and teach the French choristers their parts.

Bobby and I hit it off immediately, and so did our wives. We all became close friends. He had recently married Vilma Ebsen, who with her brother Buddy made up a featured dance team then performing in the hit revue "The Bandwagon." Children of parents who ran a dance academy, hoofing was in their blood.

One day I met Bobby by appointment at the cubbyhole Romberg had in the Broadway warrens. The Boss was absent, but a score on which he was working was spread out on his desk. I couldn't help peeking. To my amazement, there was one beautiful score in small, dainty notes in ink, then right beside it a half-finished score page with heavy black-as-black notes, somewhat messy but readable.

I pointed to the pages and said, "Looks as if somebody's copying this elegant score...somebody in a hell of a hurry."

Bobby explained, "That's Romberg. You can't write as fast as he does and have it look pretty."

"But why is he copying somebody else's score?"

"He hasn't time to score all of "Rose de France" himself, so he's hired Hans Spialek to do part of it."

"But why is he copying Spialek's score?"

"Oh, that's because of those nosey French musicians. In France, in fact, in all Europe they still hold to that old-fashioned doctrine: that a composer isn't really a composer unless he orchestrates the music he creates. Rommy has the ability to score every bar of this show, only he doesn't have the time to do it."

"But he has the time to copy it."

"He can copy five times as fast as he can score. You should see the ink fly around here." He pointed to the fat blots.

I was still confused, asking, "How would the French musicians know whether or not he scored a number?"

"He's going to conduct the opening night of this show, so he'll have to rehearse the orchestra himself. He'll come to that first rehearsal and put the scores on the podium. At the first break a musician who knows Romberg's handwriting will nonchalantly wander near the podium and take a quick gander at the scores. If he goes back and tells the rest of the orchestra that our boss didn't write everything himself...well, Rommy won't get the attention and respect he needs."

I was shocked, saying, "I can't believe that a man with the credits possessed by Sigmund Romberg would have to sink to such a cheap deception."

"It's not so cheap," replied Bobby. "Hans Spialek isn't cheap, especially when he isn't getting credits, I'm not cheap and you...if you ever squeak this story I'll see that you're sent back to Lambertville, New Jersey, to arrange for the Fleetwing Fire Company Fife and Drum Corps."

Which could still happen!

....

So Romberg and Dolan went to Paris to rehearse and open "Rose de France" without me ever meeting the composer, although I seemed to know a lot about him. In preparation for Bobby's return, his wife, Vilma, bought an extra large box of soft pencils and a conductor's baton. She said, "I'm sick of him going down into that orchestra pit eight shows a week and hacking away at the ivories. I'm going to meet him on the pier when he gets off that boat and hand him these pencils and the stick. He's simply got to become a composer or a conductor or maybe both...forget that anonymous piano playing!" I thought it was fortunate that she was working in a hit show. It certainly influenced the attitude!

I was very busy, turning out as many orchestrations as I could possibly write in a new, larger apartment in Jackson Heights, opposite that legendary par-3 golf course, now long gone and covered with buildings. The aftermath of George M.'s summer programs had brought me many offers of radio work. The money coming in from the ones I had accepted was necessary and nice, but I was still uneasy, knowing that I was not getting any closer to my main objective, the musical theatre.

One day in the late winter of '33-'34, I received a phone call from Al Goodman, asking me to meet him at an address in the heart of the theatrical district. The address sounded familiar. I was still working for Al, who was in his second year on the Lucky Strike Hit Parade with his virtuoso orchestra, for which I scored a big number every week. I was accustomed to attending a weekly conference with Al in his apartment of fond caloric memory, but this was different, and why did the new address ring a distant bell?

When I reached the designated meeting place, I recognized the same hole-in-the-wall where I had met Bobby Dolan before he went to France: It was Sigmund Romberg's working hideout! To confirm my guess, after I knocked and was admitted, here was Al introducing me to the famous composer.

He said, "Rommy, I want you to meet my star arranger, Don Walker."

Romberg queried, "Dan Vawker?"

Al said, "That's right, *Don Walker*."

"Veil," said Romberg, extending a carefully manicured hand with long, pianist's fingers, "It's a pleasure to meet you, Dan Vawker." And for the next seventeen and a half years, in spite of constant corrections, that's what he called me, *"Dan Vawker."*

When we met that day, he was about forty-seven years of age, on the bottom leg of one of his eternal diets, looking a bit gaunt while remaining rotund and rather paunchy. A man of medium height, he gave the impression that once he had been much taller. Having lived a number of his formative years in Vienna, it was no wonder that he looked like the kind of man for whom Sacher invented the tort. He loved good, rich, expensive food, his worst enemy.

Behind his rather stern outward appearance lay a kindly, thoughtful gentleman with a healthy sense of humor, all of which I was to discover as I grew to know him better.

Al explained the purpose of our meeting. He said, "I have known Sigmund Romberg for a long time and have conducted several of his shows. So when he got an offer to do his thing on radio, I was the first person he called for help, since he knew that I had successfully made the leap from show biz to airwaves. I explained to him that I was so contractually tied up that it was impossible for me to participate in his projected program…except for a little free friendly advice from time to time…but I could give him the man who brought George M. Cohan out of the nineteenth century into the twentieth with his orchestrations. So that's the reason for this powwow."

Romberg explained. (I refuse to try to write out Rommy's patois using conventional symbols. It was never very heavy, and he turned it on and off. One regular feature was the interchange of double-yous with vees and vice-versa.) He said, "I have been approached by executives of the J. Valter Thompson advertising agency. I understand that it is one of the leading agencies…."

"It is," I said, "very reliable and successful."

"They vant me to make a trial one-hour concert program…."

"A pilot."

"Dat's the verd…a pilot, and if they like it and their sponsor likes it, I vill go on the air next fall, presenting twenty-six veekly programs, von after the other."

"Just music?"

"I'll have a commentator, I tink his name is Phelps…."

"Billy Phelps! Sounds terrific!" approved Al.

I, the practical worrier, asked, "How big an orchestra?"

"Around thirty, a couple more or less."

"Singers?"

"A chorus of eight and the usual four principals."

"And with all that, what do you play?"

Rommy said, smiling, "Vatever I vant to play."

I was incredulous. "Doesn't the sponsor or the agency have any program control?"

"Not really. All they tell me is vat they *don't* vant. Like lowbrow jazz and highbrow opera in foreign languages. That's why they got me, a middlebrow, to play middlebrow music."

Al asked, "Who thought up that term, 'middlebrow music'?"

Rommy answered demurely, "I guess I did."

Al hooted and said, "I can tell, right now, that you're going to be a hit!"

I still wanted details and asked, "When do they want this one-hour pilot?"

"Within a month. If the program is going to go on in the fall, the agency needs at least six months to prepare their end."

I looked at Al. My participation in Romberg's program depended on him releasing me. I said, "I never could score Mr. Romberg's audition while working on Lucky Strike."

Al said, "I know. You're a single-purpose character. Why do you think I asked you to this meeting today? This is the biggest chance you've ever had, and I'm ready to do without you for a month in return for the great, honest work you have done for me...and if, God forbid, this audition you're talking about isn't picked up, I'll welcome you back to George Washington Hill."

I was overcome. While trying to voice my gratitude, I began to retrograde to adolescent stuttering. Al stopped me.

"Don't blow your top," he advised. "You see, I owe Rommy a favor, but don't ask me to tell you why." He moved toward the door. "You two have plenty of problems to solve together, and I have another important meeting to attend. Just to satisfy my incurable curiosity, Rommy, would you mind letting me know who is the sponsor of your beautiful program, or is it a secret?"

"It's been in the trade papers...it's Swift and Company, of Chicago."

"Swift and Company! The meat packers! Beef and lamb and...Rommy...PORK! So how can a good Jewish boy like you go on the air advertising pork, Rommy?"

Rommy smiled and answered, "I'm hiring a private rabbi to sanction every program."

Exit Al.

....

Working together with Hershel Williams, the account executive from the J. Walter Thompson Agency, Rommy and I fashioned an audition dripping with massed strings and other reminders of turn-of-the-century Vienna. Rommy knew nothing about broadcasting music, that was my field, but when it came to selecting felicitous songs, that was his field, strengthened by the fact that he had lived in and loved Vienna when it was the capitol of the waltz. He introduced me and eventually millions of other Americans to music by Lehar, Friml, Kalmann, Herbert, Kreisler, and others, not to forget the single-s Straus (Oscar) and the double-s Strausses (Johann and sons). Added to all that wealth of material were Romberg's own copyrights, many of them substantial song hits of recent years. We were loaded with excellent program candidates, which spoke well for our ability to produce twenty-six different programs throughout the coming '34-'35 season, but first we had to select the very best of the crop and arrange them into a program that would encourage dear old Swift & Co. to buy the whole series.

The agency gave us the perfect writer for our audition script in Robert (Bob) Simon, a well-known music critic, but in the end it was Rommy himself who insisted on the "middlebrow" approach and the Viennese atmosphere. After about three weeks of thinking and writing and orchestrating and organizing, we were ready to go into a studio and wax a one-hour program.

At that point there was a large question mark, of which all the creative people, including yours truly, were well aware. We all knew that Rommy was a famous composer whose fecund imagination and European roots had been a determinative factor in the building of our program, but did he have the technical ability to conduct it effectively? None of us had ever seen him swing a stick, much less lead a large orchestra accompanying vocal soloists and chorus!

Rommy soon calmed our shaky nerves. His stick technique was essentially conventional, with the occasional addition of some highly individual gestures that were, nonetheless, readily understandable. He knew exactly what he wanted and how to get it, requisite talents for good conducting. Hard-boiled, skeptical instrumentalists took to him at once and did their cooperative best.

I can see Rommy now, conducting the majestic introduction to the "Emperor Waltz," which is not itself in 3/4 time. He explained to me that the original purpose of that lengthy, formal preparation was to summon the glittering couples to the ballroom from wherever they had been socializing, giving them time to get poised and ready. Then the conductor would start the famous oom-*cha*—cha vamp with the slightly rushed and accented second quarter-note and off they would go waltzing!

Rommy performed the whole routine, using hands, arms, and a swingin' tummy to emphasize the beat. Television's loss (it wasn't ready till after the war) was radio's gain, for just the way he brought in that three-quarter-time immediately created a mental picture of that bygone ritual of Hapsburg days.

Viennese waltzes are a fascinating study. Each one has its own idiosyncrasies while they all use, on broad melodies, that curious after-pulse. Rommy knew all the traditional tempos, the retards and accelerations, the holds and the hurries, the lifts and the spins. Best of all, he knew instinctively how to convey to his musicians and singers, inspiring them, the illusion that live dancing was occurring. He waltzed on the podium!

Years later, orchestrating Bock and Harnick's "She Loves Me," my experience with Rommy and his waltzes stood me in good stead, helping me create a nostalgic echo of Old Vienna.

....

Swift & Co., represented by the J. Walter Thompson Advertising Agency, did not hem and haw over Sigmund Romberg's terms for his program. Within a week after we had made the audition a jubilant, Rommy called me with the good news that he had signed for twenty-six Programs, starting in October '34 airing every Saturday night at 9 P.M., on NBC from Studio 8-H. He wanted to settle my business relationship with him, a matter we had never mentioned in the heat of battle. In his typical manner of conducting business matters, he invited me to lunch at Robert's (pronounced Ro-*bair's*), a famous haunt of serious epicures. When I asked him where it was located, he replied, "Thirty-three West Fifty-fifth Street." After he hung up, I realized that the address of the restaurant was the same as that of Rommy's apartment and I thought, *Oh, you bad boy, living in the same building with temptation...You'll never get your weight down!*

There was another guest at that so-called luncheon. I was introduced to Rommy's lawyer, Howard Reinheimer, a handsome, impressive man with a plentiful head of tight curly light brown hair, an adornment that was rather unusual in a New York lawyer.

Rommy said, "Howard settles all my contracts. That way I keep out of trouble."

We all had a good laugh and immediately put aside the pressing business that was the purpose of our meeting.

As we sat down, a waiter in livery appeared carrying a tray with three tall glasses containing a pale, bubby, pinkish tan iced liquid. My companions started to sip their drinks, but I held back.

Rommy noticed and exclaimed, "You're not touching your aperitif! I hope you're not a teetot'ler!"

I quickly disclaimed being such an unsocial person. I explained, "I can't take an alcoholic drink and orchestrate. Since I'm generally working in the middle of the day, I'm not used to having a snort at lunchtime."

"Umm...," said Rommy, I vouldn't call this drink a snort." He asked the other guest, "Howard, vill you have another wermouth cassis?"

Howard had had barely time to take a first sip. He shook his head, "I have plenty, thank you."

Rommy spoke to the hovering waiter, and pointing to my glass, he said, "The soda in that drink has stopped bubbling. Bring him a fresh one...and while you're at it, I'll have another."

As time went on, I learned that the incident of the aperitif was standard procedure with Rommy. He tried, without much success, to restrict himself to the foods on his doctor-supervised diet, but then he usually doubled or tripled the given quantities.

He announced, "Now I don't want either of you to worry about a menu. This is a day of celebration. Swift and Company have signed for twenty-six veeks, and all we have to do at this time is get organized to do the job. Already I have ordered the lunch, so ve don't have that problem to hold us up."

But we did have his idea of a light lunch to confront. It started off with escargots. Somewhere I had read that those alleged delicacies were actually deshelled snails, and my mind went back to my mother's War of the Nasturtium Beds, in which murderous conflict I had been an unwillingly drafted private. I had been taught to hate snails and to kill snails; now I was expected to chew and enjoy snails! Only by concentrating...hard...on Rommy's beaming face was I able to ward off regurgitative disgrace, that unthinkable, involuntary menace.

Suddenly our table was invaded by waiters who practically tore out of our hands the remains of our aperitifs, making room for the contents of a pale old bottle of wine that had been reverently brought into our presence by Robert, the propriétaire himself. He opened the precious flask with great ceremony and poured Rommy a sample. Receiving enthusiastic approval, he half-filled our fresh glasses. Apparently the vino in that bottle was so valuable, Robert wouldn't let any of his employees even touch it. When he set it down in an ice bucket, I saw the label, "Château Pavillon Blanc." I wondered if it was really worth all that fancy performance.

At about that time, I had begun to realize that Rommy was doing his best to please and impress me. If I hoped to have a continuing relationship with him, the least I could do would be to show him that I was enjoying his fabulous luncheon. So I started to lift the wineglass and the elbow at fairly regular intervals, while restricting myself to the tiniest sips possible.

The soup came. It was a marvelous homard (lobster) bisque that wiped the memory of the escargots from my vitals. Where I had been nauseated at the thought of more food, in a flash I was ravenous! I began to sample the interesting rolls and real butter.

My empty soup bowl was replaced by a delightful "salade vert," mixed as only a Frenchman knows how. I found that the rolls and butter went as well with the salad as they did with the soup.

The entrée arrived. I was informed that it was "Tornedos Henry IV." It looked big enough to satisfy Henry VIII. It was an extra-thick cut of tender beef fillet, wrapped with a strip of pork fat and set on a round of French bread, the whole creation drenched with hot (I think béarnaise) sauce. As I looked at it, my hunger deserted me, replaced by a feeling of fullness. The arrival of a red Château Dauzac in another fresh glass helped a little, but try as I did, I could not give that fantastic entrée the justice it deserved; there was no space left to shove it.

His tornedos a happy memory, Rommy asked to have the pastry cart brought to our table.

How pretty it looked! Loaded with fabulous concoctions, only one of a kind. Gateaus, tartes, éclairs, timbales, heavy with apricots, cherries, figs, and strawberries, all out of season. Not to forget the essential petits fours, which Rommy always ordered in large quantities because, obviously, they were non-fattening, being so little. Dessert selected, Rommy gave the waiter his customary order for coffee, which was: "Demitasse mit cream, mit sugar, and leave the pot right here." He needed plenty of liquid to wash down all those petits fours.

Howard had kept an intermittent conversation going between courses: anecdotes of the law, exploits of his young sons, scandals of showbiz. Now he looked at his watch and said, "Rommy, I've got to get back to the office. I came here hoping to help you settle your arrangement with Don Walker, but you haven't even started to discuss it. We'll have to set another date, and don't make it lunch or we'll never get organized!"

He left.

Rommy, pouring his fifth demitasse, said sadly, "Business, business, all the time business, that's our Howard. I don't remember ever hearing him laugh…that is, to really laugh *hard*. It's a shame; otherwise, he's a wery nice man."

I suggested that the two of us might try to arrange our money matters ourselves and no time was better than the present.

"No," Rommy said, "that vould only upset Howard. Tell you vaht, let's think about our deal overnight. You get together all the facts: the bars, the pages, the vorking time, the copying costs…all that. Tomorrow I'll call you and set a time for us to meet. *Then* we'll settle our problem!"

Putting off a hard decision to an agreed settling time pleased him as much as getting rid of the problem itself.

………………………………..

The next morning, while I was completing my summary of the complicated music costs of the Swift & Co. pilot program, Rommy phoned me. He was in a joyful mood.

He said, "Dan Valker, I think I've got our problem solved. I vas avake most of the night vorrying about it. Then I fell asleep for a vile and voke up as dawn vas breaking mit de answer!"

I said, "That's wonderful, Rommy. What is the answer?"

"Ah-hah, my young friend. I'm not going to tell you over the phone, I'm going to show you! Are you free this afternoon?"

"As free as can be, at your service. I've just finished my music cost papers."

"Goot. Meet me at 4 P.M. in the office of Harms and Company, 62 West 45th Street, Manhattan."

He hung up before I could start on the mob of questions his instructions aroused. Harms, Inc., was a well-established music publishing company that specialized in the scores of musical shows, having under contract the Gershwins, Rodgers and Hart, Jerome Kern, Romberg, Cole Porter, and numerous other quality composers and lyricists, most of whom had been substantially aided in their theatrical careers by the legendary Max Dreyfus, the head of the company. Harms was large enough to maintain an orchestration department headed by Robert Russell Bennett with Hans Spialek and Hilding Anderson, plus a heavily Italianate copying crew whipped by Signore Combattente. To that date, my only contact with Harms had been to employ a couple of their copyists when my old trusty Romo Falk got swamped by some last-minute changes.

Arriving by elevator on the floor where most of my personal "greats" had trod, I diffidently approached the receptionist and said, "I'm here to see Sigmund Romberg."

Puzzled, she looked me over and said, "But Sigmund Romberg does not have an office here."

"I know he doesn't," I said. "But he publishes here, doesn't he?"

"Not all the time," she said. "Sometimes with Witmark."

"Well, he said he'd meet me here."

She was looking at her pad. "He did say that he had an appointment with a Dan Vawker."

"That's me! *Don Walker*."

She picked up her pad and went to an unlettered door, opened it, and announced to those within, "There's a young man out here who won't admit he's Dan Vawker."

I could hear Rommy saying enthusiastically, "Send him in!"

She came out and with a toss of her head indicated that I could enter that holy of holies. "It's all yours, Dan," she said.

As I went by her, I silently mimed *DON, DON*. She stuck out her tongue at me.

Within, Rommy introduced me to Dreyfus, saying, "Max, here is my new discovery, Dan Vawker. He knows more about orchestrating for radio than any other arranger in New York. Besides, he's a wery nice fellow vit a nice family."

Mr. Dreyfus, the famous Max who had a tentacle in nearly every worthwhile musical in New York, at first sight was not a very impressive man. Rather small, looking like one of a thousand husbands taking the subway in the late afternoon from the garment center to upper Broadway, it wasn't until one was close up and could see his sharp, clever eyes that one could believe the scuttlebutt that he was a self-made millionaire. A shock of pure white hair added to his grandfather image, which usually turned out to have been less benign than foxy.

Shaking hands with me, Dreyfus said, "We've been playing parts of Rommy's radio audition. I want to complement you on your job. For a man who I have heard is a jazz arranger, to hear him come up with impeccable Viennese waltzes is surprising."

Embarrassed, I said, "I like an assignment that calls for a definite style, one that takes some research. Then the challenge is to stay within that style, eliminating the tiniest anachronism while keeping the orchestration interesting to present-day listeners."

"You set yourself a difficult task, but I must admit that you accomplish it. That sound you get! Those strings! That isn't just Viennese style, that's something special!"

I explained, "It's the result of a collaboration between the sound engineer and the orchestrator. As of now, I haven't met a single sound man who can read music, and I'm just as ignorant trying to puzzle out the diagram of a sound system. But we're both learning, and in time we'll speak the same lingo. Meanwhile we both need the other and we have to collaborate, especially on mostly musical programs, such as Rommy's."

"How do you collaborate?"

"First we jointly agree on the physical placement of the members of the orchestra, the singers, and the commentator. Then I am admitted to the engineer's jealously guarded control room, where I act as a general critic of balance and quality. Reading from a copy of the score, I follow the rehearsal, cueing entrances and effects for the engineer, things Rommy would be doing himself if he wasn't out in the studio, conducting."

"Isn't there a clash of personalities between you and the engineer? It's his control room."

"It's part of my job to avoid wrangling. It's a touchy situation, but I'm only there to help the whole production, not just to protect what I have written. For instance, I am never in a control room when a program is on the air; the engineer has enough on his plate without me bothering him about details. I go home and try to evaluate the program as an average listener."

Dreyfus said, "It's a whole new world, this radio business." He looked at Rommy. "Old timers like us had better learn to live with it. I think you've got winners here, Rommy, both in your radio program and your arranger. But where do I fit in? Why did you want me to meet Dan Vawker?"

"Because I vill be writing a new show," said Rommy, his diction betraying his roots as he became somewhat excited, "a show you vill be publishing, I hope, and a show Dan Vawker vill be orchestrating, I also hope."

"Won't he be too busy with your radio program to score a full-scale musical?"

"Ve'll find our way around that...remember, the radio program is on only twenty-six veeks and then we have twenty-six off. Plenty time to prepare a musical."

Max was getting nettled. He said, "What are you getting at, Rommy? Are you asking me to put another arranger on my staff while I've got Robert Russell Bennett and Hans Spialek twidling their thumbs?"

"But Max, you need Dan Vawker, he's the waif of the future."

I felt like a real waif, up on a block in a slave market.

Giving in, Max said to me, "I hope you don't mind a personal question, but it's something I must know if I'm going to make this Hungarian fiddle-player happy. Tell me, in all confidence, how much money do you need a week to keep you and your family going? Don't rush: Go over to that window and see if you can carefully come up with a reasonable figure."

I did as told while they quietly conversed about social matters. Somewhere I had heard that Max Dreyfus asked that kind of question to candidates for drawing accounts, so I wasn't completely unprepared. After a decent interval I rejoined the duo.

"Well," Max said, "have you come to a figure?"

"Yes, sir. It's one hundred fifty dollars per week."

"Good. With two children you won't be rolling in funds, but neither will you starve."

I said, "I have a very economical wife."

"Fine! And from what I have seen of you, I am sure that you know the value of a buck yourself, having been graduated from Wharton School with honors!"

Aha! I thought. *He's been checking up on me for I don't know how long. I'll have to step very carefully in his vicinity.*

Max continued. "I am proposing that Harms...that's my company...put you under the same type of drawing account contract as Bennett and Spialek. I'll give you a blank copy of that contract to take home and study. Briefly, it provides for a certain amount to be sent to the orchestrator regularly...every week...and at the end of every quarter, if there is any credit balance in your account, that is paid to you in a lump sum."

"But Mr. Dreyfus, sir," I said, "where's the profit to Harms for handling my billings, collecting my receipts, giving me a drawing account...?"

"For which we charge you nothing? That's the way we work. It is well known in show business that if you are producing a musical and wish to get the best orchestrators for it, you have to come to Max Dreyfus and arrange for him to publish your score. That's where Harms makes its money…not out of charging its arrangers an agent's measly ten percent, but out of publishing hits from hit shows!"

Rommy stood up, his immediate business finished. He signaled me to do the same.

Max said to me, "I'll have your contract ready in about a week, then we'll have a signing celebration. By the way, who is your lawyer?"

I was embarrassed, not having one. But Rommy answered quickly, before I could admit the deficiency.

He said, "Howard Reinheimer."

"That's too bad," said Max, "because that means we'll have to put off the signing ceremony for God only knows how long."

Everybody laughed, and then Rommy took me for lunch to that once-upon-a-time male-only refuge, now the female-invaded Oak Room of the Plaza Hotel.

Over a celebrative cocktail, I gently chided Rommy, "You knew you couldn't afford to keep me on salary for the six months until the Swift program starts, so you cooked up this Max Dreyfus deal for me. HEY!" I suddenly saw another twist that I had overlooked. "You've told me that you want me to score your next show. Now you've contrived to have me do it through the customary Harms system…and if it turns out that the job is too much for me to handle while arranging the Swift radio program, I'll have Russell Bennett and Hans Spialek available to help me!"

I looked at him finishing his drink, grinning and signaling the waiter to bring another round. I said, "Oh, you're a tricky one, Rommy. Fred Waring once accused me of being Machiavellian, but now I've met the real Niccolo. But why didn't you brief me?"

His eyes twinkled as he said, "I tought it vas more fun to let tings blossom naturally."

....

Things developed but not quite the way I had expected. It took about a month (which I heard was a speed record) for the Reinheimer office to agree to the contract Max Dreyfus offered me. Harms was to provide me with a drawing account of $150 per week, which gave them a preemptive call on my professional services and the right to collect my business income. As Mr. Dreyfus had explained, at the end of every quarter I would be given a statement of my account and if it showed a credit balance of more than $1950 (the amount I had drawn), I would immediately be paid the difference. It was an excellent arrangement for a young man, being certain of a fixed weekly income that could be budgeted for regular living expenses, while as a reward for hard work there was the promise of a quarterly bonanza that could be invested or spent for pleasure or emergencies.

I was mildly surprised to find that the Harms contract extended for only one year. *So they're not sure of me,* I thought. *Well...I've got a year to show them what I can do. At the end of it, they'll be glad to sign me for a longer term.*

But then, as soon as I had signed the one-year Harms contract, I was presented with another set of similar contracts that would go into force the day after the Harms contract terminated. These later contracts were with the British music publishing firm of Chappell & Co., Inc. I puzzled, *What are they planning to do with me? Send me to England? For how long?* I checked the length of those later contracts. They were for three years! I wondered, *What the devil's going on?*

After being sworn to absolute secrecy, it was explained that Warner Brothers, the motion picture giant, was going into the music publishing business in a big way, a natural development from making so many musical pictures. They were buying up famous companies such as Harms, Witmark, Remick, and others, planning to put them all together in a super music-publishing corporation. Max Dreyfus was willing to sell Harms and its precious copyrights for I forget how many skillion dollars, but he refused to sell the contracts of the men who were the creative heart of Harms, that is, the composers, the lyricists, the orchestrators, and even the copyists. Owning, with his brother Louis, the English music-publishing firm of Chappell and Co., Ltd., was planning to extend that company's operations to the United States, where its new offices would provide a headquarters for his creative people.

As advised by Rommy and Reinheimer, I signed with Max Dreyfus for four years, not worrying about the name of the company that held my contract. I was sure that wherever Max settled down would be the place where opportunities to orchestrate for the theatre would develop, the kind of activity that was my primary ambition to pursue.

A satisfactory income assured for at least four years, Audrey and I decided to move from our second Jackson Heights apartment to one of a row of small houses on the other side of that postage-stamp golf course, our main purpose being to separate the girl child from the boy child at night, so that if one cried it didn't necessarily require the other to join in the nerve-shattering chorus.

I remember that underfurnished house very well: I mixed my first cocktail in it. We had been given a handsome silver cocktail shaker the previous Christmas, and before going to dinner at the Don Bryans, dressed in our very best, we decided to christen it.

I prepared a lethal mixture called a "Green Dragon," a recipe gleaned from the Food & Drink section of the weekend *Sun*. As I remember, the dangerous ingredients included rum, creme de menthe, and brandy (Wow!). Worried by the heavy alcoholic proof of the potpourri, I thought to thin it out by adding some innocent water. Unfortunately, said water came from a bottle labeled "Seltzer," which I calmly poured into the shaker, clapped on the silvery top, and shook.

While cleaning up after the detonation in our second-best clothes, I thought, *What a powerful weapon could be fashioned out of soda and ice cubes! And a lot cheaper than cold steel and gun powder! Especially handy in Arctic combat!* Our kitchen smelled rather nicely of Puerto Rican rum and stale mint all through the year and a half we lived in that house. Since that demonstration of the power of compressed and agitated carbon dioxide, I have been particularly careful while handling drinks for the kiddies and as far as cocktails are concerned, I am a steadfast member of the Enlightened Mixers' Union, whose watchword is "*stir*," never "shake."

....

In the summer of 1934, Rommy, always open to offers that would bring him extra cash, accepted a proposal by a motion picture company to go to Hollywood for ten weeks and write a score, in collaboration with Oscar Hammerstein, for a film entitled *The Night Is Young*. Although, when released, the picture was an instantaneous flop, one song that was written for it has become, through the years, a greatly loved "standard." The writing of the sparse but inspired words of "When I Grow Too Old To Dream" is described in some detail in Oscar's book, unimaginatively titled, *Lyrics*.

Rommy returned from California in early September, excited by the prospect of soon conducting his own network radio program. He called me at once, making a quick date for the morrow, which was, as usual, lunch at Robert's. He said, "Dan, it vill be vonderful to eat a decent lunch mit you."

I hastily replied, "Rommy, pl..eee..se, don't make a banquet out of it. There's nothing to celebrate. Let me select from the menu as much or as little as I want." I added, "Doctor's orders," as an afterthought.

"Vy? Are you sick?" he asked, concerned.

"No," I answered, "not really, but my doctor doesn't want me to take any chances."

"But Robert's is a fine restaurant. After those hash-houses in Hollyvood it vill be superb!"

"I know, Rommy. I haven't spoken a word against it. Just let me order my measly little lunch myself, that's all."

He grumbled a bit but agreed. I realized that he got almost as much enjoyment from ordering fine food as eating it. When I met him the next day at lunchtime, he was nursing a Vermouth Cassis.

His face lit up when he saw me. He said, "I tought, from your phone call yesterday, that you vere sick, but now you look healthy, tank Gott. Have an aperitif."

He signaled a waiter and ordered a Vermouth Cassis for me and another for himself. I let it ride because I didn't want to irritate him after our long separation. Moreover, I had some bad news that I would have to ease into our conversation.

He gave me the opening, asking, "Vere are the new scores? You didn't leave them by the hatcheck girl, did you? They are too waluable!" His short fuse started to light up.

I said quietly, "As a matter of fact, Rommy, there are no new scores. I know, before you left, we laid out a full list of instrumentals featuring various soloists in the orchestra, but all summer long Max Dreyfus has kept me busy out-of-town, troubleshooting."

"Vhat dis trrrouble-shooting? Mit a gun?"

"No, no, Rommy. It was to help shows that were in trouble on the road. As usual, they were all blaming the orchestrations. I've been to New Haven, Boston, Philadelphia, and Washington. Rescoring, fixing, making sick numbers work, spreading happiness. Mr. Dreyfus says that all this experience will be a great help to me when I score your next show, when I am trusted with the whole responsibility."

Cooling off, Rommy said, "I thought Max vus my friend."

Thankful that the Romberg hurricane had gone out to sea, I said, "He still is...very much so. He wants to see you become a big success on radio. Then he'll sell a lot more copies of your songs and get a bigger slice of ASCAP. He's definitely on your side. When you win, he wins."

"So vhat do we haf to do to keep vinning? Ve've got a whole month before the program starts. Vhat do ve do wif it?"

"It isn't what we *want* to do with that time," I said. It's what we *must* do with it. We should be at least four programs ahead when we start, and we've got about four weeks to build them in. I'm assuming that we're playing the pilot *as is* for the first program."

"Ve are. Vith some little changes in the commercials."

"That's to be expected. Tell you what we have to do, Rommy: Ask for a phone and call Hershel Williams at the Agency. Have him set up an emergency conference tomorrow…no…make it the day after. Tomorrow just the two of us…nobody else…will figure out what *you* think the next four programs should be. Then, at the full meeting the next day, we'll be ready with *your* ideas, all worked out, no hesitations, no impossible formats to be attacked."

Rommy thought for a minute. Then he said, "You are right. It's a goot scheme. If the program is to be a hit, it vill be because Bob Simon carries out my ideas in the script and you follow dem out mit the orchestra. If a lot of people put in their outside ideas, ve have no style, no nothing. Vhat time vill ve meet tomorrow?" He called a waiter and asked for a phone.

I said, "Let's meet at your hideaway off Broadway at 10 A.M. That gives both of us time to think."

"And ve'll come back here for lunch?"

"Oh, no, ve von't." (I was beginning to talk like him.) "If we get hungry, I'll go around the corner to Lindy's for sandwiches and coffee."

"Vell…at least ve can have the big meeting the day after tomorrow here at Robert's."

"I'll grant you that…if you promise not to have any preordered festal board. Each person will order whatever they feel like eating, from the regular menu."

As he reached for the phone, he said, "You know, Dan Vawker, sometimes I tink you vant to take all the fun out of vorking."

…………………………..

Rommy's Swift & Co. program was a solid success. It demonstrated that there were a large number of meat-loving "middlebrows" out there in the hinterlands. We sailed happily through the rest of '34 and into '35 without any nerve-wracking problems, sticking to our format, always staying a comfortable number of shows ahead of the current one. We were on the air every Saturday night, on Sunday the production staff rested and met every Monday for lunch at Robert's, each member ordering his individual needs, frustrating Rommy, but getting the work of the meeting done.

My job, which included being Rommy's right-hand man as well as sole orchestrator, turned out to be far more lucrative than I had anticipated. Since the income from it would have to go through Harms, I asked Max Dreyfus to handle the negotiations for my weekly services. He made a deal for me that was far beyond my wildest dreams: $700.00 per week, an unheard-of stipend for an orchestrator in 1934. Yet my drawing account remained at $150 per week, which kept the old noggin from swelling and squandering.

When our twenty-six shows were over, there in Rommy's hand was a signed contract for twenty-six more, starting in the fall of '35. It was comforting to know, facing the unprofitable summer, that a lucrative job would arrive in October.

There was more than a Swift & Co. radio show waiting in the autumn. Rommy, an omnivorous reader, had come across a novel, set in Vienna, that begged him to put it to music. In addition to the obligatory romance, it went heavily into psychiatry, normal for Vienna but a bit odd for 1935 showbiz.

Oscar Hammerstein, who in 1935 was Rommy's customary collaborator, was not as enamored of the "MAYWINE" project as the composer. Anticipating problems with the script, Oscar agreed to write the lyrics for Rommy's tunes but did not wish to take on the responsibility of providing the book. Rommy enlisted Lawrence Schwab as producer, and he dug up an acceptable bookwriter and most important of all, THE MONEY! For reasons obscure to a lowly orchestrator, an opening night of December 5, 1935, at the Alvin Theatre (now the Neil Simon) was announced long before the musical went into rehearsal.

Thus, in the spring of 1935, as the first Swift radio series ended, I was committed to orchestrate, simultaneously, two large Sigmund Romberg musical projects in the fall.

There was only one way to satisfactorily serve the two assignments: I would have to work hard on the radio program during the summer in order to be at least eight weeks ahead on it when "Maywine" went into rehearsal. In my role as Rommy's advisor on the Swift Hour, I could certainly order the orchestrator (me) what to score in advance, especially when the boss was planning to once again spend the summer in Hollywood.

Desiring to find a haven where I could work in peace, away from the "Waring Wives" and midnight alerts to travel to Boston, etc., to rewrite some other arranger's orchestrations, Audrey and I hit upon the idea of finding a house we could rent for the summer, near to Lambertville, New Jersey, my parents' home and my place of birth. (It was also the location of a good tennis club, of which I was still a member.)

Enlisting my mother as a real estate scout, she found for us a rental that had everything we desired. It was a pre-revolutionary stone farmhouse with a recent, thoughtfully conceived addition, two miles south of New Hope, adjacent to the northern section of the Washington Crossing State Park and its famous "House of Decision," where on that Christmas Day in 1776 Washington and his generals resolved to abandon the defensive, cross the ice-choked river, march nine miles in the snow, and attack the mercenary Hessians, sleeping off their holiday debauchery in Trenton.

The property was owned by a big shot, one Horace B. Tobin, President of the Crescent Wire Company of Trenton. He had two mansions, one in Trenton and the other on the Jersey Coast, using the Bucks County farm only for parties. What kind of parties was not explained, except that Mrs. Emma Tobin, concerned about her husband's health, was trying to get rid of both the farmhouse and the parties.

We rented the furnished homestead for five months, with an option to buy it and its surrounding ten acres for ten thousand dollars. We moved in, children and all, on April 15, 1935. I will never forget that day, driving our essential belongings from Jackson Heights, Queens, to Bucks County, PA, in a rented open truck. Against all history and weather reports, that day it *snowed!* A whole inch! April 15! SPRING?!

Safely settled in Bucks for five months, there was yet important New York business that had to be disposed of before I could immerse myself in scoring for Swift #2. The day was at hand when my one-year contract with Harms expired and my identical arrangement with Chappell & Co. became operative.

On that fateful day when Harms turned into a subsidiary of Warner Brothers, I tested the facilities for commutation between New Hope and New York. I found that at the best of "on times," from country door to city desk, one should allow for at least two hours…and if that was all it took, one was lucky.

Being first-time-fortunate, I cleared my locker (I had never been assigned a desk in that crowded office) at Harms 45th Street and carried my working paraphernalia five blocks north on recently renamed "Avenue of the Americas" (formerly 6th Avenue) to the Radio

City Music Hall Building (then called the RKO Building), took the elevator to the third floor, entered the virginal offices of Chappell & Co., and jockeyed for desk space.

The cubical assigned to "Arrangers" was just large enough to house a small upright piano, its bench and two flat-topped desks, placed back-to-back. Since there was no one about to say no, I put my things in the desk nearest the window, which was to become recognized as my personal demesne for the next fifteen years. The other staff arrangers had apartments in Manhattan where they lived and worked, using the desk that faced me only for late changes and fixes that required them to be near the copyists, who were handy and sometimes noisy, just across the hall.

That day I met most of the staff of the new American "Chappell." There was Larry Spear, the "professional" manager, in charge of "plugging" the most promising songs. Dr. Albert Sirmay, a naturalized Mittel-European, who made all the piano arrangements of the firm's publications, was theoretically in charge of all the orchestrators, but if anyone was "in charge" of our group of zanies, it was Selma Tamber, who handled our billings and almost anything else connected with our work.

At the top of this truncated pyramid stood Henry Spitzer, Max Dreyfus's personal representative. As is usual in similar "buyouts" of active corporations, Dreyfus had to agree to not personally participate in the active management of a music publishing firm for a certain number of years (which I believe were not less than five or more than ten). He solved that problem by moving from his home in Bronxville to an extensive estate in Brewster and appointing a trusted underling, who he had raised from an office boy, to sit in his large office in the new Chappell quarters in Radio City, where he would receive all his orders by phone from Brewster.

Watching all this complicated structure for him, spending half her time in Brewster and the rest in the office, was his personal secretary, Rose, who still called me Dan Vawker.

This was the atmosphere into which I had been thrust by the benevolent machinations of Sigmund Romberg. In the future Chappell was where at least 75 percent of the newest Broadway musicals would be orchestrated. I believed that if I worked hard and as well as I could, I would get my share of those productions. I went back to Bucks County, happy in my work, looking forward to being with my family, and pleased with the place where we would be spending the summer.

....

For once I was scoring without the handy pressure of an *imminent deadline*, too inexperienced to know that if extrinsic forces have not provided that work-prod, the ambitious artist must create it, believe in it, and live by it.

. This effort does not always contribute to domestic harmony, especially where very young children are involved; the concept of a self-imposed deadline is too complicated for their unsophisticated minds to grasp. Only by heartlessly barring them from "Daddy's Den" were those dubious "gems of orchestration" inscribed, every one of them a notable victory of concentration over chaos.

During that summer of '35, in spite of an occasional crying crisis, I was able to get far enough ahead on Swift #2 to make possible a concurrent orchestration of "Maywine." Helping was my experience on Swift #1: The cast was nearly the same, the only fundamental change being the replacement of commentator William Phelps with Deems Taylor, a change that did not affect me or my work.

It was a pleasure to write for an orchestra that would have almost the same personnel as on Swift #1. Artie Shaw would be there, again playing 1st (legitimate!) clarinet beside Larry Binyon, handling the 2nd (legitimate!) flute, while Oscar Levant fingered the piano between quips and Veralee Mills caressed the harp. Bill Johnson would be preparing our small but elite choir, which contained great singers like a very young but notably rich contralto answering to the odd name of Rise Stevens.

Then there was our "truants from Toscanini" string section, the glorious heart of Rommy's kind of music that gave his program its special, romantic sound. Familiarity with my musical resources made it possible to prepare, far in advance, the orchestrations for the first two months of Swift #2.

Rommy returned in early September with Bobby Dolan, with whom he had been working on the coast. Bobby was to be making his debut as a theatre conductor with "Maywine," on the same occasion as I submitted my first complete Broadway orchestration to the unmusical ears of the dramatic critics.

Mrs. Lillian Romberg had been busy all summer, commuting from Beverly Hills to New York in order to supervise the decoration of the Rombergs' new duplex apartment in the Ritz Towers, the lower floor of which would house an arranging and copying department for the Swift #2 program. Rumor had it that Rommy's doctor had told Mrs.

R. that he could do nothing more about her husband's embonpoint as long as he lived in the same building with Robert's.

Rommy submitted to his relocation because he enjoyed working in close proximity to his arranger and copyists, which was impossible at 33 West 55th Street. His carrot for compliance with his wife's wishes was her permission for him to continue having his regular Monday business lunch-conference at Robert's. On those occasions, he valiantly attempted to make up for the "Off Limits!" his missus had metaphorically placed on his favorite restaurant all the rest of the week.

With the passing of Labor Day, 1935, Audrey and I faced a momentous decision, one that was to shape the rest of our lives. We had until September 15 to exercise our option to buy the country house that we had come to love. There was no question that we wanted it, but could we swing the deal?

Rommy's sensitive antennae told him that I was worried about something, and he questioned me. I reluctantly explained. He was interested and thought the house sounded like an excellent investment as well as being a nice place to live. He said, "If you can't sving the deal yourself, Dan Vawker, I'll co-sign the note mit you."

I was thrilled by that declaration of faith in me. To those he cared about, Rommy was a very warm, kindly person.

As it happened, I did not need to obtain his signature; exhibition of my three-year contract with Chappell was sufficient security for the local banker to extend the necessary credit. (He had known me from childhood.) Within four years, Audrey and I were able to pay off and burn the mortgage, owning the property outright, with all its assets and liabilities.

Today, as I type this history in "Daddy's Den," enclosed by 20-inch-thick, 200-year-old walls, I know that a walk through the lower floor of the house would bring me to the large living-room with its exposed beams. There, sitting by the big fireplace, dominating the ambience, will be the king-sized overstuffed chair that was Rommy's Christmas present that first year the Dan Vawker clan celebrated the holiday in its own house in the country. Rommy could have fitted into that big chair very nicely.

....

During the summer of '35, I studied the means of commutation between the New Hope area and New York City. With the very best of connections (a rare occurrence), one had to allow two hours plus from

Bucks County home to Chappell desk. It was clear that come fall I could not afford to squander four to five hours a day traveling, while trying to orchestrate two large musical projects. So we gave up the Jackson Heights house and sublet a modest apartment near 72nd and Central Park West.

I remember well one chilly fall morning when I had arisen before dawn, eaten my self-prepared breakfast, and walked across the park as the sun came up. Arriving at the Ritz Towers I was checked, then allowed to take the elevator to the penultimate floor. I opened the apartment door with the key that Rommy had given me, eager to get scoring a number from "Maywine." To my amazement, there was the boss himself, sitting at my desk, writing with ink-stained fingers a nearly finished orchestration.

He looked at me sheepishly and explained, "I vus trying to get this finished before you came in, but I didn't quite make it."

"But what is it, Rommy?"

"A long story, Dan. Just as I was getting undressed for bed last night, I thought of that spot in next veek's program, vere ve need someting lifely, and I remembered a peasants' dance I haf seen as a boy. I couldn't get it out of der Kopf (my head). So I came down here and started to write it out. Now I haf only eight bars to go and you show up. I vanted to surprise you."

"You surprised me, all right. But you've been up all night, Rommy. You can't take that kind of beating. Get some sleep now; finish your score later today."

"Look over vaht I haf written. I'll finish it vhile you're looking."

I studied his score. In the rare times when he orchestrated himself, he always gave me his work to check out before handing it to the copyists. This one was simply titled "KOLO." (In Webster's Dictionary, "kolo" is defined as: "a central European folk dance in which dancers form a circle and progress slowly to right or left while one or more dancers perform elaborate steps in the center of the circle.") Rommy's orchestration was raw, rough, and rather sloppy, but no one could deny the sheer energy, the primitive authenticity of the piece. I thought, *This is just what the Swift program needs…a shot in the arm.*

Rommy had finished the score and asked, "Vell…vhat do you tink?"

"I think it's terrific, Rommy. Wild and wonderful. Just the sort of a number to wake up the sleepers. I don't want to change a single note."

"Not a single note?"

"Not one. Not even the place where your pen sputtered and sprayed some spots that look like notes."

He went up to bed, exhausted but happy. I was pleased, too, for that particular program was heavily loaded with schmaltz and sure could use a spot of authentic excitement.

....

"Maywine" was not a solid hit, neither was it a flop.

It received that kiss of lingering death known as "mixed notices." The critics were uncomfortable with the musical's potpourri of romance, psychiatry, and melodrama. Yet it had an outstanding performance by Walter Slezak, a fresh, surprisingly different score by Romberg with brilliant lyrics by Oscar Hammerstein and purely by chance, in that dull theatrical season of '35–'36, not much competition. So it limped on, held up, as the Broadway gossipmongers whispered, by Sigmund Romberg's constant injections of Swift radio program profits, an early example of the beef bolstering the backers.

The burden of keeping "Maywine" flowing led Rommy to accept an offer to take his radio program to the West Coast that summer of '36, directly following the last program of Swift #2. The Dan Vawker family went right along with him, complete with Audrey, our two little children, a nursemaid, and my tennis rackets. We traveled the famous railroad route: 20th Century overnight to Chicago, a four-hour layover, and then the Chief for two more nights to LA. We played interminable bridge games with Rommy, who was a wiz, and his secretary. Fortunately Audrey ("Dollink" as Rommy called her) was an excellent player or we would have been public charges on arrival in California.

The advertising agency that was handling the necessary details of Rommy's summer program had, to our dismay, located the Walker family in a large, expensive suite in an old, famous hotel quite near the hectic hub of Hollywood and Vine. Surrounded by concrete and asphalt, our lodgings did not represent the California we had traveled three thousand miles to enjoy. Something had to be done and quickly.

Before leaving the East, I had made up a list of phone numbers and addresses of acquaintances who I knew were living on the West Coast; the first name on the small roster was Ebsen, Buddy. His brother-in-law, Bobby Dolan, had said, "While you're out in the Wild West, try to contact Buddy. He's on one of those seven-year film contracts and is going crazy waiting for a part. A friend from New York would be manna to him."

I dialed the number and it was, sure 'nough, Buddy, with the Florida drawl.

"I've been expecting you," he said. "Vilma," (his sister, Dolan's wife), "in her last letter mentioned that you were coming. Welcome to Horrorwood. Where you staying?"

I told him, adding, "We're very unhappy. There isn't a blade of living grass within a couple of miles, and this doughtel is the kind of place you have to get all dressed up in your best for breakfast."

"That won't fly at all, 'specially when you've got to grind out twenty pages of score by lunchtime. Tell you what you ought to do, right now. Go out and rent a car."

"Rent a car? Why?"

"'Cause if you walk along a sidewalk here, you're liable to end up in the pokey. Nobody walks…only criminals!"

"But how can a car help us? We can't sleep in it…not with a husband and wife, a nursemaid, and two small but inquisitive kids!"

"All you have to do is drive out this way on Sunset and meet a very nice real estate lady who happens to know. She'll take good care of you."

He gave me directions to a realtor whose office was on Wilshire in Westwood. As instructed, I rented an auto and with Audrey set out to find the "very nice real estate lady." She was as advertised and took us to an integrated circle of furnished garden apartments.

She said, "There is an apartment here that has just become available. I hope the cleaning women have finished their work and left. If not, and you like the place, you may have to wait till tomorrow to occupy."

She opened the door, and we entered and were delighted.

After our unhappiness with that formal, urban hotel, our joy was hard to restrain upon finding this new-pin-shiny gem of a temporary home. We immediately closed the deal and our realtor left, smiling.

As we were examining our new toy in depth, there came the sound of door chimes.

"Have the magazine subscription boys discovered us so soon?" Audrey asked.

I cautiously opened the door. There was Buddy and his wife, Ruth, Walter Winchell's "Girl Friday" before Buddy wooed her away from the tabloid environment.

"Where's your car?" I queried. "You told me it was dangerous to walk in California."

"Well, seeing as we're only a hop of a skip away, we thought we'd chance it."

"A hop of a skip…you mean you're…."

"Right next door."

"So you managed this whole thing!"

"Let's say I had my teeny-weeny little finger in the pie. Now, are you happy?"

"Deliriously. Come on in and let's start Old Home Week in our new hangout."

"With a shake and a shim-sham-shimmy!"

....

The 1930s was a wretched time for theatre people. In those ghastly depression years, formal entertainment came to be regarded as a dispensable luxury, the first item to be eliminated from the family budget when squeezed.

Through all that discouraging period, Rommy kept cheerfully composing musical shows. What is more surprising, he constantly found producers with backers willing to finance the presentation of his brainchildren. His list of flops and unlucky failures, amassed during those hard times, is awesome. There was:

"Nina Rosa," '30. A modest hit slain by the market crash.

"East Wind," '31. No one could afford to go.

"Melody," '33. Opened 2/14/33. Banks closed 3/8/33.

"Rose de France," Fall '33. Mild hit in Paris but no interest in bringing it to the United States.

"Maywine," '35. Mixed notices. Ran six months by breastfeeding. (Mostly by Rommy himself.)

"Forbidden Melody," '36. Star a flop. Closed quickly.

"Sunny River," '41. Embarrassing bomb. Sudden death.

In between the theatrical defeats of the thirties, Rommy composed the music for a number of films, none of which were conspicuously successful. In that miserable period, only one great song ("When I Grow Too Old To Dream") and his radio programs can be deemed winners. Yet he never gave up working and scheming on theatrical productions, trying to rediscover the magic that had formerly produced a seemingly unstoppable flood of twenties hits. It was my happenstance to be close to him during his extended drought.

In the seventeen years I worked under and with Sigmund Romberg, I occasionally heard criticism of his compositions by members of the musical fraternity. The most frequent indictment was that "he deliberately steals themes from composers whose works are no longer protected by copyright." I always defended Rommy, pointing out that such criticism was unfairly based on the music of a single hit show, "Blossom Time," whose libretto was based on the life of Franz Schubert. What could be more appropriate in a musical story about Schubert than the use of his music in the score? Rommy never attempted to conceal the facts of his participation in the music of the show. On published song copies and phonograph records, when the material was based on a Schubert theme, the credit was always: "Music by Franz Schubert, Adapted by Sigmund Romberg," or, when space was a problem, simply "Schubert-Romberg." (As in "Song of Love.") When he wrote a number unaided, he correctly took all the credit (as with "Tell Me Daisy").

Only once was I suspicious of a theme when Rommy handed me to score. The incident occurred in Rommy's house in Beverly Hills, where he kept his vast library of operas and operettas. It was a week when the advertising agency was introducing a new product of our sponsor and thought that our radio program should also do "something different." They suggested that we present an original one-hour operetta, "Music by Sigmund Romberg," that had never before been exposed to the public, which would "tie in" with the introduction of the new product.

Bob Simon came up with the book and lyrics of our mini-operetta, entitled "Ma'mselle Bébé." Its imagined locale was Paris, and everything about it was very, very Frahnnnch.

Rommy approached the composition of his new mini-operetta with confidence. The job was right down his alley, and for a while all went well. On the Monday our six-day rehearsal began, he played the whole score for the cast, with the exception of the theme song. There was even an excellent Bob Simon lyric ready for that, crying out for a creamy Romberg waltz, my boss's musical meat and potatoes.

He must have written at least twenty waltzes during the next five days, all of them dull, derivative, or both. The lyric was perfect, but Rommy couldn't find the damn tune! All involved became more and more apprehensive as the week flew by; finally, on Friday, frantic. I left him late that night at the piano in his great basement music library, surrounded by torn-up scraps of manuscript and no "I Found You In Three-Four Time."

I arrived at his residence on North Rexford Drive in Beverly Hills at 5:05 the next morning. It was Saturday, the broadcast would be on at 7 P.M., Pacific Time, that evening. I let myself into the music library with my own key. Rommy was there, still at the piano, bleary-eyed and fretting.

"You're five minutes late," he complained.

"At this hour, you're lucky I could find a cab," I retorted. "By the way, how are you doing?"

"Vell, it's been a vorrysome night. First, I got out fourteen scores of French operetta composers and played trough all dere valtzes, just to get in a goot mood. Den I took a nap on de couch. Ven I volk up, I had some coffee. Den I found some French operas and played trough some of dere valtzes. Den I tried to write 'Ma'mselle Bébé'...no dice! Ev'ryting lousy, so I had a sandvich...and another nap. Ven I voke up, it's just starting to get light. So I studied Bob's lyric for one more try...and...*Zing! Subito!* It all happened! Here's de tune, I just finished it ten minutes ago!" He handed me a very messy penciled manuscript and said, "You vill know vhat the harmony should be...nutting fancy till de fifteenth bar."

I studied the hen-scratchings, putting the music together with the lyrics, playing it all the way through in my head as ideas for its orchestration grew and blossomed.

Impatient for the jury to file in and voice a decision, Rommy queried, "Vell...vhat do you tink of it?"

Pulling myself away from the exciting orchestral possibilities of the new song, I answered, "Rommy, it's gorgeous! All by itself it's a marvelous tune and in the context of the script, with Bob's lyric, it's perfect. In fact, it is so good, so Parisienne, it worries me."

"Worries you? How?"

"You know well how people have accused you of lifting other composers' themes. This chanson is like nothing you have ever written before. It doesn't feel like a Sigmund Romberg song. If it's truly your own invention and you're willing to defend it as such, more power to you. I'll shut my big mouth and get started on orchestrating this wonderful melody."

Rommy could look thunder clouds when angered, but now the dangerous flush was fading. He said quietly, "Thank you, Dan Vawker, for your honest concern for me and my professional reputation. Most men would be afraid to speak to me so frankly. To calm your fears, let me promise you that I made up, out of my own head, every note of 'Ma'mselle Bébé.' Playing all that French music undoubtedly affected my style; that's why I went through it. But I can swear to you on my father's beard that there isn't a single phrase of 'Ma'mselle Bébé' that has been consciously lifted from another composer's verk. Understand?"

"Case dismissed," I said. "Verdict for the defendant, who better get upstairs and snatch some sleep; he's got a long, hard day ahead."

He did as suggested while his intrepid interrogator thanked his lucky stars for giving him such an understanding boss.

Relieved, I tackled the complicated job of inserting the new song into that evening's program:

8:30 A.M.: Copyists waiting for score in office near studio.

10:00 A.M. Male soloist must have copy of song to learn.

12 noon: Total cast call. Must have vocal parts of new number.

3 P.M. Orchestra call. Must have all music <u>except</u> new number.

4:15 P.M. Deadline for orchestra parts of new number.

5 P.M.: Dress rehearsal.

6 P.M.: Theoretically a rest and refreshment period before the show. Usually the most feverish hour of the week.

7–8 P.M.: THE SHOW? Orchestrator in the booth cueing the sound engineer and trying to be tactful.

8 P.M.: Congratulations all around. Went to dinner with Rommy and Mrs. Romberg. They call each other "Bunny." All very confusing.

....

The Westwood summer of '36 was a pleasure for all members of the Walker delegation. Even Anna, our dour German nursemaid, was in seventh heaven. When we hired her in New York we didn't know she was silver-screen-struck; when she agreed with surprising alacrity to take the long journey west, neither Audrey nor I got the message; once we were there, finally settled next door to Buddy Ebsen, she was in cloudland. Every Thursday, her inviolate day off, she would take a guided tour to gawk at "Homes of the Stars." When she had seen all that had been advertised, she'd start again at the top of her list, a seasoned veteran.

On two of Anna's Thursdays, fate and the advertising agency scheduled functions that Audrey and I were forced to attend. On those occasions our babysitter was...believe it or not...the most accommodating Buddy Ebsen. Childless, he adored our two little devilkins and the regard was warmly returned. His famous dance with Shirley Temple was not solely a superb professional performance; Buddy loved kids.

He had a small circle of close friends, one of which was the comedian Jerry Lester, whose humor I could never seem to fully appreciate. Buddy's favorite hangout was a bistro on Melrose (or was it Beverly?) where Audrey and I occasionally went with the Ebsens to hear another friend, Louis Prima, play his terrific trumpet, backed up by his combo, which included Slam Stewart, the famous string bassist who sang husky jive syllables in unison with his vigorously bowed improvisations.

For a while, Buddy and I had a little game we played at Prima's. We both thought that in the convenience of our homes we could make top-notch daiquiris, that newly popular Cuban cocktail. When we ordered a round in Prima's joint, its taste was sensational, so far better than our amateurish swizzles that Buddy and I were humiliated there before the eyes and taste buds of our critical spouses. That night we solemnly swore to steal the secret of Prima's bartender.

On our next expedition to Louis' dive, we let the ladies be seated while we barreled up to the bar and ordered our tipple from a position where we could observe the mixing. As customary, the Jamaican took a large glass, into which he put cracked ice, lime juice, powdered sugar, and white rum. All that was normal. Then he suddenly dipped down under the bar with the half-filled glass and, we thought, added another ingredient. It was all very swift and mysterious.

Next he clapped a large, nickel-plated bar-shaker onto the mixing-glass and vigorously agitated the contents. Then he rubbed the rims of four cocktail glasses with the rind of the squeezed limes. Removing the mixing-glass from the bar-shaker, he poured from the latter four perfectly measured frosty cocktails of Caribbean nectar.

"Two dollars, please," he said, handing us a small tray for carrying our purchases back to our table.

Prima ran a rather casual place, and such a procedure did not cause the brouhaha it would spawn today.

The daiquiris were as superb as the act of their construction. When our ladies went where Ladies often go, I said to Buddy, "Did you see what he did, crouching under the bar?"

"No-oh," he sighed. "I haven't a clue. Ricardo sure does something down there under the bar, but I don't know what it is."

"Think we'll ever find out?"

"We've got to keep trying. Can't let a simple problem like this lick us, can we?"

"Never! We'll fight to the last daiquiri!"

"That's the stuff!"

During the next month, about once a week, we dropped into Prima's, partly for the music but mostly to pursue our "Battle of the Bar." Trying every watching angle, we hung around the damn dispensary, irritating our neglected wives, left grousing at a table while we stretched our necks at the bar.

One unusually quiet night, Ricardo, the bartender with not much to do, said to Buddy and me, "You characters slay me. Why do you come here? You don't listen to the music, you bring your own women, you just sit around the bar and order daiquiris. Just what the hell goes on with you?"

Buddy broke down and explained, "We think your daiquiris are the greatest. Right now, my ambition in life is to be able to make them like you do...not better...just as well. I can put the cocktail together like you, except when you're almost finished you crouch down under the bar and do something top-secret. We're convinced that whatever you do down there is the difference. We're going gaga, dedicated to solve the damn mystery!"

Rikky looked Buddy over and said, "Big Boy, what's it worth to you to find out?"

Buddy painfully took out his jealously guarded wallet. Until that moment, I hadn't realized how serious he was. With a sigh he extracted a fiver and, with an even longer sigh, placed it on the bar. Buddy was always very careful about money.

Rikky acknowledged Buddy's finnif and turned his dark gaze to me. "And you," he questioned, "what's it worth to you?"

Pulling out a sigh from even deeper down than Buddy's, I dug out another franky and placed it beside the first. Ten dollars disappeared into Rikky's ready pocket in a flash as he knelt down behind the bar and came up with an unimpressive-looking bottle half-full of a colorless liquid.

"This is the big secret," he said. "It's Falernum, a liqueur made in Diaquiri, Cuba. It adds something great to any rum drink."

He took two shot glasses and poured each of us a few drops. It was very sweet and pleasant, tasting of a host of aromatic ingredients: almond, ginger, lime, rum, and who knows what else?

"Where can you buy this?" Buddy wanted to know for his five dollars.

"Any high-class liquor store," said Rikky. He warned us, "It only takes two or three drops per cocktail; you can ruin a daiquiri with too much."

Armed with our expensive knowledge, we had no trouble finding a liquor store that carried Falernum. We were happily surprised that its price was so modest. We each bought a bottle and hurried to our homes to practice duplicating Rikky's masterpieces. That agreeable task called for a certain amount of sampling, in which chore Audrey cheerfully cooperated. Just as we had agreed that perfection had been attained, the doorchime pinged: The Ebsens were reporting for the usual cocktail hour, and that day it was the Walkers' duty to entertain. When our neighbors entered, it was obvious that they were as well lubricated as their hosts.

Offering Ruth a chair, I remarked, "I've been trying to duplicate Rikky's daiquiri for the last two hours, and Audrey thinks that now I've got it right. Are you ready to be a member of the jury?"

She snorted and replied, "Buddy's been fiddling around with that fancy drink ever since he got home with his magic bottle. Who do you think was drafted to be his handy tester?" She pointed her thumb to her chest and moaned, "His Girl Friday."

"That should have been fun."

"Some fun! After those Cuban confections, I would like a restorative, also from an island. Could I have a nice, hot cup of coffee? No cream, no sugar, straight java, <u>please!</u>"

....

The pleasant summer was drawing to a close and so was Rommy's radio program. I had managed to get two weeks ahead with my scoring, and he didn't really need my physical presence to wrap up the series, so Audrey and I decided to make a large side trip on the way back East. So we bought a shiny new Ford convertible roadster and worked out two traveling itineraries that were planned to merge in Philadelphia in two weeks' time. Audrey and I would take the scenic route in our car, touring Sequoia, Yosemite, Salt Lake City, Yellowstone, Montana, and North Dakota to Pipestone, Manitoba, where Audrey's grandma and uncle lived, running the Ellsworth family wheat farm. After a quick visit, we would be off again, driving through Manitoba, Minnesota, and Wisconsin, taking the big auto ferry across Lake Michigan from Milwaukee to Muskegon. Then we would cross Michigan, Ohio, and Pennsylvania to our home near New Hope. While all that was unwinding, our dear friend Buddy Ebsen would wait ten days and then put nurse Anna and our two kids on an express to New Orleans, where they would change to the Crescent Limited, which we would meet in Philadelphia.

I have to admit that the double continental crossing, Group I to the North, Group II to the South, with calm expectation that we would all meet in the East at a certain place at a designated time had in it the seeds of madness. But we were young and inexperienced in long travel. We were also very lucky, for when the Crescent stopped at Philly, Audrey and I were waiting on the platform. Shepherded by Anna and helped with their luggage by their slaves the trainmen came Ann and David, two weeks older and three thousand miles wiser. It was a tearful, thrilling reunion, the memory of which has warmed these inadequate words.

....

There was no time for a rest in the country. Sigmund Romberg had written the score for a musical dangerously titled "Forbidden Melody," starring a famous singing actor with substantial European credits, scheduled to open in New York late in October.

August '36 came to an end, and so did Rommy's summer radio program. Audrey and I heard his final show on an Atwater-Kent radio set in a motel in eastern Ohio. After the last chord faded away, Rommy took a plane to New York in order to be present at the first rehearsal call of "Forbidden Melody," so he could play his score for the assembled cast and staff. I reported only one day later, before there was a number staged that could be orchestrated. As is usual at such a stage in a show's development, only an Overture, Entr'acte, and Exit March can be scored, for all other numbers involve the synchronization of action and music.

In the meantime, Audrey had found a satisfactory sublet in the same general area where we had located in '35–'36—that is, on the West Side near transportation and Central Park. This was to be our last season together as a family in New York City, for by another year Ann would be of school age and we wanted her (and later David) to attend a superlative Quaker-run school not far from our country home.

Our landlords that '36–'37 season were an elderly couple named Brouse, who regularly fled to Florida in the cold months, as Audrey and I do now. My son David always referred to that apartment as "Missus Brous-ez House." That was where I scored most of "Forbidden Melody" with the remainder at my desk in the office of Chappell & Co.

At this point, I must explain that my memory, previously labeled "skittish," is also very "convenient," for it can quickly "forget" data that another part of my brain considers "not worth remembering." A "two-tiered" memory is possessed by many individuals: one level being able to remember for a limited time a mass of recently acquired details, while the other level is capable of recalling striking events far in the past. With respect to "Forbidden Melody," I find that for me it might as well be dubbed "Forgotten Dissonance" as far as my memory of details is concerned. On the other level, there are three of its happenings I cannot forget. There is:

(1) The Case of the Unprofessional Pro.
"Forbidden Melody" was in its second and final week in Boston, with only a few days remaining before the justly feared New York City opening. Morale was at its lowest ebb. Boston critics had gleefully disemboweled it, and the loudly heralded foreign "star" wasn't drawing gnats.

The scene was the bare stage of the Colonial Theatre, sans decor, filled by the entire cast in work clothes. The time was mid-afternoon, and the rehearsal of a new Act I Finale was in progress. The entire staff, including Rommy and this reporter, was gathered in the front seats of the house, watching, listening, and occasionally suggesting improvements.

In the middle of an ensemble refrain, our center-stage "star" began waving his out-stretched arms and yelling, "STOP!" There was an abrupt, shocking silence, during which he began the most embarrassing vitriolic diatribe that I have ever heard from an angry actor. There before the entire company he excoriated the book, the music, the costumes, the scenery, the direction, the choreography, the lighting, and even the orchestrations. He was just starting on individual members of the cast when two beefy bass-baritones, signaled by the director, approached our gift from Europe and lifted him up by the armpits, carrying him backward, kicking and screaming off the stage, depositing him in his handy dressing room.

The cast never forgave that humiliating, unprofessional incident when our presumed "leader" spilled his guts before the whole company. If that was his real opinion of the show, how could he play it with any semblance of sincerity eight times a week? He wasn't that good an actor.

The cast of a new musical, out-of-town and preparing for an imminent opening on Broadway, is amazingly loyal and hardworking, often suffering far beyond the call of duty (or shop steward) in order to polish what may be a hopeless affair. They are pros and understand that it is not their function to produce new scenes or songs; their responsibility is to put the material they have been given before an audience as best they can. As long as the lights are turned on properly and the orchestra plays in tune, there is always a chance: History lists a number of musicals that were lemons in Boston miraculously becoming sweet tangerines on Broadway. The Great White Way is the ultimate taster.

(2) The Case of the Curious Clarinet.

One day, when "Forbidden Melody" had been in rehearsal for over two weeks, Bobby (Robert Emmett) Dolan, our conductor, came to me privately and said, "Don, you've got to help me, I think I'm going bats."

"I'm available. How can I help?"

"It's our singing star...he can't sing."

"There's lots of entertainers who can't sing. But they talk their way through a number and make audiences think they're singing."

"I wish he would do that, but he keeps trying to vocalize and he can't. We've been rehearsing behind locked doors, but I'm afraid that some of his most horrible sounds must have leaked out. I think the cast is wise to him. What's driving me nertz is guessing what Rommy's reaction is going to be when he finds out that his canary is a crow. There'll be hell to pay!"

"And the devil will be around to collect his dues any day now...just as soon as the run-throughs begin and our headliner starts to honk his way through Rommy's best tune."

"The boss'll explode!"

I tried to calm Bobby down, offering, "I'll try to prepare Rommy for the blow...so it doesn't come out of the blue...a hint here and there...."

Bobby thanked me. He agreed, "I'll do the same. We've got to watch out for Rommy's blood pressure. It's better to let it rise gradually, rather than all at once."

A few days later, the show moved from the group of rehearsal rooms it had been using to the "dark" theatre that would be its home during the prospective New York run. That afternoon the first run-through of Act I was scheduled.

When I entered the empty house that day, I seated myself unobtrusively in the rear. Rommy was down front, with his secretary behind him with her memo pad, ready for his notes. Bobby Dolan was in the deserted orchestra pit, preparing to conduct the cast and his hard-boiled rehearsal pianist, whose thankless job was to make the beat-up eighty-eight give the impression it was a full complement of twenty-five musicians.

After a couple of false starts, the run-through got underway with our rousing opening number, which employed the entire cast, with the exception of our star. Although that curtain-raiser did not disclose any trace of the plot, at least it set the time and place of the coming story as "late nineteenth century in Mittel Europa, where the peasants are cheerful and vigorous." Then the stage emptied, leaving on our young leading lady, playing a simple local beauty. Enter our leading man, a dashing vagabond who was really a prince. Then followed the obligatory "Instant-falling-in-love" scene, underscored with playful, then tender, finally amorous music that led into one of the most bewitching tunes that Rommy ever wrote. This was the song that for some obscure reason, later in the story, got itself "forbidden," a foolish thing for a beautiful melody to do.

Our star got away with the introductory part of the song, which was mostly light "singspiel," playful talk hiding serious intent. But when our strangulated baritone reached the principal theme, he attempted to vocalize, filling the theatre with strange, unpleasant sounds.

That was when Rommy stood up and calmly stopped the proceedings. "Ve vill haf to pass this number," he announced. "Ve haven't had enough time to vork on it." Raising his voice, he called, "Dan Vawker! Vhere are you?"

I stood up and waved, "Right here, Rommy!"

"Goot. After this run-through, ve vill have a conference mit Bobby here. Members of the producing staff are velcome."

With that surprising turnabout to equanimity, Rommy sat down and let the rehearsal continue. Wherever our lead had any singing to do, Rommy arose and had the director skip to the next sequence. Because of the large cuts, the run-through was over early.

On the way to the men's lounge, where Rommy had called his conference, I remarked to Bobby Dolan, "The old man sure crossed us up with his sudden composure."

"And how!" he agreed. "That's what makes working for him interesting...you never know which way he's going to turn."

The producer, the director, and the stage manager came to our music department meeting, that's how serious the matter was deemed to be.

Rommy opened the discussion by stating the obvious, saying, "The only simple vay to solve our problem is to get rid of our leadink man."

The producer groaned, explaining, "But that's impossible. He's got a rock-ribbed contract. If we fired him, his manager would impound so much of our money, I couldn't open the show. Think of something else, we've got to go with the bum."

The director asked, "How the hell did we ever get into such a bind, with a singing star who can't sing?"

Rommy said sadly, "His European records vere goot."

I suggested, "Maybe someone else made them."

The stage manager conjectured, "Maybe he's had a debilitating illness."

"Like changing a good ear into a tin one?" asked Bobby.

Rommy took over. He said, "Have your jokes, boys, but this is serious. Ve're stuck vif Mister Foghorn. Ve...and I mean *us,* the music department, must find some <u>vay</u>...*any* <u>vay</u>...to make our *yarble yarble!*"

Bobby said, "Let's stop dreaming. A singer he'll never be...but I think I could coach him to talk the number."

"But my melody!" cried Rommy, stabbed in the heart. "What happens to my best tune?"

"It will be there, if I know Don Walker. Under the voice in the orchestra, note for note exactly as you wrote it, Rommy. The audience won't realize that he isn't singing it."

Rommy, still unconvinced, looked at me. He asked, "Vhat do you tink, Dan? Vill this trick of Bobby's york?"

"It's got to work. It's our only chance. My problem is to find the right instrument to carry your melody. Its best sound will have to lie in the normal register of our man's speaking voice."

"A cello?"

"He would drive a cellist out of his mind, trying to play in our hero's register. We need an instrument with fixed keys, not one with an unfretted fingerboard."

"A bassoon?"

"Too comedic for a love song."

"A bass clarinet?"

"Too ominous."

He was desperate, asking, "Isn't there an instrument that has the right range that can be played softly?"

"Rommy, it just came to me. There *is* such an instrument. I've never used it, but it exists. It's an E-flat *alto* clarinet, pitched a fifth below the common B-flat clarinet and a fourth above the bass clarinet. It's 'Chalumeau' lies in our man's speaking frequencies. Now please understand, I have never handled or played the instrument myself....All I know about it has been gleaned from books on orchestration. I understand that it is a fixture in full concert bands and is often used in marching ones, so it shouldn't be too difficult to obtain a specimen."

"Who would play it?"

"Our first clarinet player would double on it. I'd only use it on our star's numbers, not throughout the show."

(I knew that the first clarinet in all of Rommy's shows was an old pal from Bustanoby days, who always played his chair as if it were an inherited right, often not to my total satisfaction. In this case, I knew Rommy would be pleased to have his friend paid extra each week for an additional double.)

Our crisis meeting broke up with the understanding that (a) Bobby Dolan would teach our star how to talk through a song like an English actor and (b) that Rommy would have his old friend dig up an E flat *ALTO* clarinet, for the use of which the production would pay him (1) a weekly rental of twenty dollars and (2) an additional 10 percent added to his salary for playing the thing.

Show folk usually place an amazing trust in the mysterious machinations of their music department, properly believing that the details of its operation are too complex for an uninitiated observer to understand. From the moment a musical goes into rehearsal until the first reading with an orchestra, commonly out-of-town, the cast and the staff have heard no accompaniment to their songs and dances other than the depressing sound of a worn-out piano. Suddenly hearing the music of the show played by a full orchestra is a tremendous thrill to all concerned, even stirring the usually blasé musicians who are creating the excitement.

On that happy day, arrangers and conductors are heroes, a joyful period that sometimes lasts as long as twenty-four hours, until individual performers and staff have had time to listen more closely to what will be taking place in the pit while numbers in which they are involved are being rendered. After that initial period of exaltation comes "fixin' time," when everyone and his/her dog has icky suggestions on how to improve an otherwise perfect orchestration.

Rommy demanded and got permission from our producer to have our star's first contact with the orchestra a private one. On that occasion, it was immediately obvious that our idea of having him talk against the alto clarinet's melody would work beautifully—that is, if we could (a) stop our man from trying to sing *at all,* for every once in a while, possibly feeling romantic, he would produce some bone-chilling noises and (b) get Rommy's old pal to play that "curious clarinet" quietly, so that an ordinary listener could understand the lyrics of the song.

On a Dolan promise that he would get our lead to abandon all desire to vocalize, except possibly the last note of the song, when the brass would cover whatever horrible sound came out of that wide-open mouth. On (b), being a clarinetist myself, I pledged that I would explain his function to Rommy's pal, correcting his mistaken impression that that any song of the star was an E flat clarinet solo. On his parts I had written in large letters: *SUBTONE!* but he had ignored that directive, maybe because he didn't know what it meant. "Subtone" is an effect indigenous to single-reed instruments, being a soft, smooth, silky sound, requiring a loose embouchure and light breath from the diaphragm. It is a special timbre that was invented by recording and radio musicians, playing in the lowest "Chalumeau" range of the clarinet.

By the time "Forbidden Melody" opened in Boston, Rommy's beautiful tunes were being presented clearly by the combination of our unmusical lead and our "subtone" clarinet. After reading the excellent Boston critics, who hated the show, Rommy said, "Vell, they didn't like our imported star, but at least they vere wery kind with the score. Of course, none of them knew vhat vas going on down there in the pit, and maybe it is better that they didn't." He continued:

"Vell…I've written a lot of shows, but this is the first time I've had von in vitch ve had to teach our singing star how to talk and our first voodvind how to blow!"

....

(3) The Case of the Available Arranger.

"Forbidden Melody," playing at the Colonial Theatre in Boston, was not alone in its musical appeal to playgoers, for tough competition had much to do with its miserable attendance. Only two blocks away at the Shubert was a new Cole Porter item, "Red, Hot & Blue," with an impressive cast including Ethel Merman, Jimmy Durante, Bob Hope, and the Hartmans. Although its reviews were modest, its producers were hoping, with such a popular cast, that it would be a smash in New York.

Early in the morning of Thursday, October 15, 1936, the phone rang in my room in Boston's Touraine Hotel. It was Selma Tamber, my supervisor at Chappell & Co. in New York City.

After the usual greetings, she asked, "How busy are you with Rommy?"

I told her, "His producers have shut down on all orchestrated changes. I think they are running out of money."

"So you're free and have nothing to do?"

"Well...I have to hold Rommy's hand once in a while. He's not very happy."

"Could you slip in an easy orchestration for another show?"

"I guess I could, but Rommy would have to know and approve."

She thought a moment, then said, "They've never been happy with Merman's first number in 'Red, Hot & Blue,' so Porter is writing a new one."

"At this late date? They open in New York next week, just after we do!"

"Porter has it almost finished, and they want to put it into the show tonight. They tell me it's simple and short."

"It would have to be...but...hey! What's the matter with Bennett and Spialek?"

They're loaded down *here* with a new revue. And you're *there,* with nothing to do. Come on, Don, this is a terrific chance for you. Porter hasn't been ecstatic about his orchestrations lately."

"I won't lift a pen unless Rommy says okay."

"Hang up! I'll get to him but *don't move!*"

I didn't. After about ten uneasy minutes, the phone rang. It was Selma, directing me to "get over to the Ritz and dig up Kessler, Merman's accompanist. He's got all the dope you will need on the instrumentation and her routine. Then get to work...FAST!"

I said, "But did you get Rommy's permission for me to...."

She interrupted, "Rommy says he will need you tomorrow. You're all in the clear today. So *GET GOING!*" She hung up.

Following her instructions, I walked across the Commons to the Ritz-Carlton, where I located Kessler and got the material and information that I would need, leaving the music staff of "Red, Hot & Blue" to organize copyists for an afternoon scramble that I insisted take place at the Touraine, handy to where I would be scoring.

I asked Kessler if I could hear Merman sing the number, now titled "Down in the Depths on the Ninetieth Floor."

He told me, "Last night, after the show, the orchestra was given a seven o'clock call *tonight,* for a one-hour rehearsal of the new Merman number *before* the show. So we have to be ready."

"When can I hear her sing the number with you and the piano?"

"She'll be rehearsing book till late in the afternoon. I won't get her until maybe 4 P.M. If you hold up scoring till then, you'll never make the 7 P.M. orchestra call. You're going to have to sail without a compass. As Durante says, 'That's the conditions that prevail.'"

I hurried back to my room in the Touraine and ordered food. I laid out my working impedimenta and began to study Porter's penciled manuscript of "Down in the Depths on the Ninetieth Floor." Food arrived and while I was charging my batteries, I familiarized myself with the song I would be orchestrating.

Immediately there was a welcome surprise. Almost all songwriters have favorite keys in which they invent their tunes, using copyists to transpose their original manuscripts to the key(s) in which their performers will use.

Not so Porter! He created his song in the proper key for Merman—a very fine point indeed, but most significant. I realized that I was working for a very meticulous man. It would be wise for me to try to be just as finicky.

Although the order of the day made it impossible for Ethel Merman to sing "Down in the Depths" for me, which I was sure she would have wanted to do, I was fairly well equipped to orchestrate for her without benefit of prior audition. In March 1931, Audrey and I had spent our honeymoon week in New York City's Barbizon-Plaza Hotel and emerged from our nuptial bliss long enough to see and enjoy the currently running success "Girl Crazy," Merman's first big hit. Ever since then I had been a devoted fan of the lady with the fabulous pipes. Now I was to orchestrate for her; that thrilling style, that commanding presence, that unique and vibrant voice were all engraved on my memory, ready to be recalled whenever I needed to write an instrumental accompaniment to support her performance.

That October afternoon, my scoring pen fairly flew. When writing for an all-purpose orchestra of twenty-five musicians, there is an "embarrassment of options"—so many different ways the basic material can be orchestrated. A great deal of time can be squandered "thinking through" those options, time that is usually very much "of the essence."

That magical afternoon, I wasted no precious minutes on alternate methods…there was only one solution and that was the "right" one. I could "hear in my head" only Merman's sound and the logical accompaniment for her marvelous bugle. There were no scratched-out and written-over notes, no torn-up score pages, no periods of staring at a blank wall in search of inspiration. By 4:30 P.M., I was finished!

The copyists had arrived at 1:30 P.M. and set up in a room adjacent to mine. It was about 2 P.M. when I gave them my first pages of score amid a great deal of grumbling. Copyists prefer (and rightly so) to be given a completed score to copy so that they can properly lay out alternate page turns, avoiding mass movement of paper. But that is a nicety that has to be abandoned when copyists are handed, progressively, a few score pages at a time, which was certainly the case they could expect with "Down in the Depths."

Having finished the score and feeling completely burned out, I lay down to rest for a few minutes and dropped off the deep end. When I awoke, it was after six o'clock and twilight without. The copyists' room was empty, and I assumed that the orchestration was complete. I grabbed a bun and a cup of java on the way to the Shubert, where I zipped by the stage doorman without a challenge. (He knew me from previous shows.)

I snuck into the back of the house and hid myself in the dark of the last row. I wanted to be available in case some trouble developed in my orchestration, some bobble that only I could unravel. Otherwise I wished to stay anonymous, for I had heard that the show was breeding all kinds of top-level acrimony and I certainly didn't want to get involved. After all, R.H.&B. was still Russell Bennett's baby, although he was at that moment in New York, scoring somebody else's musical.

Praise the Lord! Everything went slick as grease, so I didn't have to arise and declare myself available to fix wrong notes. Even when Merman came in at 7:30 to sing with the new orchestration, there was no hitch, she loved the arrangement and said so, asking, "Who scored this?" The conductor mumbled something, I couldn't tell what.

After Ethel had sung the number a couple of times and felt secure, it was 8 o'clock and the house had to be opened to the public. The rehearsal was over and seat-holders were entering. I went to the "Standing Room Only" area behind the seats and stalled around until the show started. I knew that "Down in the Depths" was Merman's first number and came early in the show. I didn't have long to wait.

I wasn't prepared for that brilliant, golden palliated gown that she wore for the number, nearly overshadowing the clever, important lyrics she enunciated so clearly. Breathless, I waited anxiously for the powerful finish I had added to the composition, knowing that unless the audience, with its applause, was confirming the orchestra's vociferous hosanna, my coda would sound forced and out of place.

Inevitably the finish came and it was beyond my fondest expectations: She stopped the show! Whether or not my "second coming" music would sound appropriate on a rainy Wednesday's matinee was a moot question. Also moot was the advisability of stopping a show so early, a premature high might make all the rest of the evening feel downhill. Those matters were not my concerns. What mattered to me was the unchallengeable fact that Merman had stopped the show with her first number, and I had written the orchestration that helped her do it.

Deliberately incognito, I left the theatre and walked to Lockober's famous restaurant, where I had an excellent, expensive meal, feeling that I had earned it, advancing my cause with people who counted. I didn't need instant recognition; the future was my main concern.

....

"Forbidden Melody" closed on the Saturday night following its opening, achieving a "run" of four performances. It deserved its ignominious fate. My trick with the alto clarinet, trying to conceal the embarrassing fact that our "singing star" couldn't sing, didn't fool even the most tone-deaf critic. That gentleman and his colleagues had an adjectival field day, dragging out vicious metaphors that they had been saving for years. Their posture seemed to be, "when you've got a show down, kick it."

On the Monday after the Saturday closing of "Forbidden Melody," I approached the stage door of the theatre, where the late lamented production had expired. I was carrying a large empty suitcase of Rommy's, intent on rescuing the scores of my orchestrations that I knew were in the music trunk near the subterranean rear entrance to the orchestra pit.

I was operating at the behest of Rommy, who wished to have those scores filed in his large music library. When one was putting together a weekly radio program, one never knew when a score from an old, "forgotten" show could be useful. Often, after a musical closes for good, the scenery is burned and once in a while the music trunk goes with it. Rommy didn't mind if that happened to the instrumental parts, but he wanted to save the scores.

As I went in the stage door with my case, I noticed a small group of vaguely familiar men grouped about the stage door of the theatre directly across the street. I felt that I had seen them all before but thought nothing of it. In the basement I found the music trunk, opened it with Rommy's key and extricated my scores, loaded them in the suitcase, and left the parts to their fiery fate.

There are times in a musician's life when he thinks that the heaviest things in the world are lead, elephants, and music manuscripts, not necessarily in that order. There is one school of thought that believes the weighty thoughts of an orchestrator, transferred to strong paper, is the true cause of the backbreaking quality of manuscript. Another school holds that it's the engrossing ink. Whatever the real reason for my burden's amazing avoirdupois, I was just about able to struggle it up the stairs from the theatre's nether regions to the stage door.

After catching my breath, I worried my millstone out on the sidewalk, only to be confronted with His Nibs, Rommy's clarinet-playing Old Buddy, carrying an instrument case and glowering. He was six inches taller and a hundred pounds heavier than yours truly, but I was much younger and a shifty tennis player.

"Where you goin' with that music?" he snarled.

"I'm taking my scores to Rommy's," I explained. Then I realized he had a right to ask, for Rommy had made him the orchestra's librarian, a cushy job paying the lucky musician an extra $15 dollars a week, in addition to his loot for playing the alto clarinet. I added, "The boss wants to keep my scores for possible radio use."

"He never instructed me to let you take any music out of the theatre."

"The show's closed, man! What difference does it make that he wants my scores? If you insist on an O.K., here's a nickel to call him and check. There's the phone, right inside the stage door!"

"You're trickin' me, Walker, just like you did with this!" He held up the case he was carrying and waved it, barking, "This goddamn alto clarinet I had to buy. Two hundred dollars worth of crap down the drain. I'll never use it, there's nobody who writes for it, I can't even sell it. You owe me the two hundred bucks I've got in it and if I have to, I'll take every one of 'em out of your lousy hide!"

He put down the case and started to advance toward me, fists clenched. His buddies across the street moved for a closer view of the expected chastisement. Orchestrators are not ordinarily popular with marginal musicians.

Somehow I lifted up my case loaded with manuscript and, as he approached me, let it fly. It caught him neatly on the solar plexus and down he went, belching out a long "Hhhuuuuuuhh!" Silently thanking the unknown person who had put the strong straps and rugged lock on my missle, I gathered it up, seeing a cruising cab turning the Eighth Avenue corner with its light on. I flagged it down, loaded on my case, and left the scene of carnage in haste.

I gave Rommy a blow-by-blow account of my unpleasantness with his friend. He laughed and said, "I'll bet that's the first time you ever knocked somebody down with an orchestration."

....

The scene shifts to the summer of 1947, when Audrey and I drove our children across the United States, rented a house in Beverly Hills (on the wrong side of the tracks), and prepared to work on Rommy's second summer radio program for Raleigh Cigarettes. As soon as I stepped into his king-sized, half-underground, music library-cum-studio on Rexford Drive, I saw that a fresh decorating hand had been dressing up the hitherto strictly functional workroom, with its whitewashed stone walls, its dark wooden bookracks loaded with dog-eared scores, and its ebony piano.

On the modest spaces between bookcases, old, retired musical instruments had been decoratively hung on the chalky walls: here an ancient concertina, there a Civil War bugle, further down the room Rommy's childhood three-quarter-size violin, and at the end of the room…Yes! Yes! There it was! The curious E-flat alto clarinet!

I cried, "Rommy! You had to buy this thing after all!"

Coming down the room, he said, apologetically, "Vell…how did I know that you vouldn't vant to use it sometime? I thought that it might be nice to have it handy."

"Did you pay your pal that two hundred dollars he said it cost him?"

"Vell…after I deducted the fifteen dollars he got for being librarian, the 10 percent extra he got for playing that instrument and the tventy dollars rental he collected, my total cost vas only a hundred thirty-six dollars to keep my friend friendly."

"But how can you *stand* it every day…up there on the wall, staring at you, reminding you of 'Forbidden Melody'?"

He smiled and said, "I vant it there. Every day I vant it to remind me to never again allow a producer to cast a star I haven't heard sing *IN PERSON!*"

....

When the debacle called "Forbidden Melody" hurriedly closed, Rommy became disgusted with Broadway showbiz and decided to accept an offer from Metro-Goldwyn-Mayer to revise, for handsome pay, his own scores of "Maytime" and "Desert Song," both musicals scheduled for film remakes. Then he was to adapt, for the same company, the score of Puccini's American opera, "The Girl of the Golden West," for use in an elaborate film. His was a valuable, exclusive contract; acceptance of its terms caused a sizable upheaval in Rommy's career.

With all that work to be accomplished in Hollywood, he decided to make his primary home in that area, keeping only a modest pied-a-terre in New York City, now that the Swift programs and their musical servicing were no more.

So he cut most of his ties to Manhattan, resigning from the American Society of Composers, Authors and Publishers and his presidency of the Songwriters Protective Association, bought a mansion in Beverly Hills next door to Ira Gershwin, acquired a useless Dalmatian, and settled down to work for the flicks.

6. Frank Black

Rommy's withdrawal from New York City did not reduce my workload. I had my constantly renewed (and sweetened) basic contract with Max Dreyfus, who kept sending me out on the road to minister to ailing shows. Then into my life came one Frank Black, an excellent musician, who was administrative head of the music department of the National Broadcasting Company (NBC).

Originally he had been the creator-arranger of the famous Revelers Male Quartet (with James Melton) and had risen from the ranks to be NBC's top "house" conductor, leading important sustaining and commercial programs.

Black's office in Radio City was less than ten minutes' walk from my closet in Chappell & Company. On the very day I had seen the Rombergs off to California, my office phone rang and it was George (can't remember his last name), Frank Black's librarian, who wanted to know if I could slip across 50th Street and meet his boss. Would I?! I was on my way at once.

I met a tall, trim man in his early forties, with a touch of gray just beginning to creep into his straight, sable hair. "Distinguished-looking" would be a good capsule description. As I was to discover, behind that impressive facade was a warm human being, a brilliant pianist, and a considerate friend.

He brushed aside small talk and got down to business at once, explaining, "Here at NBC, our oldest sponsored musical program is Cities Service, which I conduct. For a long time the show, featuring high-class standard music and legitimate singers, has been constantly successful, but recently its ratings have begun to sag a little…a gentle warning, not a fire alarm…as yet.

"I believe in anticipating and eliminating sponsor trouble before it happens. I freely admit that 'we'…and I confess that I am one of the 'we'…have let the program become too routine, too cut-and-dried. I want to change all that…but not suddenly…only quietly and gradually. Would you be interested in helping me rejuvenate good old Cities Service?"

"Of course!" I said excitedly. "It sounds like the kind of interesting challenge I enjoy facing. But—"

"If you've got any 'buts,' spit 'em out."

"You have a famous arranger, Steven Jones, who I know works on Cities Service…why can't he help you make this subtle change you desire?"

"Don't worry about Steve," said Frank. "He is an excellent, well-schooled, *legitimate* orchestrator. You would be no threat to him; I can keep him busy every minute he wants to work. But for the refurbishing of Cities Service, I need a new approach, a fresh mind…and with all that, an appreciation and respect for the values that exist. Somebody like…Don Walker."

I was temporarily stunned, at a loss for words.

He continued. "Part of my job here is to keep aware of what is musically happening in NBC's broadcasting. I couldn't help noticing that George M. Cohan and Sigmund Romberg were both presented at their best on our network, so I asked questions and found out why. It was the general opinion that it wasn't only your excellent orchestrations, but your overall influence that had a lot to do with the success of those well-established names. That is why I would like to enlist you on behalf of Cities Service, a good program that needs to become better."

"You flatter me, Mr. Black."

"Call me *Frank*, for Pete's sake!"

"You must know, Frank, that I'm on a long-term, weekly drawing-account contract with Chappell & Company. Everything I earn, inside or outside 'the house,' has to go through that account. They don't charge me any commission for the service; eventually I receive every penny that comes in or is credited to me. All that Chappell gets is my exclusivity, the right to decide who employs me. If it's radio work, they don't seem to care who I work for, as long as my bills are paid regularly to 'the house.' But if some theatre producer tried to hire me without publishing his musical score with Chappell...well...there'd be instant screaming and waving of an exclusive contract!"

Frank said, "I would like to arrange for you to have some kind of long-term involvement with me. Who do I talk to at Chappell? Max Dreyfus?"

I laughed and told him, "If you asked for him there, they would tell you that he doesn't work for Chappell. By his sales contract with Warner Brothers for Harms, he isn't supposed to be running a competing company. If you want to talk to him about me, here's his private number in Brewster."

Frank had his secretary put through the call. From the one-way conversation, it was hard to tell what was taking place, although it was obvious that the conversation was friendly.

After profuse "thank-yous," etc., Frank hung up and reported, "Max suggests that you develop and orchestrate one big number for the 'new' Cities Service, to be paid for at the going rates. Then, if all goes well, we'll discuss and negotiate a more lasting connection. Do you agree?"

"What can I do? My master has spoken...all the way from Brewster. Have you any ideas for my trial orchestration?"

"Yes. For some time, I've been toying with a plan to present every week a medley from a show that is playing on Broadway. That will bring Cities Service up-to-date in a hurry. Thinking through that plan led to you, Don. Even when you write for radio, there's a theatrical touch in your work. A listener can imagine that he's in the front row of the audience with the orchestra in his lap, accompanying a stage full of dancers and singers."

"It's my ambition to write for the theatre, Frank, but if along the way I find that Mama and the babies need shoes, I'll take profitable work where I find it, even if it means orchestrating for that upstart entertainer, the wireless. So which running show will we 'salute,' as the scriptwriters call it?"

Frank said, "I lean toward that show with the Cole Porter score. I know the drama critics don't like it much, but that music...and those lyrics...I think that classy material is perfect for our purpose."

"I agree. There are a couple of other reasons why 'Red, Hot & Blue' is a good selection. It is a Chappell publication, and I'm sure Max Dreyfus will clear the playing rights for us. Also, the show isn't a complete sellout and our broadcast of its best moments should be a big lift to the box office."

I called Selma Tamber at Chappell, and she rushed us copies of all the songs from "Red, Hot & Blue." Then and there we laid out a routine that included "You've Got Something," "It's De-Lovely," "Goodbye Little Dream, Goodbye," and the title song. Looking over the layout, I observed to Frank, "We've forgotten to include Merman's big number."

Frank hadn't seen the show and said, "We've just got to have that one; what is it called?"

"'Down in the Depths on the Ninetieth Floor.' But do you have a Merman-like singer who could handle it?"

"I think so...but is it absolutely necessary?"

"Ethel stops the show with it."

"Oh? Then we *must* include it. Who scored it? Bennett?...Spialek?..."

I said, "Hold on to your seat, Frank. To answer your reasonable question as to who scored Merman's barnburner, it just happened that I did. It went in the show just two nights before they closed in Boston. It happened that I was the only available arranger in Beantown in that emergency."

....

The medley from "Red, Hot & Blue," based on a going Broadway show, was a shot in the arm for the Cities Service program. It scored high on the charts and was acclaimed for being timely, interesting, and musically flawless. There was a healthy reaction at the box office of the Alvin and Vinton Freedley, and the producer was satisfied that he had traded the rights for that one performance for what was actually a free, fifteen-minute radio commercial.

Frank Black was so pleased with my work on the R., H. & B. medley that he immediately attempted to fashion a contract with Max Dreyfus, whereby he would have the right to my professional services whenever Chappell did not need me for theatrical orchestration. When the lawyers got hold of that one and all its endless permutations, it soon became obvious that no such contract, fair to both sides, could ever be invented. So I worked for Frank Black until his retirement from NBC in the late forties without a word of our accord on paper, with only a handshake supporting our "Gentlemen's Agreement."

On Cities Service, the success of my first show medley led to demands for more. The only problem was the paucity of musicals with the necessary quality and reputation. At times we had to use revivals and even "salute" composers in order to produce our theatrical selections. The personnel of Cities Service's advertising agency hated me, for my show medleys were very close to what lawyers call a "grand right," which producers of musicals are loath to release for broadcasting without payment of ridiculous amounts of boodle.

Another backfire from my inventions was the understandable desire of Frank B. to capitalize on my involvement with the musical theatre: when I had worked on a new production from its inception, doing preliminary research, spending approximately four packed weeks orchestrating it in New York, then nursing it through all the interminable tiny changes made in its agonizing weeks out-of-town, when I thought that with the arrival of the scheduled New York opening night I would at last be relieved of the burden of endlessly revising that pawed-over score, that was when I would discover that dear Frank had scheduled, for Cities Service, one of my typical "show medleys," based on the music of the stage show that I was longing to forget for a while.

Working for Frank Black was not all agony. Being initially an arranger-orchestrator himself, he knew very well how to challenge me with fascinating and broadening musical projects. There was a summer sustaining program where I had to work with an orchestra that was a facsimile of the late Classical, late Mozart combination with its double everything: two flutes, two oboes, two clarinets, two bassoons, two horns, two trumpets, and two timpani, plus a reduced but complete string section. There was a symphonic series featuring odd items such as Don Walker's orchestration of a Godowski piano transcription of a composition by Von Weber! Frank even went so far out as to have me orchestrate, for the full symphony, portions of Beethoven's late string quartets!

Musical madness of that sort requires the collaboration of a superb orchestra of near virtuosi, playing at times tongue in cheek. Frank Black acquired the use of such an orchestra shortly after I started to work for him; it was available to him throughout the rest of his career at NBC.

In the spring of 1937, the halls and offices of NBC were all abuzz with the news that David Sarnoff, its Chairman of the Board, had signed Arturo Toscanini to conduct a new NBC Symphony Orchestra, yet to be organized. The first scheduled concert of the infant ensemble, with Toscanini conducting, was to be broadcast on Christmas night, that aging year of 1937, from Studio 8-H of the RCA building in Radio City.

All through the spring, summer, and fall of that year, NBC's contractor of musicians, H. Leopold Spitalny, labored to form the brand-new symphony orchestra that Sarnoff had promised and used to entice Toscanini. One can easily imagine the problems and pressures accompanying such a task. At the beginning of the year, Spitalny had been in charge of seventy-four "house" musicians, of which at least half were unusable in the symphony, being standby pianists, saxophonists, guitarists, trap-drummers, etc. At first the hasty formation of a great new sinfonia seemed doomed, but as the word spread Spitalny was surprised to discover that so many top-drawer players were available, motivated by the desire to experience the excitement of playing under the legendary baton of the famous conductor.

Underwriting the staggering cost of a full symphony orchestra of over one hundred musicians, signed to yearly contracts, was not a normal, or even a possible procedure for a broadcasting company, rich as NBC happened to be. So the contracts that Spitalny's recruits had to sign gave NBC the right to designate for whom and for what the individual musician would perform.

That is why, for the next seventeen years, the sustaining and often the commercial programs broadcast from NBC benefited from the availability of the select musicians recruited for Toscanini's use.

As long as the Maestro had "his" orchestra complete and handy for his rehearsals, concerts, and recording sessions, he didn't mind having them work for other conductors while he was elsewhere. It was good for their technique to have to play a certain number of hours per week for someone else, for that would keep them in shape for when he returned. At that point they had to be razor-sharp and ready!

Others at NBC profited from the constant presence of the superb musicians who had been recruited for Toscanini. Frank Black and his arranger-orchestrator, Don Walker, were among that lucky group of beneficiaries.

....

For approximately ten years, starting in 1937, I orchestrated Broadway musicals as assigned to me by Max Dreyfus. In the gaps between those stints, I arranged and scored music for Frank Black and his NBC radio programs. Switching from radio to the theatre was easy, for the sounds of a pit orchestra were forever printed on my mind. Executing the reverse, living stage to electronic studio was always difficult, for broadcasting was a new audio technique that was still very much in the process of physical development. Many times, while making the transition from theatre to radio, I would go to a silent speaker and, pressing an ear against the fabric over the horn, try to imagine what the notes I intended to write would sound like coming out of that mute box. Any uninformed person catching me in the middle of that act would surely think that I had gone bananas...and maybe they would have been right.

In the country one weekend afternoon, I was operating on an orchestration when the phone rang. It was Frank Black. He said, "What are you doing right now?"

"Working for you," I answered, pleased that it wasn't necessary for me to twist the truth a bit to show my dedication.

"That dreary business can wait," he said. "You'll never guess where I am."

"I'm afraid to try," I admitted.

"Do you know where Mechanicsville Road is?"

"If it's the Bucks County Mechanicsville Road, I sure do. It crosses Aquetong, the road I'm on, about four miles from here."

"Well, get in your jalopy and rattle north to that junction, turn left and, at the third driveway, turn right. Got it?"

"Yep! Is it safe to bring Audrey?"

"Of course."

So I recruited her and off we went, following Frank's directions, leading us down a tree lined lane to a large homestead, obviously old but rebuilt and extended fairly recently. And there was Frank greeting us, introducing his beautiful young wife, Eve, with her absolutely authentic Georgian accent.

"How do you like it?" he asked.

We were stunned, not only at the size of the manor but from the unexpected shock of finding the urban Blacks in our rustic surroundings.

"It's...it's awesome!" I stuttered.

"We just bought it!" exulted Frank. "All this and one hundred ten fertile acres!"

"You're going to farm it?" I asked in surprise.

"We don't have to worry about tilling the land," explained Frank. "There's an adjacent farmer with four grown sons and all the necessary machinery; he wants to rent the acreage."

Eve suggested that we come in, see the house, and have a drink before Frank showed me around "the ranch" while she and Audrey talked women's talk.

When Frank gave me the grand tour, we were accompanied by his gorgeous red setter, who seemed devoted to him. We saw the well-kept barns and outbuildings, then going back to the house we came to an enormous oak tree.

Frank patted the great trunk, saying, "I've been told that this titan was a good-sized sapling when Columbus discovered America."

In a farmer's field, between my property and the "House of Decision," stood a similar giant oak: solitary, symmetrical, in the locale, famous. Experts had figured its age to be at least five hundred years. As far as girth was concerned, Frank's patriarch could have been its twin brother, with one exception: Frank's tree had a big, bulky, low-level branch almost as portly as its main trunk, sticking out at right angles toward the barns. How that unbalanced, poorly propped-up branch had remained intact and fastened to the trunk, through all those hundreds of years, was a major mystery, but there it grew and prospered, denying the laws of gravitation, full of leaves and life.

I could see that Frank was understandably proud of his model farm, his red setter and, in particular, his great tree. I was happy for him to have his vibrant Eve, supporting him in his daily struggle with the backbiters that prowl the inner hallways of great corporations.

To dilute my excessive altruism, I must confess that I was pleased to have a trusty messenger handy to carry my scores into New York to be copied; it meant I could do more work in the peaceful country, instead of sweating it out in that un-airconditioned closet in the RKO building, with that saxophone teacher, also with his window open, honking with his pupil in that hungry studio directly across 50th Street.

....

After Toscanini's first season with the NBC Symphony ('37–'38) was successful, the Maestro, now having confidence in the personnel, began to lengthen his season with it, even taking it on tour. The threat of war in Europe was also a factor in reducing his appearances overseas.

In spite of his increased schedule in the Western Hemisphere, there was still about half a year during which the members of the NBC Symphony were available for sustaining and commercial programs. There were a number of summers when Frank Black was the anchor conductor of the NBC Symphony's broadcasts, sharing the podium with single appearances of guest conductors, some of them quite famous.

I was hired to attend all the rehearsals of those summer symphony programs, working in the control room, close to the sound engineer, reading the orchestrations and cueing him for significant changes of dynamics. Today we have engineers and directors who have been trained to follow orchestral scores, but in the forties there was "no such animal" and the sound controllers had to depend on score-reading musicians like yours truly.

The normal human ear is a marvelous sound receiver, detecting frequencies from the threshold of audibility to the threshold of pain, a far wider range than the electronic instruments of the forties possessed. A full symphony orchestra of one hundred musicians, with its tremendous variety of quality and levels of sounds, was a constant headache to the engineers. Their greatest fear was being caught napping when the orchestra made a sudden violent explosion, as it is often likely to do, knocking the dial needle into the red range and sometimes taking the program off the air. The only way to forestall that disaster was to have somebody available to read the score and warn the engineer, at the critical second, to "down the pots!"

After participating in such rehearsals, my regular routine was to go home and, taking notes, listen to the program on the air, leaving the men in the sound booth the job of controlling the orchestra, getting myself out of their hair.

It was a great experience for me, increasing my knowledge of symphonic scores many-fold, while being handsomely paid to do it. The individual little quirks and foibles of the guest conductors were interesting to observe and discuss. I remember one program when Stokowski was the guest conductor, rehearsing a very modern work. (I think it was an Arthur Bliss Concerto.) There was one irritating passage where that great orchestra had a tendency to fall apart. Whether the trouble arose from an inherent defect in the scoring or from Stokowski's beat is impossible to pinpoint, they were very uncooperative bars. Stokowski rehearsed them over and over, making sure.

That night I listened to the program at home as usual. As the orchestra approached those perverse bars, I felt a growing apprehension and sure enough, when they got to them, that super collection of sterling instrumentalists became as disorganized as a junior high school orchestra at its first concert. Over the air waves, I heard Leopold Antohi Stanislaw Stokowski yelling, "STOP! CUT!" and then, "Start at letter K!" There was a pause until everyone found letter "K" and then the concert was resumed. Mercifully, television had not yet arrived, or there would have been a beautiful picture of red faces accompanying the continuo.

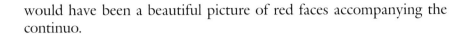

One Sunday in '43 Audrey, I had been invited to a Sunday brunch at Frank's messuage. When we arrived, no dog, nor Frank, greeted us. I pulled the rope on the exterior bell several times before Frank appeared.

He said, "Sorry, but Eve and I are rather busy right now. Come in and see what we've got to contend with."

We entered and followed Frank to his interior kitchen door with the glass insert. "Take a look," he said, "and see the brouhaha that's going on inside."

We looked. At first it seemed that the Blacks' grand country kitchen was a mass of writhing red. Then Frank's setter could be distinguished, rushing about, trying to take care of ten...count 'em if you can...TEN RED SETTER PUPPIES! We had heard that the breed often produces abnormally large litters, but we hadn't expected to find proof of that canine trivia in Frank Black's kitchen!

But there they were, chasing each other, chasing Mama, sniffing, barking, biting, stopping to pee-pee and excrete while poor Eve vainly tried to mop up the multiple messes that the excited animals kept making.

Frank made the understatement of the year, apologizing, "I'm afraid we won't be able to give you brunch...our cook's upstairs in her room and we can't even get to the stove."

So he took us to Colligan's Stockton Inn for brunch. At one point, after we had enjoyed the Maryland Terrapin, Frank seemed to fall into a brown study, being abnormally quiet for a while.

Finally I said, "What's on your mind, Frank? Are you with us or somewhere else?"

He shook his head and answered, "No, I was just thinking that maybe we'd be better off with a *male* dog."

I said, "Maybe a nice black Labrador."

"That's a *very* good idea...*Black*...all-black...Frank Black's all-black, all-male Labrador!"

In the middle 1940s, there was a late August weekend when Bucks County was battered by a savage series of damaging storms. First were two days of tropical rain, softening the ground, loosening roots. Then came the windstorm with gusts up to forty-five miles per hour. Lastly, to top off the bitter dose, there was a violent electrical storm that came circling back, time after time. Cornered by the elements, I retreated to my back room and dug into a job previously handed to me by Frank Black.

Finally the sun peeked out and I emerged from solitary with a completed orchestration, anxious to get it into Frank's valise so he would carry it to New York to be copied.

On the way to his farm, I was forced to make several short detours around large fallen trees that blocked the road—trees that the overwhelmed highway crews had not yet reached to clear from the roads. Along the way I began to wonder how Frank's precious patriarch had fared in the recent monsoon.

Driving down his tree-lined long lane, I could note some minor damage, but nothing abnormal or irreparable. Getting out of my car at the front of the house, there was Frank's cherished oak proudly lifting its majestic head over the rear of the mansion.

Thank Heaven his revered tree is intact, I thought, patting Frank's Labrador, who had appeared to check me out. His master was not far behind, and I greeted him with congratulations for his property's survival in the recent holocaust.

"Hold the hurrahs," he said."Wait till you see the rear view."

He led me around to the back of the house. It appeared that a bolt of lightning had hit exactly where that great lower off-center branch had grown out of the main trunk. That enormous limb now lay on the ground, extending nearly to an outbuilding. Where the dismembered branch had grown out of the rear of the tree, there remained a monstrous open wound in the trunk. One could still smell the brimstone.

"My tree is ruined," said Frank sadly. "There it stood for five hundred years, defying the elements, the timber harvesters, the fungi and insect pests. Then Frank Black comes along and whoever it is up there decides Frankie needs a good kick in the pants. There goes my tree, all buggered up."

"But Frank, it isn't ruined," I argued. "Tree surgeons can fix that injury to the main trunk, clean it up, and paint it over. Without that cockeyed limb, your tree looks better than ever…now it's symmetrical, better balanced."

Frank shook his head. "My tree's been terribly hurt," he groused. "It will never be the same as it was for five hundred years...never ever the same...now...."

....

I know it would be foolish for me to ascribe too much importance to "the incident of the tree" as marking a crucial change in Frank B. and his musical career. After that fateful day, I was immediately engulfed in theatrical orchestration, assigned to me by Max Dreyfus, who held my basic contract. Then Sigmund Romberg reentered my life (he had never completely left it), and I was too busy with him and other theatre personalities to orchestrate for Frank Black.

All I am certain of is the following: When I returned from California in the fall of 1947, after having worked for Rommy on the second Raleigh summer program, there was a short hiatus in my usually clogged schedule. I wondered about Frank and tried to find out what had happened to him.

Apparently he had taken advantage of the RCA pension plans and, being eligible for retirement, decided to take the leap. His address was in Georgia, where his wife, Eve, had property. I never followed up that information, meaning to try, but never finding the time.

(This page is held open in case further research on Frank B. is done and found sufficiently interesting to include here.)

7. <u>Cole</u> (Cole Albert Porter)

O ne slushy day in March '38, while I was working at home in
Bucks, scoring an arrangement for Frank Black's Cities Service
radio program, I received a phone call from Selma Tamber, my
dispatcher at Chappell & Co. in New York. After the usual salutations,
she advised, "Don, hold on to your crew cut; I have exciting news for
you, a real spine-shaker!"

Accustomed to Selma's normal hyperbole, I answered calmly,
"Dollink, when you call me here, it's usually to order me to pack my
pen and rush to Detroit or Hartford to fix up somebody else's idiot
attempts to orchestrate."

"Not this time, fella," she crowed. This assignment will be your
baby from the start. An important composer has asked for you and he
wants no one else!"

"And who is this madman?"

"Believe it or not, a gentleman named Cole Porter."

(I knew that in October of '37, a skittish riding horse with Cole in
its saddle had suddenly reared and fallen back on both of Cole's legs,
smashing them. Doctors had recommended double amputation, but
Cole's wife, Linda, had found a specialist, a Dr. Moorhead, who was
willing to try to save the limbs. In spite of his agony and the effects of
massive sedation, Cole had been able to finish the songs for a musical
version of "By Candlelight," retitled "You Never Know," on which
Porter had been working before the dreadful accident had occurred.
One waggish critic, reporting on the musical's New Haven "break-in,"
thought that "Never Know No! No!" would be a more enlightening
title for the Shubertian mess, which was "in big trouble.")

"Please, Selma," I begged, "don't send me out on the road to rescore 'You Never Know.' I read that Lupe Velez has sworn that she will murder Libby Holman; that the Shuberts, J.J., Lee, and even son Johnny, are making silly suggestions that the director, Rowland Leigh, is taking seriously. Please, don't get me mixed up in that bust with Porter unavailable."

Selma was laughing so hard she could barely talk. "Don't worry so, Don," she gasped. "I'm not sending you out to that cat-ass-trophe. Porter can't be on the road to protect his score, so he is washing his hands of the whole mishmash. He's going to allow the Shuberts to bring in other songwriters if they so wish. No...you can forget 'You Never Know.' I'm calling you now about Cole's *next* show, giving you plenty of time to arrange your schedule before it goes into rehearsal this coming September."

My knotted innards began to relax. "Thank Heavens, Selma," I breathed. "You had me scared that time. Now tell me all about this *new* Porter show."

"Vinton Freedley is producing. It will go into the Alvin. Gaxton and Moore are signed, and Vinton expects to get Mae West. I think the choreographer will be Alton."

"Great!" I broke in. "I've had a lot of luck working with Bob. Who's the overall director?"

"I'm not sure...I think it's the male part of the husband-and-wife team who's writing the book."

"Now who would that be?"

"I've forgotten. I know they had a big straight comedy hit not long ago: 'Boy Meets Girl.'"

"Now wait a moment, Selma, you can't mean the Spewacks."

"That's the pair, Sam and Bella! Do you know them?"

"No, I don't. But they happen to be living within a half-mile of where I am sitting, talking to you. That passes for 'neighbors' out here in the wilds."

"I think it would be a good idea for you to get to know them, since you'll be working with them come September."

"Forthwith, Selma. I will put your excellent suggestion into action, insinuating myself on the Spewacks so that by the time the show goes into rehearsal we will be, more or less, bosom friends."

Not to be outdone, she replied, "And I hope that your orchestrations for their show will be more concise than the dialogue you are spouting these days. You are getting wordier and wordier."

"You'll have to put up with me, Selma," I replied. "I just happen to be in my gray, garrulous period at present. I promise that it will not be extravagantly overextended."

She rang off, as they still say in England.

"And what was all that?" Audrey asked. "I know it was Selma on the line, but your one-way conversation sounded as if something important is happening."

"It is that," I said. "I'm to be given sole charge of the orchestrations for Porter's next show, and she wants me to get friendly with the scriptwriters, the Spewacks."

"The new people up the road?"

"Check. But how am I going to get to meet them?"

"Call them on the phone...get an appointment."

Of course the Spewacks had an unlisted number. I turned the problem over to Selma, who called me back without it, saying, "The Freedley office has their number but can't give it to anyone. The Spewacks are working on the book and don't want to be bothered by anyone less than Franklin Delano Roosevelt."

So there was no way to phone them, yet I was too excited to go back to work on Cities Service. I said to Audrey, "I think I'll ride up there and introduce myself."

She said, "I think you're out of your mind. If you're bent on going up there and horning in when they're stuck on a tough line, you'll make enemies, not friends. If you're hopelessly determined to gate-crash, you'll have to do it without the car. I have to go shopping or else we'll be starving tonight."

Not yet being a two-car family, I went hunting for my galoshes, obstinately resolved to contact the Spewacks in person and find out more about the coming Porter musical.

....

Slushing up the hilly road on the melting snow and ice, I thought about a man I had never met: Cole Porter. I had heard that when he had finished composing "Down in the Depths" on that Thursday night in Boston, he had gotten into a bitter argument with Vinton Freedley, going angrily off to New York. Somehow, after Merman had stopped the show with the new number, Freedley had wooed the composer back to the production, where Cole had plenty of opportunity to hear and become familiar with my single orchestration.

A year and a couple of motion picture scores later came Cole's appalling accident with the horse. With constant pain, recurring operations, and massive sedation, how was it possible that in the poor man's endless agony he had remembered my small contribution to "Red, Hot & Blue" and apparently wanted more of the same, enough to offer me the entire score of his new project?

In my previous Broadway experience, I had once before been assigned to orchestrate all of a musical. That was for Romberg's "Maywine," whose rehearsal period coincided with the second Swift radio program. Rommy, worried about the excessive pressures I was undergoing, gave one unimportant number in the second act, mostly music under dialogue, to my colleague Robert Russell Bennett to orchestrate. I scored all the rest of the show myself. But Russ was famous; he had to be given proper credit, so the line in the program read: "Orchestrations by Don Walker and Robert Russell Bennett."

In New York, there were more newspapers and therefore more theatre critics in 1935 than there are today. The treatment of that dual credit was diverse. Some reviewers gave sole credit to an embarrassed Bennett. Others reversed the program credit while some simply gave no credit at all for orchestration.

To a person with a steady job, it may seem picayune for showpeople to put so much emphasis on the procurement of proper credit. One should realize that the night a show opens on Broadway, a substantial number of the creative people, who have made that opening possible, are simultaneously out of work and looking for employment. To aid them in their quests, they have nothing but unreliable "word-of-mouth" and whatever credits, in black and white, that they can garner from the reviews of dramatic critics. Such mentions are gratefully hoarded as necessary equipment for landing fresh positions in that precarious profession called showbiz.

If I could orchestrate every note of Cole Porter's next musical, if the show was a hit, if I managed to score an outstanding job, if a couple of critics...even one!...noticed my contribution and mentioned it, if...if...a whole raft of IFS!...then maybe I would become established as an orchestrator of Broadway musicals and have producers going to Max Dreyfus, desiring to enlist my services.

All these "ifs" and more passed through my mind as I slogged up Aquetong Road until it reached its sharp left turn, where the Spewacks' private road led straight ahead. The mushy snow was even deeper as I struggled toward the big house, noting the capacious barn, a chicken house, a full corncrib, and a couple of nondescript small buildings. It was obvious that once the property was a working farm and surprise! part of it was still working, for I heard a horse neigh, a cow moo, and Plymouth Rocks were about, shaking their brilliant red wattles as they pecked in the snow.

I approached the main house, uncertain which of its numerous doors was the official entrance. Many of the old Bucks County farmhouses, like my own, were "railway trains" of single rooms with their own outside doors and fireplaces, added onto the "train" as the family grew and prospered. There was one door that had fancy glass inserts, a small roofed porch led to it. I guessed it was the main entry, for hanging from the little roof was an old brass firebell with a short length of rope attached to its clapper. I grabbed the rope and made the welkin ring.

There was a brief response from the farm animals, but that was all. I rang again. Still nothing but neighs, moos, and clucks.

I was about to give up and mush home when through the glass in the door, I discerned shadowy movement. Someone was there! A closer look through the glass told me that within a tall man was struggling with a so-called "burglar-proof," Manhattan-style, shiny new chain-lock.

His mouth moved, but the door was so tightly sealed I couldn't understand him any more than he could comprehend my hurried self-identification. Suddenly the door became unstuck. Restrained from opening further by the chain, a two-inch rift appeared, making vocal communication possible.

He yelled, "Whatever you're selling, we don't want it!"

I yelled back, "I'm not selling anything!"

"We've donated to the Eagle Fire Company, the Red Cross, the Boy Scouts, and the Girl Scout Cookies!"

"I'm not collecting! I don't want any money!"

"No money? Then what the devil are you here for?"

I thought it was time to try to break through his exurban paranoia by throwing some heavy names about, even if I had to stretch the truth a smidgen. So I announced, "My name is Don Walker. Cole Porter and Vinton Freedley have agreed that I shall be the orchestrator of the musical whose book you and your wife are working on right now. Max Dreyfus, head of Chappell and Company...."

Sam cut in, "Now wait a moment! How do I know you are what you say you are? Where's your car? You barge in here and—"

"Mr. Spewack, please…All you need to do is contact Vinton Freedley and he'll vouch for me. I would have called you earlier, but you have a carefully guarded unlisted phone number."

"All right, all right…I'll check you out. Don't go away mad."

He dropped his chains and disappeared. I waited.

Soon he was back and working on the lock again. He said, "Sorry to keep you waiting like this, but I'm not much of an expert with mechanical things…by the way, where *is* your car?"

"Audrey, my wife, is using it. So I walked."

"Do you mean that you live that close?"

"That's right. Mr. Dreyfus thinks it's a lucky break. I'll be able to answer any technical musical problems for you, without bothering Cole."

"There's some truth in that." All at once he solved the chain problem, the door opened all the way, and he beckoned me in, saying, "Enter Wuthering Heights."

We went through a small vestibule into a capacious living room, passing a closed grand piano with a violin resting on its lid. Across the room a mature fire glowed on the king-sized hearth, toasting the small, compact lady who sat on a long davenport, facing the warmth. She held a reporter's yellow pad, on which she had been making penciled notes.

"Bella," said Sam, "this is Don Walker, who lives down the road a piece. He's going to orchestrate our show."

"He is!? Do you mean to tell me that Freedley has to reach out to this God-forsaken corner of the Revolution to find an orchestrator? When Broadway is crawling with known tune-benders? What does Cole think about it?"

"As a matter of fact, Cole picked him out."

"Under sedation?"

"No, Bella, in cold blood. Cole *wants* him, *very much,* so Vinton tells me."

She looked at me askance. I felt like an unwanted slave, naked on the auction block.

She said to Sam, "He doesn't look like a musician to me…that sly phiz…more like a crooked accountant."

I said, "Mrs. Spewack, you've got me skewered. I have to confess that I studied four long years at Wharton School to be a C.P.A. Then I threw all that away to scribble music notes."

"I'll bet your bills are beauties."

"They are. Because my wife, Audrey, makes them up, sends them out, writes all the checks, and balances the bank account. When I switched to music, I went all the way."

"Stop! You'll be giving my husband ideas. I know he'd just love to get rid of business matters so he could dream about the shape of the next scene and how he intends to direct it. Don't infect him! He'd love to be diverted."

Sam said, "Running this place takes a lot more effort than we had expected. In our New York apartment, we were getting so many interruptions we couldn't get any work done. There was always somebody at the front door. Friends, agents, producers, actors, welfare workers, window cleaners…we couldn't get in an air-hour's writing without some kind of an interruption. So we decided to get out into the country where no one, except the absolutely necessary contacts, could bother us. Praying for peace, we found this farm, sixty miles from the city…."

"…And look what happened," griped Bella. "It takes us damn near every minute to just *exist* in this place…this…time-killer!"

I said, "I'm a sort of a native here, born across the river in Lambertville. As I remember, your property here has always been a working farm."

"That's right!" affirmed Sam. "That's how we bought it: crops in the ground, machinery in the barn, fruit on the trees…."

"…And a cow giving milk, damn her," added Bella.

"…And you bought it just the way it stood?" I asked.

"That we did," admitted Sam. "And then crops grew, along with the weeds, fruit ripened, machinery broke down…."

"…And the cow went dry," reported Bella.

"And then it was harvest time," sighed Sam. "Harvest time plus a solid ten days of heavy rains: fungi-growing, insect-multiplying…."

"Insect multiplying?"

Bella explained, "When it's raining, the insects stay home and make more insects, like people."

"That's an interesting theory," I remarked.

"It's true," said Bella. "But the squeeze that pinches me the most is that damned Molly, the cow. We kept her so we'd have fresh, unprocessed milk…you never know what chemicals they put in store-bought stuff. We have a farmhand who knows how to milk her, so why not have our own mini-dairy?"

"But you say she's gone dry."

"And do you know what we have to do to get her making milk again? They tell me that we've got to take her to a bull, or have the bull come here (which is more expensive) and let her have a time for herself! I feel like a procuress!"

Sam was fussing with the fire, renewing it.

I said to Bella, "I know what you're groaning about. Early in our Bucks County life, we had three goats: two nannies and one billy. What went on with that trio was unbelievable. Then old billy-goat ate a tin can and died. We sold the nannies at Rice's Sale and got out of the goat business before the children were old enough to ask embarrassing questions."

Sam said, "Nell, we enjoy whole milk. So I guess we'll have to get Molly laid."

"And I've got to get back to my orchestration," I said, "or else Audrey won't have the chips to buy our bottled milk. I'd like to ask one question before I leave." I gestured toward the big piano. "Who plays the violin in this house?"

"That's Sam's," Bella explained. "When he's stuck on something we're writing, he picks up that fiddle and goes far away...that's why we need such a long dwelling...there he practices playing sad songs. It's nauseating but, I guess, necessary. When he comes back to Mama, he usually has his creative problem solved."

"It's wonderful to have the writer-director of a musical something of a musician himself."

"That's quite a statement," replied Bella, "but be careful how you throw that word, *musician* about. It could very easily get bruised in these quarters."

It was past time for me to leave them to their job. I handed Bella a note, saying, "I don't want to keep you away from your work any longer. Here's my local and New York phone numbers. If there are any technical musical matters on which you might want my advice, don't hesitate to call me. Maybe we could save bothering Cole that way. I'll always be available to you people."

So I put on my galoshes and mackinaw and sloshed back to my Cities Service orchestration, hoping that my contact with the Spewacks might save Cole Porter some worry over minor musical matters.

The hike was easier going home, downhill all the way.

....

The theatre news in that summer of '38 was constantly enlivened by the efforts of Vinton Freedley, his PR people, his authors, and even the Alvin Theatre's maintenance men to find an audience-catching title for the coming new Cole Porter musical. The story was based on an early Spewack unmusical comedy, "Clear All Wires," which had been moderately unsuccessful, so that name was unlucky, not to be considered.

The plot was mainly concerned with the faux pas of an American Ambassador to Russia (Victor Moore), his corn-fed wife (Sophie Tucker), an American publisher (William Gaxton), his doxy (June Knight), and other assorted Americans embroiled with various Russians in Moscow.

In the spring, the production was announced as "I Am an American"; in the summer, it was called "First in the Hearts." At the absolute deadline, as the show went into rehearsal in early September, the cast was informed that they would be preparing a musical to be known as "Leave It to Me." That appellation was certainly no gem, but it remained, in want of anything better.

Contributing to the general apprehension felt by all who were involved in the musical, in early June, Cole slipped upon a stone staircase and again broke a leg that had been healing nicely. Once more he was immobile, an awkward and dangerous plight with a new score about to go in rehearsal. At the first cast call, with its traditional reading of the script by the actors, interspersed with the songs, Cole was unable to be present and others had to demonstrate his work. It was not an auspicious beginning.

Although Cole Porter's most obvious gift was his witty way with words, to me his musical endowment was even more impressive. Much has been whispered and some of it written concerning Cole's musical relationship with Dr. Albert Sirmay, his European-born long-time friend, adviser, and editor. Cole wrote his songs by himself, first a general idea, a rhythm, a title, then the lyrics. By that time the tune followed easily and finally, the basic harmonization, all carefully written out.

The next step was a conference with Dr. Sirmay about the new song. The good doctor's main function at Chappell & Company was to prepare all new songs for publication (not only Porter's), seeing that the printed piano parts were playable by the fingers of an average amateur. It was in this process that Sirmay could influence the composer, making sure the latter saw all the harmonic options that were available. But if such minor changes were ever adopted, one can be sure that it was Porter's decision. I was there. I saw the process and truly believe that all the published music with Porter's name on it was invented by him alone…except one! That silly one will be revealed in good time.

One day Robert Russell Bennett, who was sitting at the desk facing me in our room at Chappell & Co., asked me, "How are you making out with your Cole Porter score?" And I answered, "I'm suffering from a grievous lack of 'come sopra.'" That was a wry orchestrator's joke if there ever was one. Explanation: "Come sopra," in Italian music, means "as above." Specifically, it is the instruction that the orchestrator gives the copyist when there are certain bars of music, already orchestrated, that can be used again, verbatim, at a subsequent place in the number. The occasion often arises from a composer's use of that ubiquitous song form: "a-a-b-a," where the "a" theme is repeated twice, usually with different lyrics sung to the same accompaniment. Porter frequently used that old form but would make subtle changes in the repetitions of the "a" melody, to adjust to the changed accents in his new lyrics. Thus the panting orchestrator, the lowly pieceworker, was denied the customary candy of "come sopra," having to write out every single note of a Cole Porter score.

....

Vinton Freedley was an excessively frugal producer, a staunch defender of his investors' dollars. Thus the New York rehearsal period of "Leave It to Me" was trimmed to the absolute minimum of three weeks, with the final Sunday a union-required day off, so that the cast could prepare to travel to New Haven on the Monday.

In the summer of '38, I had spent some time planning how I was going to be able to orchestrate "Leave It to Me" without any help from my colleagues. I realized that during those hectic twenty days of rehearsal in New York, I would be spending a great deal of time traveling to and from the theatre to see numbers that were ready for me to orchestrate. There would be staff conferences requiring my attendance; sufficient hours for decent meals and sleep would have to be allowed; coffee and doughnuts might fuel me through a twenty-four-hour arranging crisis, but I was facing a grueling three-week drill! During that limited period, I would have to keep myself in top condition, mentally and physically, to be able to orchestrate the entire show.

"Leave It to Me" was a typical "book" musical. At the out-of-town opening of such shows, as Chappell & Company's records revealed to me, there would be, on the average, 3200 bars (or 800 score pages) of orchestrated music played. (Long ago, lost in the mists of time, the custom of calling four bars a score page originated, no one knows how or why.)

Dividing 3200 bars (or 800 pages) by 20 days gave me an estimated daily production average of 160 bars (or 40 pages) of score, a killing pace, especially when I knew that at the beginning of rehearsals there would be nothing staged and ready for me to see, making my daily quota, when things got going, even more difficult, if not impossible, to achieve. I had to find a way to beat the statistics.

There was only one way: write a lot of those 3200 bars *before* the show went into rehearsal. There is a substantial amount of scoring in a musicomedy that does not accompany "staged" action: the overture, change music, the entr'acte, and the exit march. In most musicals, such numbers require 150 to 200 heavily scored pages that accompany no voices. If one man desires to orchestrate a musical, employing no extra help, he should score those purely orchestral numbers before the commencement of rehearsals.

"Leave It to Me" was purported to be a "small" show, but by the time the production was ready to go on the road, the cast had mushroomed to include fifty more or less discontented performers. None were happy with the show and their assigned roles, in particular, June Knight, who had recently married a millionaire and naturally felt quite independent. She was appalled by the paucity of her lines and hated the second act song she had been given. June begged the authors to let her switch songs with Sophie Tucker, who had been allotted "Most Gentlemen Don't Like Love," while June had been saddled with "My Heart Belongs to Daddy," in her estimation a sure loser. When the movers and shakers all turned a deaf ear to her pleas, she quit.

Less than ten days remained before the trek to New Haven. It was panic-time and every theatrical agent on the Main Stem had an instant candidate for the miniscule role of Dolly Winslow. Desperately needed rehearsals were held up to audition the flood of hopefuls.

Lawrence (Larry) Schwab, a theatrical producer who occasionally served as an actor's agent, brought in a young woman he had recently put under personal contract after seeing her perform her singing-dancing act in an amateur contest in California. He had been planning to put her in a show, "Ring Out the News," that he was trying to assemble. Its prospects had seemed sufficiently promising for him to summon her, train fare advanced, from her family's home in Weatherford, Texas, where she had been resting.

What Schwab didn't know, until being presented with a fait accompli, was that his discovery had discovered that she could bring along her companion-secretary-nursemaid and her young bratscal of a son, the product of a very early, soon defunct marriage, all for that cash first-class train fare, provided that they all traveled on a Houston-Manhattan cattle boat!

The sea voyage took a much longer time en route than the train. The group arrived in New York just in time to find that "Ring Out the News" was kaput. But "Leave It to Me" was having auditions for the role of Dolly Winslow, so Schwab sent his find to the Alvin Theatre, praying that she would win the part and take an expensive obligation off his hands.

I have a vivid memory of the odd trio standing in the back of the theatre while the young lady awaited her turn to audition. How did I know I was looking at two of the most important entertainment stars-to-be of the twentieth century? Mary Martin and Larry Hagman? Nellie Forbush and J.R.Ewing?

....

In the world of the theatre, there has long been a heated controversy concerning Mary Martin's historic rendition of "My Heart Belongs to Daddy." Much has been written (and printed) on the question: "Did she or did she not fully understand the salacious allusions that Cole had so amusingly slipped into his seemingly guileless lyric?"

Although Mary has denied in print that "she did not," I have always been enlisted in the "she dids." Mary was too smart and experienced not to grasp the subtle implications of those devilishly clever remarks. To say that she didn't understand what she was singing is an insult to the artist.

To me the unsung hero of "Daddy" was the choreographer, Robert (Bob) Alton. Gifted with a wry sense of humor, Bob was far more than the creator of set dances. His great talent, unique in those days, was in the detailed direction of vocal numbers, giving the participants the proper movements and gestures to enhance the songs. In the thirties, it was considered amusing for the orchestra to emphasize funny motions, so I had to work closely with Bob, making sure that my orchestrations faithfully produced the accents and musical comments he desired.

"Daddy" was a difficult problem for Alton. Placed deep in the second act, in no way essential to the development of the plot, sung by a minor character, it had all the attributes that cause a song to be cut in Boston. On top of that, he had prepared the number for June Knight. She was gone and in her place he had an unknown recruit.

On the other hand, there were six slick male dancers available to support Mary, including Gene Kelly in his first Broadway show. That roguish sextet could be counted on to leave no juicy double-entendre unexploited.

From his first hearing of "My Heart Belongs to Daddy," Bob Alton recognized the promising potential of the satirical song and labored to make it work. Frustrated by June Knight's dislike of her material, his faith in it was restored when June was replaced by Mary, who had the ability and sense to execute faithfully, every performance, the movements that Alton had designed, while singing Cole's masterpiece in a clear, carrying voice. It has been told that Sophie Tucker showed Mary where to "raise her eyes to the skies" on certain ambivalent phrases, and if that is true I am sure that *first* Sophie had to clear her suggestions with Alton.

In my department, the orchestration of "Daddy" was deliberately made as simple and as unobtrusive as possible, while being sufficiently sturdy to support Mary's upper voice. I had to make certain that every word of Cole's brilliant lyric was heard and allowed to register with the audience. Musical comments were unsuitable, the scoring had to be an exercise in orchestral restraint, rather than manifesto.

Somehow the song, the staging, the orchestration, and the superb performers all joined together to create a sure show-stopper at a most unlikely moment in the play. It was one of those occasional miracles of showbiz.

....

Because I had scored a substantial amount of instrumental music prior to formal rehearsals, I was able to orchestrate all of "Leave It to Me" without any help from my colleagues at Chappell. On the Saturday afternoon preceding the Monday morning, first orchestra reading in New Haven, I put down the last notes of the men's dance to "Most Gentlemen Don't Like Love (they just like to kick it around)." I turned over the completed score to the copyists and took the subway to Penn Station, the train to Trenton, where Audrey met me and drove me home for a for a few free hours. The next day, a very hot Sunday for late

September, I took the family to the Doylestown public pool and we had a wonderful splash. Late in the day I was driven back to Trenton, where I caught an express to New Haven. Settled for the night in that city's Taft Hotel, I looked forward eagerly to the first orchestra rehearsal on Monday morning, when all of those thousands of little black notes would at last sound in reality as they had resounded in my head....(I hoped!)

Monday was the orchestra's day by itself. They read and rehearsed the new music, unimpressed as usual. I corrected a few wrong notes; we seemed to have the right number of bars. On Tuesday the cast came in and heard the orchestrations, singing and dancing with them. There was the usual fever of excitement, followed by puzzled questioning, the sound was oh! so different from those worn-out rehearsal pianos.

On Wednesday we were supposed to have a run-through in the theatre, but the scenery and lights were not ready, so the company and orchestra had a workout in a Yale gymnasium. On Thursday we had two dress rehearsals in the theatre, the first with piano only, the last with full orchestra. Friday, up to curtain time, was for innumerable "touch-ups." At 8 P.M. we opened to a mixed audience of Yale students and curious theatre buffs from Connecticut and New York. On Saturday we all read the nifty notices and two shows were played to enthusiastic houses. Immediately sets were struck for the move to Boston.

....

Throughout that hectic week in New Haven, in addition to my customary efforts to make sure that my orchestrations properly fitted the show and its performers, I was harried by an unlucky personal problem that kept intensifying as the week progressed. I have related how, on the preceding Sunday, I took my family to a public swimming pool. After returning home, while packing for my road trip, I remembered that my left foot had picked up a small splinter from a rough boardwalk. So I found what was left of the little offender, drew out the remnant with tweezers, treated the tiny wound with a household antiseptic, covered it with sterile gauze held in place by adhesive tape, and thought no more of the insignificant injury until the middle of that busy week in New Haven.

That Wednesday morning, taking my customary shower, I noticed the dressing on my left foot and realized that it had been almost three days since I had checked out that little wound. Stripping off the gauze, I was shocked to see that there was now a red halo about the size of a quarter around the center pinpoint. Instantly my left foot began to feel quite different from my right foot. Disturbingly so!

Later in the day, I was able to get to a pharmacy and, advised by the druggist, bought a liquid that was supposed to be most effective against…yes, I had to admit that I had a touch of what was probably…athlete's foot!…although at that point I felt anything but athletic.

The rest of the week was marked by my losing fight against a creeping, sanguine infection. It took over my left foot and began to blush its anarchistic color over my ankle. Next its salute to the revolution was celebrated on my calf. Meanwhile I had purchased every over-the-counter guaranteed eradicator of athlete's foot extant. To no avail! They all struck out, giving my fungi nothing but encouragement!

Saturday morning I became truly scared when the spreading rubescence moved over my knee and headed north toward you-know-where. Threatening to die in the lobby in front of all the weekend guests, I got the Taft front desk to somehow find me a doctor, no small feat on a Saturday in the football season. The medico gave me hurriedly useless advice and ripped off a prescription before dashing away to see the kickoff. When I got the precious directive filled, it only seemed to add fuel to the frightening flame.

On Sunday, by grim determination, I managed to catch the first express east, well ahead of the company's train. I didn't want them to see me in my embarrassing agony.

Arriving in Boston, I taxied to the Ritz Carlton. In Beantown I usually lodged at the much cheaper Touraine, close to the copyists, but on this trip Selma had insisted that I stay at the Ritz in order to be handy for Porter. Cole had told her that he was determined to go out-of-town with this show, no matter how difficult the physical problems. He didn't want another "You Never Know."

As it turned out, my obligation to be in the same hotel as Cole was fortunate. In those days, the Ritz kept an attendant on each sleeping floor, a great help when one was bedridden.

When my cab reached the Ritz that Sunday, I had to recruit both my driver and the doorman to help me reach the checking-in desk. My reservation was in order, my room ready. With a bellhop bracing me at each armpit, I was assisted to an elevator, causing a minor sensation in the lobby. We rose to the fifth floor, where I was deplaned and whisked down the corridor to a nice room, which I would learn to hate during the coming three weeks. At the door, I gave the leading bellhop a tenner with instructions to share it with the rest of my considerable entourage.

Entering the chamber, the eye was instantly caught by a whopping vase of red, red roses. They were standing on top of a mirrored dresser, whose reflections gave one the impression that the entire room was crammed with glowing flowers. If there was one thing, of which I didn't need to be reminded, it was the color RED! And here it was in overwhelming quantity! A modest card lay in front of the florid gift. It read:

Rest your foot on these…Cole.

I sat down and laughed and chortled, chuckled and sniggered at Cole's charming malapropism. I swore to myself that I would never let him know that his precious present was such a bobble! After my black humor abated, I realized that I was now forever enlisted in the army of Cole's devotees. Here was a man with both legs broken, worrying about my foot! I wished that I could meet him and express in person my fervent thanks for the posies, but for the time being I feared that I was going to be even more immobile than Cole, lacking the strong orderlies he could summon whenever he desired to move.

Alone, I forced myself to undress and examine my aching leg. Now it was pink to red and hurting all the way from my toenails to my pelvis. Most terrifying was the appearance of a rubbery lump, painful and expanding, at the very top of my inside thigh, not far from very important equipment.

The phone rang. It was Cole, who had been brought to Boston on the previous Saturday and was established in a suite on the sixth floor. I thanked him profusely for the flowers.

He said, "For the last year, I've been the recipient of so many blossoms, it's a thrill to send a few myself. How's your old foot?"

I replied, "I hate to have to report that my trouble is no longer limited to my foot, now it concerns my whole left leg. The infection has reached the top of my thigh and is raising some nasty swellings in my crotch. I desperately need a doctor, but the people downstairs tell me that their house physician won't be available until tomorrow. That may be too late. I'm scared, Cole."

"Say no more," said he. "I'm sending you my personal doctor. What's your room number?"

I told him and he hung up. In about ten minutes, Dr. John J. Morehead knocked on my door. This was the man who had given up his practice to dedicate himself to the saving of Cole Porter's legs.

He looked over my leg, being careful not to touch it. He said, "It is obvious that there is a virulent pathogen at work here, one that has not been identified. Is it bacterial, viral, or fungous? Whatever it is, I certainly don't want to carry it back to Cole. I'm sorry, but I'm in unfamiliar depths here. I'm purely a bone specialist."

"So what am I to do?" I asked as I saw him heading for the door.

"Hold the fort," he advised. "Cole has connections here in Boston and so do I. Sooner or laterm we'll find a man who'll know what to do with your problem."

"You better hurry," I said, "or else when he arrives I may be singing soprano."

....

Cole called me about 7:30 that evening, cheerfully reporting, "I think we have found the right doctor for you. Years ago I was a graduate student in Harvard Law School. I made a lot of friends here in Boston and some are still around. They have helped me find a young doctor who is in charge of medical matters connected with Harvard's athletic programs. If anyone in Boston is up-to-date on athlete's foot, he is. Tomorrow morning he has to be at the University at nine, so you will have to be ready for his visit about eight, when he wishes to take blood samples for analysis, to find out exactly what bug is biting you. How's that for service?"

"Wonderful, Cole, and thank you again and again for your help. Now you've given me hope…real hope that I can recover from this infection with no permanent damage."

"I need you, old boy, back at your desk and writing those dandy orchestrations. I've been asked to compose a new first-act number for Mary Martin, and I want you ready to score it. Everybody hates the coloratura mess she's pulled out of her old vaudeville turn, that thing she's warbling now. It hurts her character and the Spewacks want it replaced. So I've got to get you back in shape to write more of those neat little black notes!"

I said, "Cole, I promise you that I'll be able to work. My leg feels better already, knowing that your efforts to help me are underway. Are you going to the orchestra reading tomorrow? I know that I'll never make it."

He said, "If Paul and Ray* feel strong, I'll be there listening for those little mistakes you never make. Moorhead wouldn't let me go to New Haven, but by God and all the little angels, I'm going to be present here in Boston. I have to be around to protect you if some idiot dancer complains that his kick music isn't loud enough."

* Paul Sylvain, Cole's valet and Ray Kelly, a dedicated friend. On many occasions, these two men carried Cole to the theatre and to other functions.

I said, "Thanks, Cole, for everything. Please be extra careful tomorrow, no more slippages, please."

On Monday morning, my crew cut doctor arrived on schedule and had a look at my problem. He seemed too young to be a full-fledged doctor, which I knew he was.

He whistled when he saw my leg and said, "Donald, you've got a beauty there, probably aggravated by all the wrong treatments. Well, let's get to work."

He had a syringe with him and took a sizeable blood sample. He said, "As of now, there are twenty-six known vectors that cause infections that are commonly called 'athlete's foot.' Most of them cause annoying but superficial lesions that readily yield to over-the-counter antiseptics. But then there are several nasty ones that attack the lymphoid tissue and travel through the lymphatic system. You appear to have picked up the worst of the lot. I won't be able to make a positive identification of your invader till late in the day at the lab. Meanwhile, there is an important step we can take."

He got the hotel to find me a metal tub in which I had to soak my leg in a solution of potassium permanganate, twenty minutes out of every hour. (Couldn't use the bathroom tub, for the chemical would stain the porcelain a permanent deep purple, a color I soon learned to detest.)

He said, "I'll be back here at 8 A.M. tomorrow. By then I'll know exactly what we are up against. It so happens that our department is associated in the testing of a new wide-spectrum drug aimed at infections similar to yours. So far the trials indicate that we may be dealing with something nearly miraculous. If I decide that it would help you, would you be willing to sign an agreement absolving the University in case there are any adverse results?"

I looked him in the eye and said, "You're my doctor, I'm in your hands completely. If you think I should sign such a release and use this new drug, I shall."

We shook on it, and he left me to my dull routine of twenty minutes in the tub and forty minutes out, during which latter period I was able to score any additions or changes the show needed.

My antagonist was identified, and the new drug (I think it was a sulfa-something) performed its magic while my whole leg turned imperial purple from the dunking. It still took two weeks of alternate soaking and working, confined to my room, before I could venture a trip to the theatre to check my orchestrations before having them exposed to the show-hardened New York musicians.

"Leave It to Me" was the first Broadway musical in which I received sole credit for orchestration. That "sole," which eluded me in "Maywine," nearly got away from me again. Mary Martin's coloratura specialty in the first act, which she called "Il Bacio," was cooked up by an arranger in California who would have to receive program credit. The entire staff detested the number. Although it stopped the show, it distorted the character of Dolly Winslow. Cole worked hard, trying to dream up a replacement for it, but had no luck. At last, near the end of the Boston run, at that critical time of the final tightening before the Broadway opening, Freedley cut the number, getting the authors to insert, in its place, a few more lines of dialogue for Dolly, thus trying to alleviate Mary's frustration. That night the show went like a breeze, and the alien interpolation was out forever. All concerned, with the exception of Mary, breathed sighs of relief.

It was only natural for Mary to be upset by the deletion of her big solo number, although "Daddy" played noticeably stronger after the cut of "Il Bacio." She was also distressed by the key in which she had to sing "Daddy," which statement requires a rather technical explanation.

The great majority of female vocalists have two singing "voices." There are exceptions but they are rare. There is the "chest" or lower voice that lies in the conversational range and the "head" or higher voice that is the property of legitimate sopranos. The differing voices are produced by disparate components of the respiratory system. The so-called "break," where the two voices meet or overlap, has been a historic battleground for most lady vocalists who are trying to pass from "chest" to "head" or vice versa, attempting to cross the "break" with no obvious change in the quality or volume of the tone.

The "break" lies on or between A440 and D576, depending upon the singer and her vocal equipment. Mary Martin had been trained since childhood as a legitimate soprano singing in the "head" voice. She had also sung, for her own pleasure and that of others, more popular music in her "chest" voice. The break in her scale came near the D natural, a ninth above middle C, somewhat higher than most female vocalists.

Mary was obsessed by the mistaken belief that her orchestration of "Daddy" had been prepared for June Knight and hurriedly adjusted when June was replaced. Such was not the case. The number had never been ready for orchestration while June Knight was available. Mary's orchestration was written specifically for Mary.

"My Heart Belongs to Daddy" has the rather large range of an octave and a third (a major tenth). It is a stiff challenge to its interpreter because important lyrics lie both at the top and at the bottom of its compass; there is no place to cheat or slough off, every word has to be bravely projected.

It was late October, 1938. The wireless body-mike was still an undeveloped idea in the brain of its inventor. Blanket amplification of the stage was as yet experimental. Our Mary was out there on the boards with no electronic wonders to help her project Cole Porter's clever words. At that time, the key in which a performer sang was crucial in determining audibility in the far reaches of the auditorium. In Mary's case, the key of B flat minor was as low as she could go in "Daddy" and still be heard and understood in the rear of the balcony.

Near the end of the refrain of "Daddy," where at a thrilling moment the minor key suddenly becomes major, Mary had to reach a high D natural...three times! After a breath and a pickup, again that high D natural had to be hit three more times! Then came the rapid descent to the final low B flat.

When Mary went after those high D naturals, no one, including Mary, knew exactly what would happen. One performance she would reach the D's in "chest," the next might shift into "head." There were even times when she gave her audience a dollop of both. No wonder she wanted to lower the key and "sing-talk" the low notes, as she did later when she performed "Daddy" on the radio. Yet onstage, backed by Alton's worldly wise male dancers, the sum total of her fight with the song was unusually effective, creating an impression of innocent vulnerability that was both charming and enticing. Coupled with the dancers' campy satire of an unfinished striptease, the number was a delicious, historic moment in showbiz.

Mary fought to have her key lowered, to no avail. Freedley, Porter, the Spewacks, Alton, and all the rest of the staff were delighted with what happened on the underlined syllables when Mary sang, "So I *want to warn* you, laddie/ Though I *know you're per*-fect-ly swell...," and they didn't want it changed in any way.

I was imprisoned in my Ritz Carlton room, unable to defend myself and my orchestration when Mary Martin was told that due to my affliction it would be impossible to have her "Daddy" key lowered. *That was not true.* Either Freedley or Cole could have ordered the copyists to make the transposition; they didn't need me for that! But my confinement was a convenient excuse to keep Mary's charming embarrassment in the show. Such are the devious devices of the musical theatre.

From that time on, whenever I encountered Mary, the thermometer seemed to drop rather suddenly. I am afraid that she held me responsible for a circumstance over which I had no control. She has reached great heights in her profession and I am content to have participated, even so modestly, in the beginning of that climb.

On November 8, 1938, there was a prior-to-opening dress rehearsal of "Leave It to Me" in the Imperial Theatre in Manhattan. Vinton Freedley chose to open in that large house instead of the previously announced, more intimate, Alvin. The production had a very large cast, and Freedley needed more seats to make it profitable. It may be of interest to report that Vinton told me that the total cost of the musical was $75,000! All of which had been recovered before the show left Boston!

Before the dress began, I seated myself in my favorite location: in an aisle seat in the last row of the first floor's center section, where unobtrusively I could slip out to the lobby during long book scenes, returning just as quietly for the next musical number. While I was listening to the new orchestra tuning up, two sturdy men entered from the back of the house, carrying a body between them. They carefully took their burden down the aisle to the sixth row, where three empty seats were waiting for them: Cole Porter, flanked by his faithful Paul and Ray.

Almost immediately the orchestra played the overture, then the curtain rose. All through the first act, Cole sat there between his transportation, laughing, applauding, and cheering like a college freshman at his first Broadway show.

Then came intermission, and I left my observation post, moving down the aisle to the sixth row, where I halted and said, "Mr. Porter, we have never met, except over the telephone. Let me congratulate you for writing such an easily orchestrated score."

Puzzled, Cole said, "Thank you very much, but who are you? Your voice…sounds familiar…it can't be…or is it?…DON WALKER! You joker, you! Correct, as usual; this is *really* the first time we have met face to face…and I like what I see." He put out his hand for me to shake.

I started to reach his hand with mine but suddenly pulled back, saying, "Sorry, Cole, but for all I know I may still be contagious. Let's put off the handshaking until the doctors tell me that I'm completely decontaminated. To change the subject, what do you think of our New York orchestra?"

"Superb! Far better than that last group. I keep hearing clever little inside voices that were missing in Boston."

"They were there all the time, but slighted. Please tell me, Cole, so far is there any spot that you wish to be re-orchestrated?"

"Don, I'll tell you exactly how I feel about your work: If I had the time and knowledge to orchestrate my own songs, I would try to write scores similar to those I've been hearing today. It has been a little spooky, sitting here and listening to my songs sounding, with an orchestra, the way I've always hoped they would sound. It's almost as if you have been reading my mind. I can't tell you how thrilled I am."

I replied, "To me, orchestrating your wonderful piano parts has been constantly thrilling; they fit so magically into the orchestra. A greater arranger's accolade couldn't be imagined."

The orchestra had returned and was tuning up for the second act. I went back to my rear seat, picked up my notebook and pencil, and resumed making memos of some minor changes in orchestrations that I wished to insert. In the theatre, nothing's ever perfectly perfect, although it's a good idea to keep trying to make it that way.

....

"Leave It to Me" was a solid hit. All the critics, major or minor, cheered its actors, script, and score. It was renaissance-time for Cole, establishing him again in the forefront of Broadway tunesmiths. I was happy with the considerable credits I received for orchestration. The reflected glory of being connected with a "smash" lit up my status in the halls of Chappell even extending the illumination to Brewster, from which aerie Max Dreyfus made his famous reckless order to his accountants in Manhattan, raising my drawing account twenty-five unsolicited dollars per week!

One afternoon in the late spring of 1939, I was working in the cell at Chappell that I shared with Bennett and Spialek, scoring an orchestration for a radio program conducted by Frank Black or Oscar Bradley or Robert Emmett (Bobby) Dolan, I forget which. Wrecking my concentration entered Lawrence (Larry) Schwab, in his double role of theatrical producer and actor's agent. He offered me, as they say in the garment trade, an opportunity I couldn't resist.

Larry had Mary Martin, currently riding high in "Leave It to Me," signed to a long-term management contract. He hoped, after the expiration of her contract with Freedley, to produce a musical in which she would star, thereby making a lot of wampum for Larry from each of his twin vocations. He had even picked the vehicle that would enthrone Mary in Broadway's starry galaxy; it would be a musical version of "Sailor Beware!" a hit legitimate comedy of a few years back, for which he had negotiated and secured "the rights." Consistent with his own assumption of twofold responsibilities, he offered me linked positions in the new production: orchestrator *and* musical director.

I was in my thirty-second year, loaded with ambition, eager to raise my almost invisible position as orchestrator to the conspicuous role of musical conductor. Then and there, I promised Larry Schwab that if and when his exciting project became a reality, he could count on me to join it in the dual capacities he had offered. We shook hands on our agreement, whose fulfillment, at that time, seemed well in the future.

But even solid hits can be fatally hurt by unexpected international events. "Leave It to Me" was sailing along, nearing its 290th Performance, entertaining an enthusiastic public, garnering handsome profits for its investors, when on August 23, 1939, Russia's Stalin signed a non-aggression pact with the Nazi's von Ribbentrop. The repercussions of that diabolic agreement were disastrous for "Leave It to Me." Instantly most of the show's humor became painfully unfunny, making the continuance of the production impossible, wiping out any hope of launching a touring company. Such is the risk of producing a show with a contemporary story. A real hit closed suddenly…forever.

The abrupt closing of "Leave It to Me" altered the affairs of a number of theatre folk, including the activities of Don Walker. Unexpectedly there was no show running on Broadway enlivened by songs of Cole Porter. Suddenly Larry Schwab had his potential headliner, Mary Martin, on his hands, drawing advances. Cole was in California, writing the score for a film, "Broadway Melody of 1940," while looking about for a script that would put him back on the real Broadway.

Larry Schwab, determined to cash in on the unforeseen availability of the Alvin Theatre, rushed about, canvassing his angels, trying to accumulate enough investment dollars to be able to put his new "Sailor" show into rehearsal. To his pleased surprise, sufficient cash came flooding in, such were the expectations aroused by a young lady who had sung a single song in a defunct musical! Larry scrambled into rehearsal in early September, before anyone or anything connected with his project was really ready.

Meanwhile Cole had been approached by Buddy De Sylva, who handed him a Herbert Fields script that would star Ethel Merman and Bert Lahr. Cole liked the story and agreed to fashion a score for

"DuBarry Was a Lady." At first it seemed impossible for that venture to open in the 1939–40 season, but Cole wrote remarkably quickly, the performers were available and ready: "DuBarry" went into rehearsal in October.

Although Cole wanted me to orchestrate "DuBarry," I was bound by my handshake to score "Sailor." It was physically impossible for me to orchestrate the two shows at the same time. Max Dreyfus turned "DuBarry" over to Hans Spialek, and he did his usual excellent job.

From the start of the "Sailor" rehearsals, my instinct kept telling me that I had made an abysmal mistake in accepting the position of musical director in addition to the job of orchestrating the score. I had not sufficiently weighted the fact that a major responsibility of a musical director is the vocal training of the principals and chorus, requiring his physical presence at all musical rehearsals, eating up over eight hours of every twenty-four. In the remaining sixteen, I had to travel to and from rehearsals, have conferences with other members of the staff, keep up my strength with three decent meals, get some absolutely necessary sleep and somehow, clearheadedly, orchestrate the show! Inevitably, it was sleep that had to take the beating.

Exacerbating my predicament was the simple truth: that the show had not been ready to go into rehearsal. The book wasn't finished; songs were missing or incomplete, not in shape to be orchestrated. Throughout the first two weeks of the three-week rehearsal, Al White, the choreographer, kept putting off showing me any of the dances. Then came the third and last week of rehearsal, then in desperation the whole show was loaded on me for orchestration.

It was impossible for me to write every note of the score. In order to have orchestrations for the New Haven reading, I had to bring in other arrangers. At one point I had nine such helpers working. I found that after briefing them thoroughly before they started to work and checking their scores carefully when they turned them in, I had hardly any time left to orchestrate anything myself. So there I was, swinging the stick at that first orchestra reading on a Monday morning in New Haven, conducting arrangements, one-third of which had been scored by Don Walker while two-thirds of the lot had been written by guys named Joe Whozis? There was nothing to be ashamed of, but neither was there anything to cheer about. Don Walker, the sensational new orchestrator of Broadway musicals, had come up with goose eggs.

A strange thing happened to the musical version of "Sailor Beware!" on the way to the forum of Broadway. In that story's previous (and successful) theatrical life, it had been a lighthearted tale about a bluejacket based in Panama, who bets his watch, a treasured family heirloom, that he can "make" a very beautiful and popular young lady. Somehow that titillating premise turned lascivious and clumsy. Maybe today, with its freer sexual mores, the musical "Sailor Beware!" would offend no one, but in 1939, in Boston, it was an anathema.

Larry Schwab, faced with a disaster, made a very wise and courageous move. He had to protect his potential star from the stigma of a ghastly flop. So he closed his "Sailor" in Boston and booked Mary into Times Square's Paramount, along with four former "sailors," where they used material from her old vaudeville act plus a "Whistlin'" number from "Sailor" and, of course, the "Daddy" song for an encore. Needless to say, Mary and her "sailors" were a sensation at the Paramount.

Larry certainly could roll with the punches. He thanked me for the reuse of my "Daddy" and "Whistlin'" orchestrations but didn't offer to pay me again.

....

Back in my cell at Chappell & Co., I accepted kind commiserations from the staff for the sudden demise of "Sailor." I was careful not to tell them that I was thankful that the mess, with my name on it, had never reached Broadway. I went back to my always available radio work, only to be temporarily diverted by a new songwriting team, asking me to orchestrate a single number that they had created for a Shubert revue. The team was Hugh Martin-Ralph Blane, the production number "The Rhumba Jumps." The idea of combining South American melodies with jazz rhythms was an interesting challenge, so I agreed to score the opus, provided Max Dreyfus permitted. He blessed the project and my orchestration was an exciting success, leading Martin and Blane to request Dreyfus to make me available to orchestrate their forthcoming "Best Foot Forward." When they agreed to have Chappell publish their score, Max made me available to orchestrate it. That's how he operated.

"DuBarry Was a Lady" came into town and was a big hit, making me wish that I had been more cautious before committing myself to a sketchy idea in the mind of an importunate promoter. I made up my mind to study closely the script and score of the next show that was offered me, for too much sweat and agony goes into the process of orchestration to have those extraordinary efforts unrewarded by basic defects in the story.

At the same time I vowed to never, never take on, simultaneously, the two jobs of orchestrating and conducting a new musical show with a large orchestra. *There just wasn't time* to perform both assignments well. One or both of them had to be slighted.

....

I never expected to orchestrate Cole's next musical, "Panama Hattie." After being unavailable for "DuBarry Was a Lady," I was sure that Cole had crossed me off his list of preferred arrangers. In the summer of 1940, to my surprise, Max Dreyfus told me that Cole had indicated that he would like to have me score his coming show. I was thrilled and most willing.

The production was to solo-star Ethel Merman, for the first time billed alone above the name of the show. I have always felt that La Merman had something to do with Cole's choice of orchestrator. The lady never forgot anything, much less the applause she received on "Down in the Depths on the 90th Floor."

Taking down a Merman solo for orchestration was a pleasure. She was the ultimate professional, knowing that the little black notes I would write in my solitude could build her or break her, making sure that when I left that rehearsal I possessed every tiny detail of her performance. She would go over and over a particularly tricky phrase as many boring times as I requested, until I had it memorized. Once her interpretation of a song was settled, it became a rock on which all concerned could lean, night after night, show after show.

In her work, she was aided by her steadfast accompanist, Lew Kessler, a patient and talented man who understood her ambition and abilities. Like her, he knew how to collaborate with an orchestrator in order to achieve the best results.

In November of 1956, my friend Jay Blackton, who was in Boston conducting "Happy Hunting," starring Ethel Merman, phoned me to see if I would construct and orchestrate a strong overture for the show, which was to open the following week in New York. I was willing, but not having written a single note for the Karr and Dubey score, I felt that I should see and hear the musical before trying to write an overture for it. So I flew to Boston, caught their last Wednesday evening performance, and was invited to attend a cast party after the show by the producer, Jo Mielziner (!), who was also the production's scenic artist.

As I remember, the party was held in the roof garden of the Bradford Hotel, adjacent to the Shubert Theatre, where the show was playing. The bash was given by Meilziner to the company as a reward for their hard work on the road. There were hardly any outsiders present; such is the fierce clannishness of a musical comedy company nearing its supreme test. I was lucky to have been accepted.

The party started with a free bar and a catered supper. A small local dance orchestra played: The show's New York musicians were guests, part of the company to be fêted.

It was approaching 1:00 A.M. when Merman appeared with her faithful Lew Kessler. She took over the entertainment. For almost two hours, she sang all her songs from all the shows she had played, from "Girl Crazy" through "Happy Hunting," after having performed two complete shows in the last twenty-four hours! An awesome exhibition, a privilege to witness, a glorious occasion never to forget, that generous display of her incredible voice.

After a while members of the hired orchestra joined in her accompaniment. In the last hour, the New York musicians got their instruments and helped to build up a sensational finish. It was a grand impromptu session with Ethel leading the whole potpourri, in historical order! A generous gift to her coworkers!

Panama Hattie, which went into rehearsal in New York during the dying days of August, 1940, presented a number of perilous challenges to Cole Porter, which he proceeded to conquer. The period's most sophisticated song writer had to compose ditties for a child actress, Joan Carroll, age eight years. Then he had to surpass his previous efforts for Ethel Merman, for the first time starred alone, above the show.

Topping those problems, he had the unwelcome job of diverting a super-smart audience from rejecting the whole unbelievable story, concocted by Herb Fields and Buddy DeSylva, the musical's producer, wherein a divorced Philadelphia lawyer, turned diplomat, falls in love with the lady owner of the Canal Zone's most popular nightery. Rejected and opposed by the hero's eight-year-old motherless daughter, Hattie thwarts a plot to sabotage the Canal, then sings to win over the child. All that accomplished, wedding bells chime.

Thanks to Merman's efforts and a talented cast that included funnyfolk Pat Harrington, Rags Ragland, Arthur Treacher, Phyllis Brooks, and Betty Hutton in her first Broadway musical, the production was a sold-out smash in New Haven and Boston. Merman lived up to all expectations, Porter topped "Down in the Depths" with

"Make It Another Old Fashioned, Please," so who could ask for anything more? Even the orchestrations got notices.

Back in New York, the Monday evening dress rehearsal was cancelled; the scenery and lights were not ready. Tuesday P.M. a dress was attempted but broke down due to mechanical failures. That night the entire house was sold out to a large charity for a preview of what was being touted as the greatest musical of the century. As I went to my free, undesirable staff seat in the balcony, I looked eagerly forward to the New Yorkers' response to the show that listed me as its sole orchestrator.

In 1940 ticket collectors were ready at the entrances of Broadway theatres at 8 P.M., the curtain going up at 8:40. On that Tuesday night, hardly a ticket holder was waiting when the doors were opened at the 46th Street Theatre; at 8:40 there might have been one hundred customers scattered about the auditorium, the result of those endless after dinner speeches that plague charity affairs. From behind the house curtain came sounds of sawing and hammering; if the audience wasn't punctual, neither were our carpenters and electricians.

At 9:00 the orchestra was admitted to the pit. Then the scanty audience was over-entertained by the masterful sounds of musicians tuning up, endlessly, as the construction concerto continued from backstage.

At last, with the auditorium half-filled, the house curtain flew, revealing the show curtain. The conductor entered and gave the downbeat that started the overture, only fifty tiresome minutes late, but at least, the show was on!

All through the first act and even in the final second, ticket holders kept arriving, full of drinks and food, causing periodic upheavals locating and reaching their proper seats, trying to catch up with the story, tormenting seated spectators. The cast, expecting a response at least as lively as that in Boston, were at first puzzled, then worried, eventually panicky. Where was the automatic applause, the belly laughs, the whistles? Was "Hattie" only a show for the sticks?

After a frantic finale that received only perfunctory applause, Merman took her solo curtain call. The tired, over-fed, and yawning audience was more interested in getting home to bed than giving Ethel her customary lengthy accolades. The house curtains finally closed on a very upset, alarmed, and angry star.

When the cast had removed the greasepaint and changed to civvies they were called, with the staff, to the denuded stage, lit by a single dreary worklight. Standing on a small box, the director, Edgar

MacGregor, addressed us thusly: "Quiet, please! You in the back, please pay attention to what I have to say. It's important!" When he had everyone's eyes, he continued. "First I want to compliment the cast for an excellent performance under terribly difficult conditions. This was the worst audience I have ever encountered, full of booze and belching catered food, sick of endless, money-raising speeches, late and naturally confused with our story. To me, it was thrilling to see how bravely you all came through such an acid test, like the smart, experienced, good troupers you are. To show you how confident I am of this musical and your performances, I am cancelling the planned run-through tomorrow afternoon. Instead you have a 1 P.M. call at the Broadway Arts Rehearsal Studios to clean up a few rough spots. * You will be released early. I want to save your energy for that all-important opening night. So now: Cast dismissed! Please try to get a good, long sleep; we are going to need *rested, confident* entertainers!"

So off the cast went to sit up until the dawn, hashing and rehashing the musical's chances.

....

"Panama Hattie," which opened in New York's 46th Street Theatre on the night of October 30, 1940, was a tremendous hit, a complete reversal from the panicky show that had bored the fidgety audience of the previous night. The thunderous laugh that followed the first modest joke was hard to believe, but it was one of those nights when everything worked and the cast's apprehension switched quickly to confident elation.

Almost all the critics had a joyful time that night and said so in their notices; a single nitpicker was swamped, along with his quibbling remarks, by the overwhelming majority.

* As a matter of fact, the stage crew needed the time to get the recalcitrant scenery working properly.

There was an immediate rush for tickets, an enthusiasm that was sustained as laudatory "word of mouth" was spread by delighted theatergoers, giving Cole Porter his longest running musical to date in New York (501 performances) and London (308 performances in that blitz-harassed city!).

"Hattie" established Ethel Merman as a superstar, able to carry a musicomedy by her name alone, above the show's title.

Before "Hattie" Cole was renowned for his clever, timely, satirical lyrics, and his musical setting of those words, it was a shock, to those who thought they knew his limitations, to find him writing, with great success, for a little eight-year-old bobby-soxer. After the charming "My Mother Would Love You" and the appealing "Let's Be Buddies" was followed by the loner's lament of "Make It Another Old Fashioned, Please," carping faultfinders had to concede that Cole Albert Porter, in spite of appalling physical handicaps, could write superb songs for any age, character, or situation.

....

Being "on the boards" of a Broadway smash automatically enhances the prestige of any staff member so honored. Having gained that billing with "Panama Hattie," I naively expected that Max Dreyfus would be swamped immediately with requests for my services in connection with contemplated musical comedies.

No such opportunities developed. Cole Porter might want me to score his next show, but at that point no one, including Cole, knew what or when it would be. Hugh Martin and Ralph Blane were auditioning a show that they, remembering "The Rhumba Jumps," wanted me to orchestrate, but they didn't have a producer or the money. So Mr. Dreyfus, who was having trouble enough carrying the drawing accounts of Bennett and Spialek, suggested that I go back, temporarily, to radio work, thereby keeping clean my record of never having overdrawn my Chappell drawing account.

Taking the broad hint, I checked with Frank Black, Bobby Dolan, and Oscar Bradley and found they were all willing to give me work, but not on a regular basis. They knew that I'd be going back to the theatre as soon as possible. I looked about for steady revenue.

At that time there was a man-and-wife team, the Hummerts, who produced and managed mostly musical radio programs. It was a large and very profitable operation, although quality was not their hallmark. The star in their somewhat cloudy firmament was something called "Manhattan MerryGoRound," conducted by Victor Arden, who had been one-half of the twenties piano duo of "Ohman & Arden." The insane truth about that program was the Hummerts' insistence that every single show had to sound, somehow, very, very, oo-la-la, *French!* The script, such as it was, always took place in Paris, France, or its environs; the characters had French names and the whole musical atmosphere had to be clearly Gallic, on something called "Manhattan MerryGoRound!" Seems ridiculous, doesn't it? That program ran for years.

I quickly exhausted all the obvious "French" effects that I could remember, find or invent, then I started to use them over and over. The Hummerts didn't seem to mind; they felt that I was establishing a perfect "style" for the program and "sticking to it" was the key to success. In pure boredom, I fell back to my previously mentioned excessive concern over internal instrumental voice-leading, trying to improve the movement of parts within the less noticeable areas of my orchestrations.

Vic Arden, the conductor of MMGR, was an excellent musician, a hard worker, and a true friend, attributes not frequently found in the same person. He understood my frustrations and tolerated them. I have never seen another man so haunted by clocks. In our broadcasting studio, there were two: one with the time of day, the other recording the sectional and composite lengths of the orchestrations being rehearsed or aired.

Vic lived by those clocks, for if a rehearsal ran overtime, budgets had to be revised. The most dreadful disaster that could occur, a possibility that hung over every broadcast, was the fear that while on the air the program might exceed, for some unforeseen reason, its rigid time allotment, thereby raising hell with the whole network. The chance of such a catastrophe ruled Vic's life. He paid more attention to those clocks that he did to his expert, mindreading musicians.

As the spring of '41 merged into summer, it appeared that soon I would be able to extricate myself from the slavery of orchestrating flaky radio programs and resume my cherished career in the theatre.

Dr. Albert Sirmay arrived from California, where he had been working with Cole on the score for the film "You'll Never Get Rich," starring Fred Astaire and Rita Hayworth. He told me that Cole had signed to furnish the songs for a coming Vinton Freedley musical entitled "Let's Face It," based on a twenties' farce "The Cradle Snatchers," to be modernized by Herbert and Dorothy Fields. Cole had expressed his hope that I would be available to orchestrate it.

I thanked Dr. Sirmay for bringing me that welcome news; it was heartening to hear that Cole wanted me to score his next musical, although that production seemed to be at least six months to a year away.

The show that appeared to have the best chance of rescuing me from the Hummerts was the one that Hugh Martin and Ralph Blane were still auditioning, the one with all the fresh young newcomers, now called "Best Foot Forward." Suddenly George Abbott became interested in it and agreed to produce and direct, announcing an opening in New York at the available Ethel Barrymore Theatre on October 1, that very year! Max Dreyfus called me immediately to tell me that Chappell & Co. was going to publish Martin & Blane's musical and he expected me to orchestrate it. I severed my radio connections as soon as I decently could. I had a revolutionary plan for the orchestra of "Best Foot Forward," and I wanted to get about making it a reality as soon as possible.

....

During the deep depression years of the 1930s, there was a gradual growth in the size of the leading American dance orchestras, when one would naturally expect, because of the ailing economy, a decrease in personnel. At the beginning of the decade, the average compliment numbered ten:

> 3 Saxophones (two altos, one tenor)
> 2 Trumpets (or Cornets)
> 1 Tenor Trombone
> 1 Piano
> 1 Guitar (or Banjo)
> 1 String Bass (or Tuba)
> 1 Trap Drummer
> 10 Musicians

By 1940 that orchestra had expanded to the following:

	5 Saxophones	(2 altos, 2 tenors, 1 baritone)
	3 Trumpets	(or cornets)
The "Big Band"	3 Trombones	(2 tenors, 1 bass)
combination.	Piano	(The four-piece rhythm section
	1 Guitar	had not increased, they just
	1 String Bass	played louder when needed)
	1 Trap Drummer	
	15 Musicians.	

There were minor variations from the above norm, especially when the leader was an instrumentalist of repute. The above fifteen-piece combination reveals a definite tendency of the times: to strengthen the "bottom" of the orchestra by adding instruments of low frequency.

There was also a desire to develop fresh colors by having saxophonists "double" on "legitimate" woodwinds, such as flutes, clarinets, and double-reeds, while the brass experimented with new types of mutes and plungers.

It was a healthy decade for developing orchestrators, for no "big band" could get along without one or more "arrangers," as we were commonly called. When orchestras grow to fifteen or more players, every man improvising on his own doesn't work very well and it's time to "stick to the sheet" that has been written by one of those peculiar musicians who claims to "hear in his head" all those diverse instrumental sounds that he seems to be able to fit together harmoniously while writing down their curious symbols on lined manuscript paper.

....

My plan for the orchestra of "Best Foot Forward" was simple but very difficult to achieve. I reasoned that a show about prep school students, their senior prom invaded by a fading movie star in search of helpful publicity, should be evocative of the popular danceband records that young people were buying at that moment. The authors of the production, along with George Abbott and his staff, all agreed that my approach was correct but left it up to me to produce the desired result.

My heavy problem was lightened by Abbott's choice of orchestra conductor. Prompted by Martin and Blane, he hired one Archibald Bleyer, well known to dance musicians as an excellent arranger of "stocks." "Archie" was trying to get away from that dreary occupation by becoming a show conductor. Without his wholehearted cooperation, immediate understanding and promotion of my orchestral plan, the music of "Best Foot" would never have become the up-to-the-minute success it turned out to be.

I wanted to score for the 1940 "Big Band" combination, as listed on the preceding page, *plus* a string quintet to accompany ballads and provide quiet incidental music under dialogue. I desired an orchestra in which each instrumental family; reeds, brass, strings, and rhythm all had a wide span of the necessary frequencies, in effect providing four homogeneous ensembles within the orchestra, a strategy I have used successfully during all of my working life.

It was well to know the kind of orchestra I desired for "Best Foot Forward," but getting it was another story. For the reeds, brass, and rhythm sections, I hoped to have men who had filled important "chairs" in "big bands," experienced players who were tired of traveling but were familiar with the phrasings and interpolations of popular dance orchestras. In the strings I longed to have, just once, legitimate musicians of high quality. I yearned for what appeared to be the impossible.

In 1941 the Shubert organization owned or controlled more than twenty legitimate theatres in New York City. To Lee Shubert's disgust his brother, "J.J.," considered the kickbacks from the four "housemen" (required in every "house" by the musicians' union) as his private oil well, pumped weekly by his collectors and bully boys.

What was even more outrageous and a sin against dulcet harmony was the unfortunate fact that in every Shubert theatre the designated leader of the housemen was by union rule also the contractor for any additional musicians needed by a show coming into his "house." The only exceptions to that rule were the musicians (about four or five) who had accompanied the show on its break-in tour on the road (prior to New York opening).

Although musicians who have to contribute a healthy percentage of their weekly pay in order to keep their jobs may have more rapid tremolos that ones who take home a full sock, it didn't appear to me to be a sensible system for promoting merit in the pit. I had several sessions with Archie, devoted to trying to find a way to beat City Hall.

Archie and I got lucky, finding out that the Ethel Barrymore Theatre owners were terminating Shubert management that coming Labor Day, 1941. They were also willing to give us carte blanche in forming what we thought was the proper kind of orchestra for "Best Foot Forward." As that holiday traditionally marked the beginning and end of musical contracts, Archie was given the power to name his own contractor for the Ethel Barrymore during the coming year. For the first time in ages, a New York musical was going to have an orchestra in which every player would take home his full pay! The stock of available and qualified musicians ballooned overnight! We were going to have an orchestra of swingin' virtuosos!

"Best Foot" went into rehearsal very early in August, 1941. I was happily scoring away about the middle of that month when I got one of those command phone calls from Max Dreyfus.

He said, "I know you are up to your ears with George Abbott, but I want to advise you, write as quickly as possible. All of a sudden, Vinton Freedley has decided that 'Let's Face It' is ready to go into rehearsal about September 5th, opening in the Imperial near the end of

October. Cole wants you to score the show. Do you think you can handle it?"

I stalled for time, saying, "Give me half an hour to figure it out. I'll call you back. Are you in Brewster?"

He was.

I hastily ruled up a chart showing side-by-side the probable schedules of the two shows, their dates for "Going into rehearsal," "Opening New Haven," "Closing New Haven," "Opening Boston," "Closing Boston," and "Opening New York." I added another column entitled "The Body of Don Walker." I put in the known dates and probable dates. At the end of a short half-hour, I called Mr. Dreyfus.

"I believe that I can handle both shows," I recklessly promised. "I won't be able to stay in Boston every minute with 'Best Foot,' but the conductor, Archie Bleyer, is an excellent orchestrator and should be able to take care of all routine fixes. If there are any big emergencies, I'll just have to go to Boston to take care of them."

"Sounds reasonable," said Max. "To make things a little easier for you, Cole's score isn't going to be quite as long as usual. Danny Kaye is to be featured, and Cole is allowing him to use a couple of borscht-circuit numbers written by his wife, Sylvia Fine, and by his guru, Max Liebman. They probably have their own orchestrations for those interpolations."

"Shades of 'You Never Know,'" I said unhappily.

"Once again Cole is in excruciating pain," Max told me. "There is a strong possibility that he may have to undergo more operations on his legs. He is going to need all the help we can give him."

"I am dedicated to serve him," I admitted.

"So are we all," echoed Max.

....

It was a pleasure working for the businesslike George Abbott organization. With my Wharton School background, I appreciated the fair frugality of Abbott's Company Manager, Charles Harris. "Charlie" sailed a tight ship. I remember a young entertainer, Kenneth Bowers who, when he auditioned for "Best Foot," used his vaudeville act, in which he played the clarinet. Gene Kelly, who had graduated from chorus boy in "Leave It to Me" to choreographer for "Best Foot," remembered Kennie's audition when there was a dull spot in the show. He dreamed up a number for Nancy Walker (no relation) wherein Kenny, playing his clarinet like a Hindu swami mesmerizing his pet cobra, induced Nancy to sing a number under feigned hypnosis. The number turned out to be a gasser, and Kenny was riding high until the leader of the New Haven musicians told him that if he was going to play his clarinet on stage, in costume, he would have to become a paid-up member of the musicians' union. Kenny worried about the modest New Haven initiation fee until he discovered that the union scale for a musician playing on stage, in costume, was $75 per week, while Charlie had been paying him only $50 per week as an actor! Kenny was molto happy with his new classification.

"Best Foot Forward" was a fortunate show. From its first rehearsal, when the book was read by the cast and the songs were demonstrated by the composers, it was clear that a hit was in the making. The book was funny and honest, and the music was sturdy and up-to-the-minute, featuring the to-be-famous "Buckle Down, Winsocki." The cast was oh, so young and fresh and vigorous. As I sat quietly listening to the reading, I could "hear in my head" the "big band" sound that would send those nubile arms and legs and bodies hoofing, hopping, sizzling. I could hardly wait to get my pen on paper.

The show opened in New York on October 1, 1941, to hit notices. Although the critics did not fully understand what had happened in the pit to make the music so bright and exciting, they applauded the score. A few even mentioned the orchestrations!

After a fine run of 326 performances, "Best Foot Forward" had to close because it became impossible to keep the ranks of the cast complete: Young male performers were being steadily drafted to fill, it seemed at the time, more important ranks.

....

I was unable to be present at the triumphant opening of "Best Foot Forward" in New York City on October 1, 1941, thus missing the excited congratulations of friends for having brought the true "big band" sound into the pit of a Broadway musical for the first time. I was in New Haven, tending to the minor musical adjustments needed by my other charge, "Let's Face It," being prepared for its out-of-town opening.

There was really nothing wrong with Cole's latest effort. His worry arose from the show being truly hilarious, so funny that the quality of the excellent score was disregarded. In addition, Cole was once again in despair from agonizing pain in his left leg. His physical condition made him hate the show and its obvious success; he hated his own score, calling it too facile; he even disliked the orchestrations, with which Freedley, the authors, and all the staff were delighted.

I tried to please him with minor adjustments, while on the other hand I saw no reason to drastically change orchestrations that show-after-show were working beautifully.

After "Let's Face It" opened in Boston, drawing ecstatic approval from tough critics who were still laughing as they wrote, Cole quietly had himself shipped back to New York and entered a hospital for more drastic leg operations. His detested show was a smash hit and ran for 303 performances. I doubt that he sent any of his royalty checks back to Vinton Freedley.

....

After "Let's Face It" had opened and established itself on the Great White Way, the careers of Cole Porter and Yours Truly1} diverged. The rift did not occur because either one desired to end a professional relationship. It was, in Cole's own words, "Just One of Those Things" that happen in showbiz.

Recovering from his operations in 1941, Cole went to Hollywood and wrote the songs for a Columbia Pictures film entitled *Something to Shout About,* chiefly distinguished by having in its score one of Cole's finest creations: "You'd Be So Nice to Come Home To."

Coming home to the East Coast in '42, he became interested in a script for a projected Ethel Merman musical, written by his familiar collaborators, Herbert and Dorothy Fields. Cole wrote a few songs for the project, and they auditioned their incomplete opus for their favorite ever-successful producer, Vinton Freedley. He immediately hated it and bowed out.

Still having faith in their new brainchild, they took it to Michael Todd, the upstart producer who had gambled his shirt on an all-black "Hot Mikado" and won. Todd liked the project at once but wanted the title changed. So "Jenny Get Your Gun" became "Something for the Boys" and Cole's next hit, while I was busy scoring a hopeless show with music by Johnny Green, called "Hi, Ya, Gentlemen," which expired on the road before facing the New York critics. The Mike Todd production with Merman only ran 422 performances on Broadway.

Back went Cole to Hollywood, where he stayed while film versions of three of his hit shows were being made by various picture companies. Then back to the East again to write a score for another Mike Todd production, "Mexican Hayride," featuring Bobby Clark and June

Havoc. It ran for 481 performances, in spite of lukewarm notices and a Porter song entitled, believe it or not, "I LOVE YOU," sung by operetta's heroic gift, Wilbur Evans. It was not Cole's most clever lyric.

While during the war years he was hard at work writing songs for one hot ticket after another, the Weird Sisters were conspiring to give Cole his greatest single song hit, without any effort on his part.

In Hollywood, during the middle thirties, Cole had written a song for a film that was never produced. The song was based on a poem written by a Montana cowboy, who had sent it to Cole, who saw in it possibilities enough to negotiate for all its rights, which he received for a payment of $150. He then used the title and a couple of idioms from the poem, inventing himself almost all of the lyrics and every note of the tune and its harmony. Put on the shelf by the picture company, there it languished for eight years until a song was needed for a country-western singer, Roy Rogers, in a film called *Hollywood Canteen*. Rogers recorded it, and Bing Crosby heard the recording and got the Andrews Sisters to record it with him. That platter was a barn burner, a powerhouse, selling in the millions; the sheet music wasn't far behind.

"Don't Fence Me In" was a welcome embarrassment to Cole. I think that in his private heart he was amused and somewhat proud that his gentle satire of country and western banalities had been "taken for real" by the general public, producing unbelievable kudos and kopecks for the lampooner. It certainly took his mind off his dreadful physical problems for a spell.

Late in the summer of '44, Cole Porter reentered my life. Max Dreyfus informed me that Cole had asked him if I was available to orchestrate the songs he was writing for a fabulous musical entitled "The Seven Lively Arts," which Billy Rose was producing to play in a refurbished Ziegfeld Theatre with an augmented orchestra of forty musicians. I doubted that I could handle such an enormous assignment all by myself. Max smilingly explained that I would have help, for none less than Igor Stravinsky was composing *and* orchestrating the ballets. I was impressed and looked forward to rubbing elbows with the famous composer.

When the massive production went into rehearsal, it had a story, based on the trials of various kinds of fledgling artists in their battle for expression and recognition in the metropolis of New York. After about ten days of rehearsal, Billy Rose scrapped the story line and the affair became a super-high-class, plotless vaudeville show.

There were too many stars: Bea Lillie, Bert Lahr, Markova, Anton Dolin, Doc Rockwell, Benny Goodman, and Red Norvo. There were too many authors: Kaufman & Hart, Pirosh, Schrank, Sherman, and Ben Hecht. There were too many young hopefuls scrambling for the limelight: Nan Wynn, Billie Worth, Dolores Gray, Mary Roche, Bill Tabbert, Edward Hackett, and Dennie Moore, to name only a few. There were too many agents, too many dancers, and a plethora of elaborate sets, as Rose discovered when the revue entrained for its trial run in Philly, leaving two large and expensive sets behind because the Forrest stage was too small to accept them.

Cole had supplied sixteen songs, taking good care of his headliners: Bea Lillie with her "When I Was a Little Cuckoo" and Bert Lahr growling his "Wow-oo-Wolf!" Hidden in the imbroglio was one of Cole's best ballads, "Ev'ry Time We Say Goodbye," which still survives as a great evergreen. Although the epic had a full-dress, free-champagne opening before a glittering assemblage on December 7, 1944, and received kind, embarrassed notices, it managed to run only 179 heavily hyped performances and was a total financial failure. Cole was very sorry that he had ever become involved in it. I never met Igor Stravinsky.

During 1945 Cole spent a great deal of his time in Hollywood, keeping an eye and an ear on the progress of his biographical film, *Night and Day,* being shot at the Warner Brothers studio. The more it deviated from the truth, the more he enjoyed it. The strange casting of Cary Grant as Cole Porter met with his hearty approval.

That film was a compendium of his better known songs, an awesome list of accomplishments that also served to remind him that his current output was not of the same high quality that marked those marvelous hits of the past. Even his recent sensation, "Don't Fence Me In," had been written a decade ago, antedating that disastrous equine accident.

Curiously, after returning to the East Coast, Cole went from one doomed theatrical extravaganza to another. It was like a death-of-success wish.

Ever since seeing *Citizen Kane,* Cole had admired the work of the acclaimed wonder-boy, Orson Welles. It was exciting for Cole, at the age of fifty-five, to be approached by the young prodigy who was inviting him to write the songs for Welles' next fabulous production, based on Jules Verne's everlasting classic, *Around the World in Eighty Days.* Cole was interested. The project promised to give him the chance to write songs for colorful characters in exotic locales, far from his topical New York stamping grounds, giving him the opportunity to get out of his imagined creative rut.

So Cole contracted to write the songs for Orson's spectacular, signing the customary collaboration agreement with Welles, the bookwriter. But as time went on, he gradually realized that Orson's involvement with the production did not stop with furnishing the script; step by step, the author became the director, then the producer, finally a starring actor. Welles bristled with important functions. As usual, in such cases, nothing functions very well. It was "Lively Arts" in another frame: too big a cast, too many scenes and songs, too complicated backstage, and everywhere too much Orson Welles. At its Boston opening, the production ran past midnight. The easiest cuts were often Porter songs.

After all kinds of agonies, the pruned production limpingly opened at the Adelphi Theatre in New York City on May 31, 1946, while Cole was on a plane flying to California, shunning the hectic performance, the insincere compliments, and the inevitable reading of ghastly notices at the routine opening night party.

After 74 performances, Orson Welles was forced to give up the fight and close his epic. It had lasted less time than it took Jules Verne's characters to circumnavigate the globe.

....

After Cole's flight from the humiliating disaster of *Around the World,* there appears, superficially, a hiatus of two and one-half years in his customary flow of songs. That gap is deceptive. It was natural for the man to take an extended vacation to help repair the mental wounds inflicted by an intractable flop. The news that *Night and Day,* his alleged "biographical" film, was a huge success did much to raise his spirits. For once his poor legs withheld their torment.

Back in Hollywood after his long trip, Cole wrote six songs for the MGH film *THE PIRATE,* based on the S. N. Behrman play. Far from revealing any decline in creative powers, that modest score contains one of Cole's greatest songs, "Be a Clown," written for and performed by Gene Kelly, the film's star, whose career crossed that of Cole's several times.

Still wanting to get back to writing for the living stage, where he believed his efforts received their warmest recognition, Cole moved back to New York, hoping there to be offered a promising script that would serve to stimulate his ever-present inventive urge.

He soon found that most of the wisenheimers on Broadway were jabbering that Cole Porter was burnt out, his period passé, his name no attractor of investors' cash. No longer was he able to pick and choose among dozens of promising projects. Cole even considered writing a score for a musical about the yearly Miss America Pageant in Atlantic City!

Among the projects that Cole promptly rejected was a story about a formerly married actor and actress, divorced, but working together in a hungry road company playing a musical version of Shakespeare's *The Taming of the Shrew*. It was a "play within a play," one of Cole's pet aversions. The only reason he had read the script to the end was because it had been submitted by Bella Spewack, his respected collaborator in their successful musical, "Leave It to Me."

Cole had understandable reasons why he had rejected Bella's project, mainly that he "didn't want to mess with Shakespeare." Gradually, bar by bar, word by word, note by note, Bell won him over. Despite a painful relapse in his legs during the early months of 1948, Cole, needing a diversion to take his mind off his distressing affliction, started to fiddle with a couple of tunes that were called for in Bella's script. They came so easily and felt so right, he became fascinated with the project and kept working on it. Presently he had accumulated enough key songs to make possible an audition for investors. Disregarding lukewarm reactions, he kept getting fresh ideas for songs, embarrassing Bella, who had no more room in her script for even one more song, so tight was her writing.

As has been well documented, "Kiss Me, Kate" was Cole's greatest success. It played 1,077 performances in New York and 400 in London. There was a "National" company, soon organized after the New York opening, that ran for a long time, playing major cities. It is a classic of the musical stage, forever revivable. In 1953 MGH made a film loosely based on "Kiss Me, Kate." The less said about that confused flick, the better. Cole's masterpiece belongs on the living stage.

....

Theatergoers have told me that they liked "Kiss Me, Kate" for its humor, others were fascinated by its exposure of backstage life, most loved the felicitous songs...but all of them agreed that "it was *different*." How little did they know how *much* it was different. "Kate" was the most "different" musical, inside and out, of the approximately one hundred ten with which I have been involved.

The "idea" for the affair was born in the busy brain of Arnold Saint Subber, who in the middle thirties was working as a stagehand for a

Theatre Guild production of Shakespeare's *The Taming of the Shrew*. He thought it amusing to observe Alfred Lunt (who played Petruchio) and his real-life wife, Lynn Fontanne (who played Katharina) squabbling at each other offstage much as they did in character on-stage. For over ten years, that interesting juxtaposition, as a basis for a musical, lay dormant in Saint's mind. When it did cross his thoughts, it was rejected as being too scenically difficult, with its necessary jumping back and forth from reality to pretense.

Twelve years after he first had the "idea," after he had graduated to stage managership, Saint happened to mention his inactive "idea" in a casual conversation with a friend, Lemuel Ayers, a young but well-established scenic artist. Interested, Ayers showed Saint the physical means by which his "idea" could be made to work on the stage. That problem solved, they immediately became partners in the production of a largish musical that had, at the time, no book, no songs, no actors, no scenery and, worst of all, no money…nothing but an "idea" lodged in two brains instead of only one.

Thus, initiated by two self-styled "producers," whose theatrical experience had been limited to the creation and movement of scenery, the fabrication of "Kiss Me, Kate" began, differing from other musicals from the very inception.

Lem and Saint had no "property," as the book and score of a prospective musical is called; there was nothing for a curious investor to read or audition. By chance the partners heard that Sam Spewack, of the "Leave It to Me" writing team of Sam and Bella, had written a play all by himself, which was scheduled for production in England that coming summer of '48. So while Sam was abroad, there was Bella with lonely time on her hands with no project to keep her jumpy synapses busy.

The callow impresarios took their "idea" to Bella. Since they were old teammates, she didn't throw them out, dismissing them, saying, "I'll think about your brainstorm."

She did and found herself starting a rough synopsis. It came easily. Throughout her first sketchy outline, she felt her growing story screaming for songs. She knew who could write the special ones to accompany "that special face." Of course it was Cole, who had written those brilliant ditties for "Leave It to Me." As has been related, she won him over after his first negative reaction, almost too well, for eventually she had to rewrite to make room for some of the flood of Cole's inventions. Even in the writing "Kate" was very "different!"

Meanwhile, Lem and Saint, the two shakers and movers, were busy building the necessary business organization for the venture. In as "different" a move as can be imagined, they named Selma Tamber, my whipcracker at Chappell & Co., the *General* Manager of their production company! That was certainly the most "different" move they could have made in those days: a *woman* General Manager! With no record of experience in the theatre! Whose office was in a music publishing company! All unheard of!

(I found out later that the reason our producers were using Selma's office was because they couldn't afford to rent one for themselves. I have refrained from calling that situation "different" because as time has passed, I have encountered other showstring producers who were as pinched as our two beauties.)

To me the appointment of Selma as General Manager of "Kiss Me, Kate" could have only one explanation: Papa Max Dreyfus had decided to support the venture and Selma was to be his on the job watchdog. (What's the feminine of "watchdog"?) There, in that cell next to mine, she would make sure that every penny spent would be for legitimate and necessary purpose. My guess was fortified by the hasty installation of a direct phone within Selma's office, one that didn't have to go through the publishing company's master switchboard.

"Kate" and its circumstances continued to be "different." Patricia Morison, an almost unknown actress from the West Coast, was hired to star opposite Alfred Drake. A leading dancer of the American Ballet Theatre, Harold Lang, was hired for a part that required very little dancing. The show was not directed as usual by Bella's husband Sam, but by John C. Wilson, regarded in the trade as a producer, not a director. "Kate" opened in Philadelphia instead of the usual New Haven or Boston. Two of the original audition crew, Lisa Kirk and Lorenzo Fuller, were in its opening cast, a very rare happening, since by the time sufficient money has been sweated out of the angels, the powers that be are customarily fed up with the singers who have helped them assemble the kitty.

There were many ways in which "Kate" was "different," but that appellation did not apply to the job of orchestration. The manner in which that essential job was accomplished was all too familiar.

....

In the summer of '48, Selma told me that Cole Porter had asked Mr. Dreyfus if Russell Bennett could be made available to orchestrate his coming show, which was full of Shakespearean references. Cole felt that Bennett was the most "legitimate" orchestrator in Chappell's stable. That belief surprised me, for I thought that my work on "Up in Central Park" and "Carousel" proved that I was, at heart, when such work was called for, as "legitimate" as a modern orchestrator could be. Nevertheless, I was glad to have been informed so early, for I had other work that would make the coming fall and winter profitable, now that I knew I wouldn't be occupied with "Kiss Me, Kate."

That autumn I was very busy, planning and arranging a phonographic history of Sigmund Romberg's career for RCA Victor.

All the turmoil and distracting confusion in Selma's office, one thin partition away, was no help to my concentration. One day, early in November, the hullabaloo suddenly died down and Selma, accompanied by the orchestra conductor of "Kate," Pem Davenport, came into the Arrangers' room, where I sat longing for some lovely silence.

Selma came to the point, saying quietly, "Don, you've got to help us. We're in a bind. Russell's bitten off more than he can chew and now he's sick. 'Kate' has an awful lot of music in it...more than any book show I can remember. This 'Kate' seems musically as big as a revue. Russell needs help!"

I knew Hans Spialek was tied up with work, but there was another chance. I asked, "Isn't Ted available?" (Ted Royal was the most recent addition to Chappell's stable of arrangers. Risen from the ranks, like myself, he was usually assigned to scoring contemporary music.)

Pem said, "There is one number in 'Kate' that's right down Ted Royal's alley. It's the opening of Act Two, the song called 'Tom, Dick or Harry.' For the rest of the show, forget Ted." He pointed at me and said, "It's you we need. There's a long, long tarantella at the end of Act One that cries out for your orchestration. And then there's at least a half-dozen vocals, mostly Alfred Drake's, that you *must* score."

I thought for a moment and admitted, "As yet there are no firm recording dates for the Romberg albums I'm committed to arrange. I could push back that work a couple of weeks. Is the tapeworm at the end of Act One ready for me to see?"

There was an embarrassed silence, then Selma explained, "Once again, Cole is in agonizing pain. In spite of it, he gets himself carried to rehearsals nearly every day. For this show, he asked for Bennett, and Mr. Dreyfus doesn't want any other orchestrator to show up at rehearsals and start Cole worrying whether or not Russell has everything under control. Don, there is no way you can see any rehearsals...no way at all!"

They waited while I gathered my thoughts.

Then I said, "You are asking me to do something I have sworn I would *never* do: score an orchestration for a dance I have never seen."

Pem said, "Don, I'll help you with the dance. I'll be your eyes and ears. Whenever you need me, I'll come to your office and go over the tarantella with you, describing, bar by bar, all the action on the stage. Would that considerable cooperation satisfy you?"

I was touched. This was fellowship above and beyond. I knew how his pledge to keep briefing me could become onerous, with him swamped by endless rehearsals and conferences. At once I agreed to score, sub-sub-rosa, as much of "Kate" as Pembroke Davenport asked me to do. There in my lonely office, with no visual or aural imprints to aid me, I orchestrated:

"Another Op'nin', Another Show"

"Wunderbar"

"We Open in Venice"

And Alfred Drake's solos:

"I've Come to Wive It Wealthily in Padua"

"Were Thine That Special Face"

"Where Is the Life that Late I Led?"

And Lisa Kirk's:

"Always True to You in My Fashion."

And then that interminable instrumental Tarantella and Pavane.

It wasn't until "Kate" opened in New York that Cole discovered, by reading the program for a change, that I had scored a considerable portion of the show, enough to have Russell Bennett, that most honorable gentleman in a slippery business, insist that the credit for orchestrations would have to read: "By Russell Bennett and Don Walker."

"Kate" opened in New York's Century Theatre on the 30th of December, 1948. On the following Sunday, its cast album was recorded, as had become the custom with hit musicals. Ever since the recording of "Oklahoma," the first of cast albums, there had been a controversy over the payment(s) due (if any) to the orchestrators(s) for the recording use of arrangements that had been made, originally, for employment in a living theatre.

At first the recording companies tried to ignore their obligation. Then, in order to have a clear title to the album, they decided to pay off the orchestrator(s). There was a series of solutions: a flat payment per song, a tiny royalty on sales, and a payment equal to that billed for a commercial recording.

The cast album of "Kiss Me, Kate" was made in the "tiny royalty" period. For years in February, I would receive a check from Russell, my part of the royalty payment that he had received from Columbia Records, covering the previous year's receipts from "Kate." Russ figured that he had scored 50 percent of the recorded show; Don Walker, 42½ percent; and Ted Royal, 7½ percent; and he was divvying up that rapidly shrinking royalty payment in those proportions.

That procedure went on for a number of years, getting down to loose change, until the company, irritated by the miniscule transactions, offered to settle conclusively for a lump sum, which was also tiny. Right to the end, Russell kept doling out the pennies as if they were gold, rigidly, unshakably honest.

He was quite a man, that Robert Russell, playing a very good game of tennis regardless of a limpy leg, a residue from infantile paralysis. I was fond of him, sitting there with his desk confronting mine, scoring away like mad while listening to the Dodgers game on the little radio he carried, while I sat there rendered inactive, concentration zero, unable to "hear" a single note in my useless head.

....

Arnold Saint Subber and Lemuel Ayers, the scenery-oriented producers of the great hit "Kiss Me, Kate," spent two years, almost to a day, trying to prove that the old saying, that lightning never strikes the same spot twice, was all wrong. They even employed Jove and a large supporting cast of Olympians to properly direct the necessary bolts.

After "Kate" the young partners were hailed on Broadway as prototypes of the new breed of theatrical genii. Avid investors, waving fat checkbooks, eagerly awaited the announcement of the next project of the S. & A. organization. It wasn't long in coming. In the late spring of '49, it was proclaimed that the second production of Subber & Ayers would be a contemporary treatment of the Amphitryon legend, with a score by Cole Porter and a book by Dwight Taylor. (Who's that again?)

In that seemingly innocuous statement laid the seeds of ultimate disaster. It revealed that the "idea" of the projected musical had not originated in the mind of one of the partners, as "Kate" had, but had been brought to them by an author with no solid track record on the Main Stem. It also hinted that Bella Spewack, without whom "Kate" would never have existed, had either been bypassed or had rejected an offer to participate in the new production. Either way it was bad news.

There was a scary augery: A show that had all its production kitty couldn't find a satisfactory name! "Amphitryon," "Heaven on Earth," and "Cloudburst" were all announced and then withdrawn. At the last moment before going into rehearsal, "Out of This World" was chosen. The massacre of titles marked the liquidation of coauthors as everyone and his dog got into the game of "fixing" the script. Dwight Taylor grimly held onto his basic credit of authorship to the very bitter end, though sharing honors at times with Comden & Green, George Abbott, F. Hugh Herbert, and at the end, allowing Reginald Lawrence joint credit.

The new musical had been planned to open on Broadway the same night as "Kiss Me, Kate" was to celebrate its one-year-old anniversary. That would have been December 30, 1949. Such were the delays and disorder of "Out of This World" that it wasn't able to open until December 21, *1950!* Two whole years after the opening of "Kate"! Its so-called "star" was a very rich lady named Charlotte Greenwood, whose heyday had been during the First World War. The fact that late in the slow second act she "stopped the show" with her contortions indicates that the bored audience was willing to applaud something...anything...that would liven up the dull proceedings.

The critics' reviews of "Out of This World" were "mixed," which usually means that the reviewee is in trouble. It was, but it tottered for 157 performances because it had been vigorously presold to theatre parties. Not a hit, not a flop, but a miserable loss to investors as it faded out of our galaxy.

"From This Moment On," one of Cole's indestructible songs, was written for "Out of This World." It was cut out of the show by George Abbott, just before the New York opening. Two years later, it was inserted in MGM's film of "Kiss Me, Kate." It quickly became a great popular hit. Today it is a sturdy "standard."

....

In the summer of 1954, working at home in Bucks on my own compositions, I had a phone call from Selma Tamber. She was back at her former position in Chappell & Co., running the orchestrators, after filling the heady position of "General Manager of Subber and Ayers Productions," a job no longer existent.

Although I was no longer under exclusive contract to Chappell, my relations with Max Dreyfus had hardly changed. He was still running the company, commuting five days a week from Brewster by chauffeured limousine, assisted in the office by his brother Louis.

In the RKO building office, Dr. Sirmay continued to edit the printed piano copies of the company's publications, while exercising honorary control over the orchestrators, though alert Selma was the real boss of the boys who wrote for the bands.

After the usual telephonic salutations, Selma, wasting no time, asked me, "How would you like to score another Porter show?"

"I would like that very much," I replied. "I have the greatest respect for Cole's music and to paraphrase the master, his lyrics are the tops."

"They're the cat's pajamas!"

"And they need orchestrations that allow every clever word to be heard and understood in the back rows of the balcony."

She laughed and asked, "Why do you think he wants Don Walker? Not for that vacant stare of yours."

"It isn't vacant. It just indicates that I'm concentrating very hard, deciding which part of the information I'm receiving is worth storing away and which part can be forgotten. The brain is an amazing organ but shouldn't be overloaded with a mess of trivial chaff."

"Well, thank you, Professor, for the lecture. But when you see Cole, keep your goofy theories to yourself. Just talk about orchestration...that's crazy enough."

"As you wish, head lady. So what's my next move?"

"Cole has almost finished his score for 'Silk Stockings,' that's the title of the coming Feuer & Martin production, scheduled to go into production this fall. It's a musical version of *Ninotchka*. Remember the film?"

"Garbo, wasn't it? A dedicated Communist woman in charge of a group of Russian agriculturists, allowed to attend an exhibition of farm machinery in Paris, France. She falls in love with a French count. Is that the story?"

"That's a good rough synopsis. Already you know more about the show than I do. It seems that there's an American Dixieland band playing in Paris that gets mixed up in the action. Cole would like to talk to you about it. How to work a unit like that into the pit orchestra and so forth. Could you see him at his apartment about eleven A.M. some morning early next week?"

"Any day, Selma," I said. "Set it up, and thanks for the buggy ride."

....

At a quarter to eleven the following Tuesday morning, New York's subway system delivered me to Grand Central Station. From there I walked north on Lexington Avenue, looking for the secondary streets that would lead me to the rear of the Waldorf-Astoria Hotel, where the private elevators that serviced the Tower apartments were located. Apparently my name had been put on the "Please Admit One" list, but I had to prove that the body presenting itself to the concierge was actually that of the admittable Don Walker. After proving that I was me, a high-speed elevator quickly lifted my carcass to the herringbone floor at the entrance to Cole's lofty apartment. There I was met by Cole's lifelong valet Paul, who apologized for my recent inquisition. He led me to Cole's handsome brass-trimmed, leather-walled music room. I could hear heavy, constructional sounds reverberating in some distant area of the nine-room apartment.

Paul explained, "We're all torn up here. The lights in Mr. Porter's bathroom were positioned badly. He couldn't see to shave, a job he insists on performing himself. Fixing that small problem seems to require dynamite and steel welding. Such a small problem with such an enormous solution! I hope he'll be happy when it's all finished."

He excused himself to tell "Mr. Porter" that I had arrived. I examined Cole's Steinway: It had a special bench with a writing desk attached, the pedals raised slightly higher than customary. I was about to inspect one of the bookcases set in the walls when Cole arrived in his wheelchair, propelled by Paul. Having not seen him at close range for almost ten years, when he attended the orchestra rehearsals of "Seven Lively Arts," I was shocked by his appearance. I knew that in the interim he had been through terrible times with his legs and not very long ago had lost his wife, Linda, to dreaded, dragged-out emphysema. Yet I was not prepared to see him visibly *shrunk* in all features except those large, liquid, intelligent eyes...eyes that summed you up and filed you away in a flash.

Paul was dismissed and the two of us were face to face.

Cole wasted no time in coming to the purpose of our meeting. He said, "Max Dreyfus tells me that you are available and willing to score 'Silk Stockings' for me."

I said, "I'll be happy to work for you again, boss."

"And I will be happy to have you," said Cole. "My new show takes place in Paris. It will be the *sixth* musical I have written that has Paris as its locale. I'm up to my eyebrows with Paris and need help."

"How can I lend a hand?"

"At the beginning of our second act, George Kaufman's script calls for an onstage Dixieland band playing a jazz number. Such American orchestras and their music were all the rage in Paris at the time of our play. The producers, Cy Feuer and Ernest Martin, say they can't afford a separate Dixieland band for that one splash; if we must have a jazz band on stage, the personnel will come from the pit orchestra and return to their chairs when the number is over. Tell me, is such a large maneuver practical?"

"It all depends: If it is in the middle of an act, it's messy. If it opens the second act, it's a cinch."

"I think it *does* start the second act."

"Perfect! During the intermission, the members of the band can put on their costumes and some makeup. My only problem will be figuring out an entr'acte that will have to be played with a greatly reduced orchestra."

"I'm sure you can solve that puzzle; it's in your department, your responsibility. I didn't bring you in all the way from Bucks County to have you write a thesis on Dixieland bands. No…it's a far more touchy matter that I have to discuss with you." He handed me a paper with a lyric on it, entitled "THE RED BLUES."

"Read it," he said, "read it carefully."

It simply informed the listener that the singer had "got the Red Blues" over and over again, ceaselessly. There was an amusing section devoted to proclaiming how the "Red Blues" was far superior to all other "blues" in the spectrum, including the "Blue blues."

Grinning, I returned the paper and remarked, "It's the most cynical lyric you've ever written, Cole Porter. You didn't tell me that the Dixieland band in your new show is *not* an American orchestra, but a bunch of *Russians pretending* that *they* were. What an ironic idea! It's great fun!"

"Do you think the audience will dig what is happening on stage?"

"It won't matter what they think. The musicians left in the pit will laugh hard enough to carry the audience with them. Let me digress: One of my most treasured records was given to me by Larry Bynion, the famous tenor sax player. It's a recording of a Russian orchestra playing what they think is a swingin' version of 'There's a Tavern in the Town.' To an American dance musician, it's hysterically funny. There are a lot of the same elements here."

"All but one," said Cole. "All but a very important one."

"What's that?"

"A tune, a simple little tune. Nothing fancy, but a string of notes that doesn't sound like somebody else's copyrighted string of notes. That is what's missing, and I've broken my ass to find it. Every solution I've come up with sounds like a steal from W. C. Handy! I'm at the end of my wits!"

"A group of Russian musicians trying to play jazz...it should be easy to lampoon their strangulated efforts...."

"Easy? Did you say 'easy'? Here!" He handed the lyric to me and commanded, "Don't come back until you've got a proper tune for these words. An ultra-jazzy *Russian* tune! A funny tune with Russian dressing!"

I promised to do my darndest, which included a procedure I had used before when confronted with a stylistic problem. I went to a good record store and bought recordings of music by Stravinsky, Shostakovich, Glazunov, and Mussorgsky. I took that package back with me to Bucks County, where I already had the Tchaikovskys, the Rimsky-Korsakovs, and the Rachmaninoffs. At home I soaked myself in Russian music, classical and contemporary, for two days, just listening, memorizing nothing but soaking in styles, the atmosphere of those superb examples of Russian composition.

I did not need to immerse myself in American jazz. That was born in me and nurtured by playing an instrument in dance orchestras. From two days of heavy Slavonic indoctrination, I was ready to write the music to accompany Cole's satirical words. Stealing nothing from the Russians but the ambience, I improvised the simple tune on the piano and hurried to get it down on paper. It sounded fine when I played it over. So I grabbed the phone and called Cole's private number.

"I think I've got it, Cole!" I spoke excitedly. "I'm *sure* I got it!"

"Got what?" he asked. "Not that cold everyone's getting, I pray."

"No, no! I believe that I've come up with the tune we need for 'THE RED BLUES'! The job you gave me to do."

"Oh, that. Pardon me. I'd forgotten I gave you that assignment."

"I know you're terribly busy, but don't you want to hear it?"

"Yes...I guess so. When can you demonstrate it?"

"Any time! Any time at all!"

He thought a moment and said, "Make it next Tuesday at eleven A.M. Just a week later than when you came the last time."

"I'll be there! Panting! But you don't seem as excited about it as you were last Tuesday."

"That's because Kaufman and McGrath, the bookwriters, don't know if they want an on-stage band at all."

That information cooled me down in a hurry, although Cole still wanted to hear the tune I had composed, probably out of kindness.

The following Tuesday at eleven A.M., once again, I presented myself at the Waldorf-Towers and was treated properly, like the familiar retainer I was becoming. Cole was in his music room, waiting for me. I handed him a copy of my arrangement of "THE RED BLUES" and sat down at his "equipped-for-the-handicapped" piano to demonstrate my work for him. In those days, I played a better piano than I do now, which is like going from "passable" to "hopeless." Somehow I struggled through the number, with Cole laughing in the right places and boosting me on. When I came to a shaky finish, he applauded, cheering me with a modest "Bravo."

Breathless, I asked, "What do you think of it?"

He smiled, replying, "It's perfect…exactly what I wanted. Although some sour 'tune detective' might claim that it's derived from some obscure copyrighted source, I am sure that allegation wouldn't hold up in a court of law. I love what you have done with a most difficult assignment. However, as I told you before, the status of the number is still in limbo. George Kaufman continues to hem-and-haw about whether or not he needs a number like 'THE RED BLUES.' Well, if he wants one, we've got it. That's one worry off my mind."

I left, not knowing if "THE RED BLUES" was in or out. Then, just before "SILK STOCKINGS" went into rehearsal, Cole called me at home.

He said, "This is your favorite lyricist calling. 'THE RED BLUES' is definitely *in!* You had better come over here so we can settle your credit, the rights and so forth."

So we arranged another meeting in the Waldorf-Towers, where the elevator operator greeted me as an old friend.

Cole played for me the song he had just finished, called "As On Through the Seasons We Sail," a moving love song, which he had resurrected from a dull comedy opus that had been cut. (Cole was a great one for salvaging discarded material.) Then we got down to "THE RED BLUES" business.

Cole led off. "I am and will be everlastingly conscious of your contribution to 'THE RED BLUES.' I was hopelessly stuck, unable to find a decent tune to my own lyric. You came along and modestly offered to help. You have solved my problem beautifully. Now comes the reckoning of compensation. I'll give you whatever you want, within reason. What will it be?"

"I've given this question a great deal of thought," I replied. "I have no illusions concerning the monetary value of 'THE RED BLUES.' It is exclusively a showpiece; I doubt that a copy of it will ever be requested or sold. Then there is the matter of the Cole Porter estate. I don't want to leave it encumbered by the necessity to pay me, year after year, some infinitesimal royalty or chase me around to get my signature on a movie contract. As I see it, there is only one way to resolve this puzzle."

"And what is that?"

"Pay me the musicians' union's hourly rate for the time I have put in on this assignment, including research and preparation. This agreement will recognize, but not include, my contract with the producers to orchestrate the show at customary prices per page.

"Upon receipt of the agreed hourly payment, I will sign a release, as prepared by your lawyers, relinquishing all rights in 'THE RED BLUES.'"

Cole said, "That's more than fair. I'm sure my legal beagles will be glad to make up such a document. It's certainly a pleasure to have a Wharton School graduate available when we have a sticky musical situation to unglue."

....

That was the last time I saw Cole in private. He attended rehearsals of "SILK STOCKINGS" in New York and followed the show on its unusually extended "break-in" road tour to Philadelphia (three weeks), Boston (four weeks), and Detroit (three weeks). During that time, the original director, George Kaufman, was superseded and Abe Burrows brought in, only to be replaced by Cy Feuer, one of the producers, who eventually gave himself the odd credit of "Staged by...." In spite of the constant upheaval in the directorial department, regardless of the female lead, Hildegarde Neff, who "talked" Cole's beautiful "Without Love"; with an understudy, Gretchen Wyler, replacing the shingles-harried Yvonne Adair, somehow "Silk Stockings"1} kept selling out on its preparatory junket.

I was spared the agony of spending ten weeks "on the road" with a show that was in a chronic state of nerve-wracking flux. In the pit, conducting, was Herbert Creene, a most competent leader, who was willing to take care of the endless little adjustments in orchestrations that familiarity leads performers to request, sometimes to demand, irritating picayune changes.

In the six New York musicians traveling with "Silk Stockings," there was a trombone player (more later about him) who was a competent arranger who could score "fixes" in cuts and make needed reinforcements. When Cole wrote a new number, I drove or flew to the location of the show and scored the necessary orchestration, returning to home grounds as soon as the piece was tested before an audience. I had come to hate sitting around in a faraway hotel room, with nothing on which to work, drawing a stand-by "day-rate," while life drained away, tedious day after unproductive hour.

....

"Silk Stockings," Cole's twenty-first musical, went into rehearsal in New York on October 18, 1954, and opened in Broadway's Imperial Theatre on February 24, 1955. Cole was not present, having flown off to Switzerland five days earlier, worn out by the protracted struggle to make the show a hit.

The extraordinary efforts of all involved paid off handsomely. The reviews were excellent, especially the credits lavished on the score. The show ran 478 performances and returned a healthy dividend to its investors. "All of You" and "Paris Loves Lovers" have become "standards" in musical catalogues.

"Silk Stockings" was Cole's last full-scale Broadway musical. In 1956 he wrote a lively film score for MGP's *High Society,* giving its stars—Bing Crosby, Grace Kelly, Frank Sinatra, Celeste Holm, Louis Calhern, Louis Armstrong, and Margalo Gilmore—plenty of classy material to sing. Songs from that film that have survived the test of time are "True Love," "I Love You, Samantha," "Now You Has Jazz," and "Well, Did You Evah!" In 1957 MGM made a film of "Silk Stockings," starring Fred Astaire and Cyd Charisse. In addition to the Broadway score, Cole contributed "Fated to Be Mated" and "Ritz Roll and Rock."

But the creative power was running out. In 1957 Cole wrote a score for MGM's *LES GIRLS.* None of the songs in that film have survived the years, suffering the same obscurity as the songs he wrote for *ALADDIN,* an original television show with a book by S.J. Perelman that aired on CBS on February 21, 1958.

The last years of Cole Porter's life are a horror story, a record of crucial operations, amputations, infections, and relapses. How any man could survive the constant ferocious attacks upon his nervous system leaves one in awe of the inherent, latent strength of the human body and, in particular, the fighting, resilient version of it that was Cole Porter. He finally gave up the bitter battle on October 15, 1964, at the age of seventy-three. His body lies in a family plot in Peru, Indiana, next to his mother and his lifelong wife, Linda.

8. Richard Rogers

The first time I shook hands with Richard Rodgers was near the end of September, 1941, in the Ethel Barrymore Theatre in New York City, directly after a special rehearsal of the string section of the "Best Foot Forward" orchestra. It was a Tuesday in a week whose Thursday would see the triumphal opening of that hit musical. Although the show possessed the first "big band sound" to reach Broadway, it also owned a minimum group of stringed instruments to provide a tender accompaniment for the few sentimental and amorous moments. That modest platoon was composed of three violins, one viola, and one cello, sometimes borrowing the string bass from the "big band."

Something had gone dreadfully wrong with the rosin-sniffers during the preceding dress rehearsal and Archie Bleyer, the conductor, had obtained rarely granted permission to have a special drill for the strings to discover and remedy the discords.

I was in the first row of the house, right behind Archie, checking the sounds against my score. The rest of the darkened auditorium was empty, with the exception of the last row, where a couple of businesslike characters were sitting in the gloom. I thought, *There's that Charlie Harris, making sure that this extra rehearsal doesn't run overtime.*

Without the "big band" blasting vociferous decibels, the little string section sounded surprisingly full and strong. Archie soon found out the cause of the trouble: A copyist had skipped a line in my score, writing notes for the viola (Alto clef) in a violin part (Soprano clef). That error was soon fixed, and Archie used the remainder of his extra hour "polishing" ballads. When his time ran out, he dismissed the musicians.

As I was packing my scores, one of the "back-row" men came walking down the aisle. I knew who it was, although I had never met him. It was Richard Rodgers.

Throughout rehearsals in New York and on the road, I had seen him drifting about, saying little, just observing. There was plenty to observe, with the likes of June Allyson, Maureen Cannon, Victoria Schools, Rosemary Lane, and a bevy of other birdies leaping here and there in minimal rehearsal tights.

Curious, I had asked Archie Bleyer, "Who is that legal type I see watching the prep every day? The theatre owner?"

"Hush," whispered Archie. "Don't take that name in vain, or even his profession. That man is Richard Rodgers."

"RICHARD RODGERS! What is he doing here?"

"He's our co-producer. I guess Abbott got worried with untested songwriters and persuaded Rodgers to co-produce, thereby being available to back up Martin and Blane in a crunch."

"Abbott's a sly one, isn't he? Do you think he got Rodgers to put money in the show?"

"Who knows? But I wouldn't be surprised if Rodgers did; he certainly looks as if he's keeping an eye on assets."

Now the great man was coming down the aisle, nearing me with his right hand out, saying, "I'm Richard Rodgers."

I gave a hand, checking in with "and I'm Don Walker."

He said, "I've been listening to your work for almost a month. I like it. You have brought a verve, a freshness, a *young* sound to the old pit, exactly right for the youth on stage. But until today, I never knew how well you can score for strings. Now I've had a chance to hear your string-writing all by itself, I find it excellent! Which of the strings is your instrument?"

I said, "Thank you, Mr. Rodgers, thank you very much. I must confess that I have never played a string instrument, except, of course, the piano. But I have spent a great deal of time studying the orchestral strings, trying to make up for my lack of intimate experience with them."

"You've studied them well, you fooled me. I was ready to swear that you were a string player. What *is* your instrument?"

"The whole orchestra. But if I must be specific, I rather favor the old 'lickrish-stick'…the B flat clarinet."

"That's interesting. Why don't we go across the street and let me buy you a drink. I'd like to talk to you about another show I'm considering."

Regretfully I said, "I'm very sorry, Mr. Rodgers, but—"

"Stop right there. Forget the 'Mister' business. Call me 'Dick.'"

"I'm very sorry…uh…*Dick,* but my job here is finished and I have my orders from Max Dreyfus to go directly to Penn Station and catch an express to Boston. He tells me that Vinton Freedley and 'Let's Face It' needs me. I hope that when I get back, you will renew your kind invitation. Maybe by then the show you're 'considering' will be a firm project."

I shook hands again with "Dick" and went off to try to make Danny Kaye and his entourage happy.

....

When I reached Boston, I found out that Cole Porter had written a new number for Danny Kaye, "Let's Not Talk About Love," to replace an inappropriate night-club specialty that Kaye had been using. As is customary, the staff wanted to hear and evaluate Cole's song before an audience as quickly as humanly possible, if not sooner. A sit-up-all-night orchestrating session was obligatory.

The following evening, the new material was tested before a paying audience and it worked! It was clearly more rewarding than the irrelevant ditty it superseded. Such small victories serve to repay an orchestrator for the loss of precious sleep, although the doubling of the page price for night work tends to deliver a more substantial satisfaction.

When I returned to Broadway, I discovered that "Best Foot Forward" was a most solid hit and Merman was still shattering light bulbs in "Panama Hattie." When "Let's Face It," a very funny show, opened to rave reviews, that made *three* successful musicals, playing simultaneously on the Great White Way, for which I had written the orchestrations. It was only natural, at the callow age of thirty-four, for me to dream that I was at the top of my profession.

The correction came at once. Max Dreyfus immediately assigned me to the task of servicing a show entitled "Hi-ya Gentlemen," which was in "big trouble" during its pre-Broadway trials in, of all places, Hartford, Connecticut. So instead of reaping the expected rewards for being the orchestrator of three concurrently running Broadway hits, I was banished to a very sick show, whose routine was fluctuating every performance, spreading predictable chaos in its music department.

Yet all was not lost. At the same time Max Dreyfus consigned me to "Hi-ya Gentlemen," he raised my weekly drawing account a handsome ten dollars a week! Without being asked! Of course I had to earn that munificent boost by scoring ever more and more pages of orchestration, but the weekly check *did* look fractionally bigger, allowing my dear wife, Audrey, to feel marginally more secure.

"Gentlemen" renewed my acquaintance with Johnny Green, who was its composer-conductor. I had met him briefly during my quick in and quicker out of the doomed Paramount Studios in Astoria, Long Island. Since that disaster, he had kept very busy leading his own dance orchestra, playing in prestigious New York hotels. In his spare time, he had composed some wonderful, exceptionally high-class songs, such as "Body and Soul" and "I Cover the Waterfront," creations that adorned the stages of the best revues. "Hi-ya Gentlemen" was Johnny's first chance to write a complete score for an integrated "book" musical.

I arrived in "Hahtfud" just after the young director, Joshua Logan, had suffered what we called in those days "a nervous breakdown" and had been escorted back to home base by white-coated assistants. In his key position, there was nobody and everybody, each as one's fancy flipped. I saw little of that confusion, being confined, most of the time, to the desk in my hotel room, rewriting, at Johnny's behest, orchestrations made by my predecessors. It was depressing to have to sit there in that unfamiliar room, scrawling those little black notes that one knew would soon be going up in flames at Cain's with the supposedly fireproof scenery.

During the abbreviated fortnight I spent with "Hi-ya Gentlemen," Johnny Green and I became good friends, each respecting the abilities of the other. I enjoyed orchestrating John's compositions, and he liked almost every note I put on paper. Having written orchestrations himself, we both spoke the same musical language.

By the time I arrived in Hartford, Johnny had accepted the unhappy fact that "Hi-ya Gentlemen" was a quiet flopola. Professional to the core, he kept striving to improve his main responsibility, the music, knowing that nothing he could do would hold off the threatening collapse of the sad production.

Johnny's distress over "Gentlemen" was somewhat mollified by a letter from George Abbott, offering him a chance to write the score for a new musical about young musicians. It sounded like a wonderful project, and Johnny could hardly wait to get back to New York and pin down an agreement for him to compose the songs for such a musicomedy. It also sounded like a good job for me, working for an outfit that had produced a "Best Foot Forward."

Not wishing to be present at the "tears in the beer," following the final closing of "Gentlemen," on that Saturday morning I took a train to Grand Central, a cab to Penn Station, another train to Trenton, where Audrey was waiting with Ann (9) and David (8) in our Chevrolet. As we drove over the Delaware bridge to Pennsylvania and north on PA Route 32 to our home south of New Hope, I could feel all the worries and tensions of a show "in trouble" dissipate, leaving me free to enjoy the beauty of the countryside, the chatter of my children, and the ever-present love of my wife.

....

The next day, December 7, 1941, the Japanese made their devastating sneak attack on Pearl Harbor, while two of their highest dignitaries were in Washington, D.C., lulling us all to sleep, pretending to negotiate a peaceful agreement with the United States. On that "Day of Infamy," I was at home in Bucks County, listening, as many other Americans were, to a radio broadcast of a New York Giants football game.

The first bald announcement of the treacherous blow sounded like a slip-up, an accidental intrusion of a children's program, possibly caused by the closing of the wrong switch by a careless technician. As shocking bulletins kept trumpeting of staggering losses, realization of the great disaster grew, all the more frustrating because no instant retaliation was possible.

The football game dragged on, the players knowing that they were prime candidates to be drafted to swell the ranks of our modest peacetime forces. Each member of the audience, in the stands and listening on radio, was speculating on how the coming war would be reshaping the individual life. No longer did it matter who won the football game; a far more important contest, an ugly business of life or death, had begun.

....

The world of theatrical entertainment adjusted quickly to the reality of total war. We had no massive ships to launch, no thousands of planes to produce, only the time and ability to temporarily divert the minds of our warriors from the horror of the conflict in which they soon would be embroiled. After the initial shock, Broadway settled down to provide its specialty: entertainment, with only the occasional practice blackout to remind everyone that German subs were nearby in the Atlantic.

In the dying days of 1941, the traditional holiday greetings, "Merry Christmas" and "Happy New Year," sounded false and futile, constantly devalued by the endless stream of bad news from distant battlegrounds. Sometimes it felt as if never again would there ever be any good news.

Production of new musicals nearly ceased. Investors shied from theatrical gambles, feeling patriotic, committed to support the government's sales of war bonds. Once again, in order to keep my Chappell drawing account "in the black," I had to "switch gears" and fall back on my friendly conductors of network radio programs.

One day late in February, I was called into the office of Max Dreyfus, who had waited out his period of contractual banishment and had assumed his rightful position as chief executive officer of Chappell & Co. He told me, "You and your orchestrations have made a very good impression on Dick Rodgers. He has asked me to make you available to score his next show, which will be going into rehearsal early in April, with a June opening in New York City."

I answered, "My radio conductors know that my main ambition is to write for the living theatre. They will be pleased for me to have the chance to orchestrate a Rodgers' show. I'm sure they will cooperate and give me advance work that I can complete before Dick's production goes into rehearsal. Then I can keep my radio contacts alive, while giving Dick one hundred percent."

"Sounds reasonable, but you will have to work very hard throughout March to clear the decks for Dick Rodgers."

I answered, "I'm accustomed to work very, very hard, Mr. Dreyfus. Somehow, the tougher the pressure gets, it becomes easier to put only the *essential* notes on a page, the superfluous ones never get written. I must confess that I *like* to be pressured, the results are clearer and more effective."

Max smiled and said, "Your philosophy is dangerously close to that of a chronic procrastinator. Make sure that you don't fall into the habit of putting off work in order to get yourself into a creative frenzy."

I admitted, "I have been tempted, Mr. Dreyfus, but so far I have been able to properly organize my work time, thus avoiding impossible crises."

"Good. The copyists will love you for that. One fact you must always remember: You will not be a lonely orchestrator up there in Boston with all the weight of the world on your back. You will be a representative of a famous musical organization, one with powerful resources. If an overwhelming amount of work is loaded on you, call me and I will see that Russell Bennett or Hans Spialek or both of them are made instantly available to help you out of the predicament. Chappell will always be behind you."

I thanked him profusely for his support and went home, determined, more than ever, to orchestrate every damn note of the coming Rodgers and Hart musical all by myself. By that time in my career I knew, all very well, that the achievement of such an objective would take a lot of pre-rehearsal preparation, plus the cooperation of the director, the choreographer, and Lady Luck. So why not woo the skittish female? Maybe she would smile for me.

....

About a week later, Dwight Deere Wiman's stage manager phoned me, giving me the time and place where Dick Rodgers would render a demonstration of his songs and a summary of the story for his next musical, entitled "BY JUPITER." Attendance would be limited to the heads of production departments. Thrilled to be included in that exclusive group, I promised to be present.

The disclosure was performed in a large room on the same floor of the RKO building as that occupied by Chappell & Co. To my surprise and gratification, the first person I met upon entering was Johnny Green!

He hailed me, grinning. "Bet you didn't expect to see *me* here!"

I cooled him off with, "Nothing you could do would surprise me, Johnny Green. Don't tell me that you are going to be connected with this production."

"Connected!?...I'm its conductor! Its musical director!"

I was amazed but pleased, saying, "That's terrific, Johnny, but what of your own creation? That Abbott show about dance musicians?"

"That's on," he said, "but not till next fall. Meantime, I'll get Dick's show rolling while training an assistant to take over when 'Beat the Band' goes into rehearsal."

Delighted with Rodgers' choice of a musical director, I was introduced to the famous costume designer, Irene Sharaff. I was greeted by Jo Mielziner, the leading scenic artist, and shook hands with my favorite choreographer, Robert Alton. I thought, *If the cast turns out to be as fabulous as the staff, "Jupiter" will be a supershow! Here are all the top creative artists in musical showbiz! Gathered together for the same project!*

At that moment, another familiar face entered the room. It was Joshua Logan, the young, yet renowned director, apparently fully recovered from whatever had laid him low. What a staff "By Jupiter" 1}would have! I was happy to be able to rub elbows with all those theatrical legends.

The meeting came to order with the arrival of Dick and his trusty accompanist, Margot Hopkins, the persevering lady who taught the songs to the singers in a Rodgers and Hart musical. After a short, unproductive wait to see if Larry Hart would appear (he didn't), the presentation of the score began.

(I have variously called the ensuing happening a "demonstration," a "disclosure," a "meeting," and a "presentation," carefully avoiding dubbing it an *"audition."* In showbiz that italicized word is always connected with an appeal for money, whether made by a performer hoping to be hired or by a producer attempting to lasso investors. In our instance, the purpose of the assemblage was to acquaint the production staff with the music of the show. It was *not* an "audition.")

That day it suddenly dawned on me why Richard Rodgers' songs were so "different" from those of other songwriters. He liked to work from a lyric, one that had an inherent rhythm suggesting an interesting pattern of accompaniment. With that essential basis invented, he would whistle (he was a gifted whistler) a tune against the established background. His method was most unusual, being the reverse of the procedure of most songwriters, who nearly always start with a tune, which they later support with rhythm and harmony. The original piano copy (not the simplified published copy) of a Rodgers song is actually a sketch for an orchestration supporting a soloist.

Everything Dick Rodgers did seemed well organized. That day, in the office down the hall from Chappell, before hearing a note of the score, all present were handed a mimeographed paper:

BY JUPITER.

A musical version of Julian F. Thompson's play "The Warrior's Husband."

Credits for authorship: "A play by Richard Rodgers and Lorenz Hart."

Music by Richard Rodgers.
Lyrics by Lorenz Hart.

Produced by Dwight Deere Wiman and Richard Rodgers.
Associated Producer: Richard Kollmar.
Director: Joshua Logan. Choreographer: Robert Alton.
Scenery and Lighting: Jo Meilziner. Costumes: Irene Sharaff.
Conductor: John Green. Orchestrations: Don Walker.

CAST

Ray Bolger
Benay Venuta
Bertha Beimore
Constance Moore
Ronald Graham
Margaret Bannerman
Mark Dawson
Ralph Dumke
Vera-Ellen
Nanette Fabray
Berni Gould
Singers and Dancers

PRINCIPAL SONGS:

"Jupiter Forbid"
"Wait Till You See Her"
"Careless Rhapsody"
"Ev'rything I've Got Belongs To You"
"Life With Father"
"Nobody's Heart"

Scheduled New York Opening:
      June 3, 1942, Shubert Theatre.

There are a number of provocative inferences that can be deduced from that staff information sheet of "By Jupiter." It admits, at the beginning, that the "idea" for the musical was originated by an author who would have no working relationship with the Dwight Deere Wiman production, for the given book-credit is simply "…a play by Richard Rodgers and Lorenz Hart." That implies that Rodgers and Hart, or their representatives, negotiated with Julian F. Thompson or his representatives and obtained the rights for Rodgers and Hart to musicalize J.F. Thompson's play, *The Warrior's Husband,* without any active participation by said Thompson, for a consideration that was probably a non-returnable advance against a healthy royalty, if and when the contemplated production was activated.

Implicating Lorenz Hart as a coauthor immediately suggests that Rodgers was trying to heap responsibilities on his partner, hoping that they would keep Larry from "disappearing" during critical emergencies.

One cannot help wondering why Richard Rodgers wanted to wear three hats: Composer, Coauthor, and Co-Producer. He certainly didn't need all those titles to assert his power over the proceedings.

And why? Oh, why was Richard Kollmar needed to help produce the show? I was there and never saw the co-host of "Breakfast with Dorothy and Dick" contribute anything co-helpful, other than running to the cooperative coffee shop at the corner, carrying back cartons of java to keep the heavy brains ticking.

There was another bothersome fact buried in that pre-rehearsal handout. With only a month to go before the start of rehearsals, there were only six...that's all...*six* finished songs. Was "By Jupiter" to be only "a play with music"? Conventional musical comedies possessed from sixteen to twenty-four songs! Would Rodgers and Hart be able to complete their score by the time "Jupiter" went into rehearsal? It was comforting to know that we would be working with a renowned songwriting team, but could they possibly finish their songs in less than a month? Skepticism was rife on the third floor of the RK0 building that day in early March, 1942, but most of us went home confident that R. & H. would do it again, as they had done it a number of times in the past, and confound those few doubting disbelievers.

....

Having successfully spoofed, in "The Boys from Syracuse," a classic Shakespearean play about Romans (The Comedy of Errors), Rodgers and Hart thought they could repeat the trick with Greeks. "BY JUPITER" is set in an imaginary Hellenic state, ruled by warlike amazons, whose domesticated husbands keep their homes spotless and take care of the children while their mothers are off conquering nearby kingdoms. Of course, true love unkinks the sexes and lackluster normalcy wins at the end. But it was great fun while the turnabout lasted!

On that day, early in April 1942, when "By Jupiter" went into rehearsal, the speaking members of the cast sat in a semicircle on the bare stage of a "dark" theater, holding their scripts. Behind them, widening the semicircle, sat the singers and dancers. Facing the cast, at the focal point of the circle, sat Joshua Logan at a small table, flanked by his assistant and a script girl. When all were seated and ready, Josh gave a hand cue to Margo Hopkins, who was positioned at a battered piano, with Dick Rodgers hovering by.

Margo, picking up the cue, played a noisy half-chorus of "Jupiter Forbid," simulating the loud finish of the still unwritten overture. Josh announced, "The curtain rises," and went on to describe the scene, after which he cued the actor who had the first speech. The reading rehearsal continued, only interrupted when the script called for a song. At those junctures there were several procedures: Sometimes a member of the cast who had been taught a song rendered it; other times Margo and Dick played a tune four-hands on the piano, the cast reading mimeographed lyric pages. Once in a while, when a lyric was not ready, Dick would describe what the absent words would accomplish, backed by Margo quietly faking on the eighty-eight.

Although it was a very spotty revelation of the emerging musical, Josh kept pushing, passing over roadblocks, trying to get a continuous flow. Gradually it became obvious that here was a very, very *funny* show, with a superior script that challenged performers to make the most of it. As for the skimpiness of the score—what they heard of it seemed terrific and as to what was missing—they were willing to trust Rodgers and Hart to fill the gaps as rehearsals progressed.

Larry Hart was not the only constituent who was missing from "By Jupiter" that first day of rehearsal in early April, 1942. Constance Moore, who was to play the feminine half of the principal love story, did not arrive in New York from California until almost a week of rehearsals had passed. Her tardiness was by contractual agreement. Previous commitments had made it impossible for her to arrive in Manhattan in time to go into rehearsal with the rest of the cast. Since her entrance in the play did not occur until the middle of the first act, the producers waived the minor problem of her enforced lateness.

I remember that day of rehearsal when she first appeared in her snug working tights. Hard cases gasped, refusing to believe the physical facts their eyes were reporting.

It wasn't that Connie was the most beautiful, the most endowed, the most enticing female in a gorgeous group of girls who had been carefully selected for their beauty, endowment, and lure (not to exclude their singing and dancing abilities, if any). What made Connie different from the others was an invisible, unconscious aura of vulnerability that hovered about her, making every clumsy male who approached her fantasize that some day, somewhere, somehow, he might partake of the bloom that was the fair Constance Moore.

One day I arrived early at rehearsal to "take down," for orchestration, Connie's first act song. All I needed for my job was an empty theatre, a worklight, a pianist, Josh Logan, and the lady herself. All of those necessities had been "called" before the regular rehearsal time in order to have privacy. To my disgust, most of the males in the production drifted in and were present, scattered in the audience seats, drinking their breakfasts out of containers.

The song that Logan was planning to direct was that lonely, lovely little plaint, "Nobody's Heart." For starters, he suggested that Connie just go ahead and sing the number the way she had been doing while rehearsing with Margot. He planned to go on from there.

Connie came down to the unlit footlights and sang the ballad in a clear, true, appealing voice, as if the piece had been written for her alone. When the song ended, there was a moment of silence, followed by vociferous shouting and applause from all sections of the theatre. I had been concentrating so exclusively on Connie and her interpretation of "Nobody's Heart" that I had not noticed the infiltration of Dick Rodgers, Larry Hart, Johnny Green, Dwight Wiman, and a trio of stage managers, who surrounded the singer as they showered her with compliments.

I gathered my papers and slipped away, anxious to get to my desk in Chappell and orchestrate "Nobody's Heart" while the memory of Connie's flawless rendition remained fresh in my mind.

....

When the New York rehearsal period of "By Jupiter" had run its course, the company entrained for Boston on the N.Y., N.H. & H. It is possible that we stopped for a week in New Haven, but my skittish memory keeps whispering to me that for once a fledgling show skipped Yale and went straight to Harvard. (Cities with colleges provided extra-sharp audiences, whose reactions were helpful when shaping a show.)

The final run-through in Manhattan had starkly revealed how much of the musical score of "By Jupiter" was lacking. There were critical places at the end of each act that screamed for music, but at such times out of the wings would pop an assistant stage manager, reading from a script describing what should be happening. Something drastic had to be done before our incomplete opera could face even out-of-town critics.

That Sunday in early May, '42, the Boston express had an extra car hooked onto its rear end. There was nothing fancy about that addition; it was just another passenger coach, but differing from its fellow coaches because it had been hired by Dwight.

Wiman was to carry the cast and staff of his new musical, "By Jupiter," from Manhattan to Beantown. Outsiders were definitely not welcome.

In another way that car differed from its near companions: It seemed to be decorated with "NO SMOKING!" signs. It may have been only the luck of the draw that dealt us that particular vehicle, but then again it might have been evidence of the tricky hand of Dwight Wiman, hoping to keep his singers' vocal cords healthy. (I wouldn't put it past him.)

It was early in May and unseasonably warm. The windows of the car seemed to be hermetically sealed to assist the air-conditioning that was sadly lacking. Within the car the fetid gas that passed for air was hardly breathable. I had to find oxygen or suffocate! I left my quietly snoring seatmate, Johnny Green, and hurried up the aisle, pushed open the sliding door, and stepped into the vestibule. There the climate was better but still not life-supporting. So I opened the last door and stepped out on the platform between the cars, gulping great lungfuls of smoke-flavored ozone.

Getting adjusted to the clinking and clanging of agonized couplers, I began to enjoy the haven I'd found. It was too good to be lasting, for my transient privacy was soon invaded by one more escapee from the "By Jupiter" car.

It was the Richard of Rodgers, there in the flesh, in search of a spot where a smoker could light up.

"Nice cozy little place you have here," he remarked, taking out Lucky Strikes and a lighter. "Have one?" he queried, offering the pack.

I had to apologize, explaining, "I don't smoke, Dick."

"You don't!" He was surprised, asking, "Am I talking to an arranger who doesn't smoke? What do you do with your nerves during all those midnight hours when you're on double-time?"

"Even then I don't smoke. Neither my father nor my mother smokes. I was brought up in a tobaccoless household and never acquired the habit. Once, when I was about eleven, my chums gave me a corn-silk cigaroot and dared me to smoke it. It tasted so horrible, I gave up smoking right then and forever."

Dick conceded, "You're a lucky one. Frankly, I don't think I could get through a day, much less compose a show, without the old coffin nails." He took a big drag and waved the stub about. "Maybe someday I'll take a year off and break this damn habit!" He changed the subject. "What kind of shape are you in with the orchestrations?"

I told him, "When we read in Boston tomorrow, the band will have every bar of the music of 'By Jupiter' that has been staged and was ready for orchestration."

"The Finale of Act I?"

"Even that late entry. Johnny finished the sketch on Friday night, and I scored it yesterday. I can hardly wait to hear it, with that E-flat, B-flat timpani ostinato pounding against your basic themes played in every key that exists."

"I'm panting to hear that number myself."

Getting serious, I said, "I know I'm going to be hard pressed in Boston, with four or five new songs to be scored, plus the long dance Alton is working on, using the music of 'Wait Till You See Her.' I pray that the fresh demands laid on me during our three weeks in Boston don't come all at once in the last week. I hope that I'll be given the time to do a careful job."

As the train slowed down for its stop at New London, Dick said soothingly, "I know, I understand, but I can't guarantee anything. I'm sorry to admit it, but the success of 'By Jupiter' depends upon our success in finding Larry."

The train had come to a grinding halt.

Taken by surprise, I queried, "*Finding* Larry?"

"We don't know where he is or what shape he's in. Even his drinking cronies are at a loss. As you must know, I've had a lot of trouble with Larry...it's been going on for years. I thought I could straighten him out by giving him important responsibilities. 'By Jupiter' was to be the ultimate test, but my plan seems to have backfired. Now he's run away...like a child who has been given too much to do."

The trainmen hadn't opened the doors of the "By Jupiter" car, for it had no arrivals or departures at New London. Now there was a lot of whistling, and off we started for the next objective: Providence, Rhode Island.

I resumed my dialogue with Dick, observing, "Larry has always seemed to enjoy orchestra readings. Maybe he'll turn up tomorrow."

"Maybe," said Dick, "and if he doesn't...there I'll be, stuck with five tunes with no lyrics."

"Call Mr. Dreyfus. He's probably got a half-dozen young lyricists handy, at least one of them able to jump into your emergency and do a good job."

"A young lyricist? I don't need to search for one with Oscar Hammerstein available."

"Oscar! Can he be had?"

"Yes. I've been talking to him about another project. I know he'd be willing to help me out...but...when the news got around, Larry would be ruined for life. I couldn't do that to him...not after all those years we've been together."

I thought it was time to stick a shaky oar into the muddle-puddle. I tentatively asked, "Dick, when the two of you got interested in 'The Warrior's Husband,' did you lay out a general synopsis for a musical based on the play, including where songs should be located and what they should accomplish?"

"When you're considering acquiring an existing property as the foundation of a musical, you have to invest a certain amount of time in (a) finding out if the property can be successfully adapted to the new milieu and (b) whether or not a sensible deal can be made for the rights."

"Did your synopsis include placement of songs and working titles for them?"

"We had oodles of titles, some good, some blab. Why all these questions?"

"Trying to find out how deeply Larry is involved in our present problem."

"I think the proper word would be 'enmeshed.' Every time I pick up a script, I am surprised to note how many words...lines...bits of business were contributed by Larry...now here we are on our way to Boston and he's not with us."

"But way down inside, you know how to handle this crisis, don't you, Dick?"

He answered, "I know damn well what you're getting at...that I should sit down and write the lyrics of those necessary songs, protecting my partner from the fruits of his unconscionable defection!"

"But Dick, that's the only way out of this crisis."

"But how...where can I find the time? You know how long it takes the best lyricists to write the words of a song. Here I am, a co-producer, beset with all the financial worries of the production, its scenic and costume problems, the musical direction, the staging of the book, the choreography…with all that spinning around in my head, where can I find the time to write lyrics? Sing me something sensible!"

"For 'By Jupiter' you have assembled the most skillful, talented staff in the history of musical comedy, all leaders in their professions, all exceptionally gifted in their special fields. Your partner, Dwight Wiman, has produced a number of excellent shows on his own and is qualified to direct that staff."

"What are you trying to say? That they don't need me anymore?"

"They need you more than ever, Dick. There can be no show at all unless you come up with those missing songs; might as well close before we open!"

"But I'm no lyricist. People will ridicule my amateurish attempts!"

"Come on, Dick, make sense. You couldn't have worked with Larry Hart all those years and not picked up a lot of his know-how while suggesting the odd word, the perfect phrase."

As our express passed, Westerly Dick was silent, puffing away, obviously doing some heavy thinking. When at last he spoke, I knew my counsel had won.

He said, "The heads of staff should meet every morning at ten in Dwight's drawing room in the Ritz so that all the moves for the day are coordinated. Johnny should represent the Music Department; you'll be too busy orchestrating to attend. I should not be disturbed for any problem less than closing the show. I must concentrate on lyrics and nothing else until the score is complete.

"When I finish a song, I want Josh to visit me and hear it. We'll discuss its staging and set a date for its first performance, which I will attend. Otherwise, I must not be distracted until all the songs are finished." He looked at me in mock disgust and said, "You and your Wharton School tricks…I hope you're satisfied."

As we pulled into Providence, I said, "I think I'll go back in the show car and prime Johnny on what to expect in Boston."

....

In 1942 John W. Green (Johnny Green) was a living contradiction in New York's musical world. He was a brilliant concert pianist who made a living leading his own jazzband. He aspired for recognition as a serious composer but gained fame from the high-quality popular songs he wrote. He was youthful but prematurely bald. Without his toupee, he looked like a middle-aged business man; with his rug, twenty years disappeared. He should have repelled feisty young women, but he attracted them like a male magnet. In 1942 he was married to Betty Furness, for whom he had composed a pretentious tone poem called "Music for Elizabeth," which required the total resources of a full symphony orchestra. What Betty was to do with the massive offering, once she had it, was never explained.

In Boston I had a room on the eighth floor of the Touraine Hotel, across the hall from the copyists' work room. Johnny, not willing to pay the Ritz-Carlton's fancy prices, had a single near mine. It has always been my practice, when working on a musical, to go to bed as early in the evening as possible, in order to be able to arise in the wee hours and concentrate on orchestration in that blessed period when no phones ring and visitors are absent.

On that particular night, my phone rang at one o'clock in the morning! It was Johnny.

He was breathing audibly, saying, "Don, can you come to my room and hold my hand for a spell? I know it's an imposition, but please…." With what sounded like a last gasp, he pleaded, "Help me! Help me!"

I could hear a phone falling and bumping. I jumped out of bed, grabbed a pair of pants, and rushed quickly to Johnny's not-so-far-away room.

A haunted J. W. Green opened his door and dragged me in. He gibbered, "Don, you're a real friend. I just *have* to tell somebody what happened to me tonight, something I'll never live down the rest of my life. You're a true pal to listen to this stupid fool."

I grumbled, "But Johnny, what's happened? Why this delirium, getting me out of bed in the middle of the night?"

"Promise you won't tell."

"My lips will be sealed for the life of 'By Jupiter.' I can't guarantee anything beyond that date."

"Okay, here goes: Last night we had a short rehearsal after the show was over and the theatre emptied. It was for a new second act number for Connie Moore and Ronnie Graham. Bob Alton directed, Margot Hopkins accompanied, I conducted from the pit. The fresh material is excellent, both music and lyrics."

"Was Larry there?"

"No, but neither was Dick; he's working on the second act finale. When after midnight the business manager wanted to close the house, we had to get out. So we all walked up Tremont Street to Bickfords and had a biteski and java. That engorged, most everyone headed for the Avery and beddy-bye, leaving me with Connie to walk across the Commons to the Ritz."

"Walk? Why didn't you take a cab?"

"There weren't any around. Besides, it wasn't that far, on a warm, full-moonlit night, almost like summer. You know the walk: practically parallel with Boylston Street.

"Well…when we were getting near Arlington Street and the Ritz, walking very slowly, I saw a single, perfect white tulip, growing all by itself in a bed next to the path. I don't rightly know why next I did what I did…one of those impulse things, I guess, but I bent way-way over to pick the posy for the lady. I had just got it free when my toupee, which was fastened down at the temples, did a complete flip-flop over my face. I must have been pretty peculiar-looking when I stood up with my hairpiece upside-down, hiding my eyes, the blinded prince trying to locate the beautiful princess so he could offer her his lonely floral tribute.

"Connie started to laugh, first a snicker, a snort, then a hee-hee, a haw-haw. A shout, a shriek, with a side-splitting belly-yell. And there I was, trying to readjust my rug with one hand, still clutching my stolen blossom in the other…Tell me, Don, have you ever been laughed *at* by a beautiful woman?"

I answered, "Johnny, Audrey laughs *with* me a lot. If she ever starts laughing *at* me, then it's time to start taking a careful account of stock."

He explained, "I'm just afraid of what might happen in the theatre some night when Connie's in the middle of a song and my baton suddenly reminds her of that damn flower. She might break up!"

"Don't worry about Connie; she's a real pro. You've got plenty to be thankful for. Did you know that there is a fifty-dollar fine for picking flowers in the Commons? You're lucky a cop didn't catch you breaking the law."

"I'll never live down the humiliation I suffered."

"Concentrate on finding a more reliable glue to hold down your hairpiece."

……………………………………

Larry Hart came to Boston, fussed around with words for a couple of days, and then disappeared again. Dick kept working on the missing lyrics, gaining confidence every time a song, for which he had written both words and music, was successfully inserted in the show. At the beginning of our third and final week in Boston, there remained only one important song that was lacking. It was the little ditty that Ray

Bolger needed to set off his famous one-way "chat with the audience," which led into the grand finale of "By Jupiter."

I was handed Dick Rodgers' manuscript of "Life With Father," Ray Bolger's indispensable song, on Monday afternoon in the third and final week of "By Jupiter" in Boston. After I had studied the piece, I tried and failed to set up a meeting with Ray for discussion of the number and to ascertain his wishes regarding its orchestration. Sometimes Ray was difficult to find.

That evening I was able to trap him in his dressing room, where he agreed to go over the song after the evening's performance. Along with the manuscript had come a schedule for its trial run: orchestra call one hour before the Wednesday matinee, new number to be inserted during that performance.

The stage manager located Hopkins, Alton, and Logan for me, who all promised to attend a post-performance rehearsal of the new number that night.

Unfortunately, Ray had lifelong friends attending the show that Monday night, friends he couldn't get away from until eleven-thirty. Once again, we had to get out of the theatre by midnight, so our precious rehearsal time was devoted to teaching Ray the tune and words of the new song. He was a quick study but not one that could be called instantaneous.

When we were bounced out of the theatre at midnight, I felt that I was sufficiently familiar with "Life With Father" to score Ray's vocal. As far as his dance was concerned, that was still unexplored territory.

At 5 A.M. early Tuesday morning, I began to orchestrate the vocal of "Life With Father." By 10 A.M. I had enough completed pages to start the copyists grinding out the instrumental parts; by 3 P.M. my vocal score was finished.

After a "stand-up" late lunch, I hurried to the theatre, where the company was rehearsing. I needed the details of Ray's dance to "Life With Father" in order to write an accompanying orchestration. I searched all over the theatre for the elusive Bolger and finally found him, dozing on a cot in his "star" dressing room, concealed behind a moveable clothes-horse. I explained my problem, my lack of details of his dance, my fear of writing a dull, all-purpose "stock" type orchestration.

Ray listened calmly to my anxieties, my urgent need of minute detail so I could match music to his movements. After I had stated my case, he said, "I understand your desire for particulars of my dance, but I'm afraid that I can't give them to you because I don't know exactly what I'm going to do when I get out there on the stage. I never, ever, perform a dance *precisely* the same way two shows in a row. I am not a schooled dancer who can execute, perfectly, a set dance routine night after night after night. I never know just what I'm going to do until I'm on stage, in the spotlight. I may be a headache to the professionals who have to work with me, but as long as the audience seems to enjoy what I do, I figure that I'm safely on top of this crazy business."

I said, "Tomorrow afternoon at one o'clock, the orchestra will assemble to rehearse your solo number. My copyists, at this moment, are writing the instrumental parts to accompany your singing of 'Life With Father.' After your vocal, you will dance to music I have been hired to provide. At this moment, I don't know what to write for your specialty; I haven't a clue. All I'm sure of is that if, by one P.M. tomorrow, I don't have the proper music for your dance on the stands, my name will be 'MUD' in the minds of a number of important people. Please, Ray, Please! Help me out of this damn bambooselment!"

"Take it easy," said Ray. "Relax...there isn't any reason for you to get the highstrikes....Tell you what we'll do: Let's cut your big problem down to small ones, which we'll proceed to solve one at a time. Ready?"

"Ready!"

"Here goes: Have three natural places in the second chorus of the vocal where the orchestra will quietly vamp while I talk to the audience. I'll need a couple of very loud bars at the ends of those vamps to go with...I hope...the laughter. Then we'll need a loud 'wind-up' at the end of the second chorus, leading into the dance proper. Now the dance itself: Remember, we're dealing with a short eighteen-bar tune, providing the opportunity to insert lots of variety of color and mood. Let's start with a whole chorus of 'soft-shoe,' with a few stings in it....You work that out with the drummer. Then I'll want a smooth, double-time chorus for my 'skating' business. Next I'll need a big, bigger, and biggest 'ride-out' chorus to make the transition to the full company finale, which we have been using for the last ten days. Have you got all that?"

"Sure have." (I'd been taking notes like a frenzied stenographer.) "I don't know how we're going to do it, but come tomorrow at one P.M., the music for your vocal, your dance, and the finale of 'Life With Father' will be on the orchestra's stands...somehow....Now I better get back to the hotel and start this tapeworm moving. Looks like a rough night for all concerned."

"Will it all be ready on time?"

"Yes, even if I have to do some copying myself."

"That's like asking a Frannnch gourmet chef to prepare hamburgers!"

"The show must go on…on time!"

"Regardless of ruffled sensibilities!"

....

As promised, the orchestral parts of "Life With Father" were on the music stands at one P.M. the next day (Wednesday). Ray Bolger sat in the first row of the house, listening carefully to the reading and polishing of his solo number's orchestration. When conductor Johnny Green was satisfied with his musicians' rendition of the new piece, he asked Ray if he wished to go up on the stage and check out the routine with his dance.

Our star shook his head and said, "The arrangement sounds fine to me…exactly like the shtick I discussed with Don yesterday."

Surprised, Johnny asked, "Don't you want to run through it once with the orchestra? Just to be on the safe side?"

"I don't need to mark it," replied Ray. "As far as I'm concerned, the orchestration is perfect. If you have the time to give it a couple of more readings, go ahead, get familiar with it. I'll be in my dressing room." He went backstage, humming the fresh melody.

It was only natural for me to desire to experience Ray's first performance of "Life With Father," but having been up all the previous night scoring its orchestration, I was afraid that if I watched the show from the start, all the way through to near the end of the second act, where the new song occurred, I would surely fall asleep, thereby disturbing paying customers with my snores and sibilations. So I hurried up Tremont Street, stopping to buy a sandwich and a pint of milk on the way to my room in the dear old Touraine, where I set my trusty alarm clock to blast off at 4 P.M.

Right on time, the ribald clamor of my drillmaster shattered my blackout, then an icy shower washed me widely awake. Soon I was present in the Shubert's "Standing Room Only," behind the last row of spectator seats.

The show was playing well; you could feel the total pleasure of the sold-out house, content and thankful for being so well entertained. As Ray's climatic statement drew near, one could sense the concentration of the playgoers shifting from interest in the story to complete belief in the star; his audience was wholly in his hands.

Basking in the carefully focused, overlapping spots, Ray gave full measure, talk-singing the ditty that Rodgers had invented, inserting jokes and whimsies in the vamps I had provided, yakking "heart to heart" to all while "tripping the light fantastic," giving Bolger's best.

"His best" was good enough to give Rodgers and Hart a very long run on Broadway. "By Jupiter" piled up four hundred twenty seven (427) performances on the Main Stem, only closing, at last, because Ray Bolger, its star, wished to travel to the Pacific and amuse the troops. No actor could be found to replace the irreplaceable Bolger, so the show had to close…for good.

....

Shortly after the triumphal opening of "By Jupiter" in New York City, Richard Rodgers renewed his anonymous partnership with George Abbott by becoming an unheralded co-producer of "Beat The Band," a musical about popular dance musicians with a score by Johnny Green, who turned over his "By Jupiter" baton to a substitute in order to concentrate on a show with music of his own composition.

Because of my work on "By Jupiter" and "Best Foot Forward," plus my record of orchestrating for Al Goodman's Lucky Strike team of jazz virtuosos, Abbott, Rodgers, and Green all wanted me to orchestrate "Beat The Band." So they negotiated with Max Dreyfus for publication of the new show's score by Chappell & Co., and he agreed to make me available to orchestrate their project when it went into rehearsal, early in September, 1942.

During the weeks of August, '42, I tried again and again to obtain an up-to-date script of "Beat The Band." I was always put off, being told that the authors were "still working on the book." When I attended the first full reading by the entire cast, it became obvious why the authors had been so secretive: The script was amateurish and confused. Johnny's tunes were top-drawer, but it didn't matter how good they were; the entire project was doomed by the embarrassing mess of a story.

It is difficult to understand why Abbott and Rodgers let themselves and their investors get involved in such a floppo as "Beat The Band." They must have had good reasons, ones to which this limited observer was not privy.

....

After approximately three and one-half weeks of rehearsal in New York City, the quarrelsome company of "Beat The Band" traveled by rail to New Haven, Connecticut, for the traditional "split-week-break-in." That's when the scenery was put together with the actors, the story embellished with orchestra music, and the whole affair lit by more lights than absolutely necessary.

I recall that pre-opening dress rehearsal on Wednesday night in New Haven. It was exciting to watch the perfection of the short Act #1, but then Act #2 went on forever with serious scenic problems, so basic they could not be tackled with the whole company milling about. So the cast was released for an optimistic hour ("but stay near, folks") while stagehands wrestled with the brouhaha. Eager for fresh air, I fled to the nearby Commons and relaxed on a handy park bench.

It was a warm October evening, lit by a full moon, rising. Instead of enjoying the pleasant prospect, I found myself mulling over the manifold problems of "Beat The Band."

In the New Haven Shubert Theatre, there was no orchestra pit. The musicians played on the same level as patrons sitting in the first row of seats. That evening Johnny Green had done a good job of "shushing" his men. But come Boston, where there was a deep pit, the singers would want their music played louder, so they could hear their accompaniment. Then I knew the singers' agents would grouse, claiming their clients were being maliciously drowned out. There was absolutely no way for the music department to win.

I wasn't worried over musical balances; kinks in that department can be routinely straightened out. I was more concerned with the pit musicians' reaction to the play, which they were hearing for the first time. The story was loaded with "inside" musicians' humor; I wondered how an "outside" audience would respond upon hearing pit men splitting their sides over alleged jokes that were not understandable to paying customers. Sometimes the nicest people, disregarded, turn hostile.

The New Haven reviews were more luke than warm; in Boston the eminent critics despised the show. Attendance, never healthy, kept dwindling. An optional closing notice, posted backstage in Boston as soon as the first scathing verdicts hit the newsstands, served to destroy any last vestige of morale. The second week in Boston was agony for all concerned, knowing that evidence of their hard work would never reach Broadway.

I have one pleasant memory of "Beat The Band." In the second act, there was a hysterical number that had no honest linkage with the plot. It was sung and cavorted by a mad trio of jellybellies, made up of two overweight actors and our beefy second trombonist from the pit orchestra. After playing the first act in the band, our slip-horn specialist put on costume and makeup during intermission. He then pranced on stage with the other two crazies. After stopping the show, our musician went back to the pit and resumed tromboning. The name of that versatile, adipose slide-man was (and still is) *JACKIE GLEASON!* Let us be thankful he soon found out that his greatest gift was the ability to make people laugh, a much more rewarding occupation than honking a second trombone.

………………………………..

By the summer of 1940, German armies had overrun and controlled the most important cities of Norway, Denmark, Belgium, Holland, and a large part of Northern France. At once they began to collect and assemble all kinds of shipping in the ports on the eastern side of the English Channel. It was clear that Hitler's next objective was England. Saturation bombing of English cities by the Luftwaffe confirmed the belief that invasion of the British Isles was imminent.

In those desperate days, many affluent British families sent their young children to faraway, English-speaking lands, hoping to save them from what seemed a fast-approaching holocaust. When Dick and Dorothy Rodgers were asked by dear British friends, the d'Erlangers, to harbor their young daughter, Zoë, they were more than willing to take the responsibility as contributing to the war effort. When Zoë, with her British nurse, arrived safely in the United States, she was immediately treated as a member of the Rodgers family.

The addition of Zoë and her nanny into the daily life of the Rodgers' modest Manhattan apartment caused a certain amount of friction, no matter how thoughtful and cooperative everyone tried to be. The advent of Zoë caused Dorothy and Dick to consider an alternate way of life, ending with a move of their entire menage from the city to an old mansion on Black Rock Turnpike in Connecticut, where they had fifteen rooms and five baths to accommodate their swollen family.

When city dwellers move to the outskirts, they always leave neighborhood friendships behind, to be replaced, one by one, in the new terrain. Not so with the Rodgers! Not far from their new location lived the heart and soul of the famous New York City Theatre Guild: Terry Helburn and the Langners, Lawrence and Armina. How fortunate! (or was it planned?)

Anyway, Dick was asked to read the script of a straight play entitled "Green Grow the Lilacs," by Lynn Riggs, which the Theatre Guild had presented a decade earlier. They now wished to produce a musical version of that play with, they hoped, a score by Rodgers and Hart. (At the time, the Guild Group did not know that Larry was on a drinking debauch.)

At once Dick saw the possibilities of a musical based on "Green Grow the Lilacs." When Larry returned from Mexico, in bad shape, "haggard and pale," Dick offered to check into a sanitarium with Larry while they both worked on the new musical.

Larry rejected that offer and added, "I don't think 'Green Grow the Lilacs' can be turned into a good musical. I think you are making a big mistake." He left and shortly after that confrontation returned to Mexico and resumed his drinking. It was a bitter end to a partnership that had lasted over twenty-five years.

Dick took the "Lilacs" script to Oscar Hammerstein, who saw, immediately, its great musical potential. He soon became not only the lyricist of "Oklahoma" but also the author of its "book."

....

On the evening of March 31,1943, "OKLAHOMA!" opened in the St. James Theatre, 246 West 44th Street in New York City. It was an instant "smash," using up, in no time, all the laudatory comments the critics had been saving for years.

The overwhelming success of "Oklahoma!1}" remains a sturdy landmark in the history of the American musical theatre. It proved that a bucolic story, well told, integrated with appropriate and melodious songs, well sung, would almost always spell "HIT!" (That is, if some extraneous disaster, like an unscheduled air raid or a careless star's necessary abortion, louses up the advertised opening.)

Happily avoiding any such handicaps, "Oklahoma!" stifled all mean detractors and became the greatest sellout that Broadway had ever spawned, not because it was the chic "thing to see," but due to it being a wonderful show for every member of the family.

Immediately after "Oklahoma!" opened, the Theatre Guild got to work on a "National" Company of the show, which eventually ran ten and one-half years on the road, playing in every important city in the U.S. and Canada.

Because of their great success, Dick and Oscar had all kinds of promising offers to write other projects, but both of them had commitments they had made prior to "Oklahoma!" Oscar had been writing an all-black treatment of Bizet's "Carmen," and Dick was once again hoping to get Larry straightened out by putting him to work on an updated "Connecticut Yankee."

Early in the summer of 1943, I was called to the office of my boss, Max Dreyfus, who had apparently lived out his period of exile from the management of a music-publishing firm, as required by his contract with Warner Brothers. He appeared to be in complete, open control of Chappell & Company.

We exchanged the usual salutations, and then he said, "This fall I don't want you to get tied up with radio programs. Dick Rodgers is producing an updated version of 'A Connecticut Yankee' and has asked me for your services as orchestrator."

I was thrilled. Although, by that time, I had orchestrated three complete shows ("Best Foot Forward," "By Jupiter," and "Beat The Band") in which Dick Rodgers had functioned as either Co-Producer, Co-Lyricist, or Composer, he had never once expressed an opinion of my work to me, good or bad. "Old Frozen-Face"was my private name for him. Now I would have to change all that to "Mister Rodgers" or "Kind Sir." Perhaps he had the same trouble I did when trying to compliment someone who had done a good job. Maybe he was really a member of the human race....

The new "Connecticut Yankee" occupied most of my time that fall of '43. It was a dreadfully cold, rainy autumn with an early killing frost. That was the year I subletted the Far-Eastern, 72nd Street apartment of my former college saxophone partner, Philip Cohan, who was in California producing the CBS radio programs of Jimmie Durante and Paul Whiteman. How I hated having to take cabs, back and forth, from that East-side apartment, where I scored my orchestrations, south-west to the theatre district, where "Yankee" had its rehearsals. Oh! what a beautiful morning it was when I grabbed my traveling clothes and writing tools, telling my cabbie to head due South to Grand Central Station, where there was a train waiting to carry me to New Haven, Connecticut, where I had a room reserved in the Taft Hotel, adjacent to the Shubert Theatre, where a "Connecticut Yankee" would be rehearsing and then playing all through the coming week.

....

Once in a long while, there comes a new musical that seems to have been a special favorite of Madame Lady Luck. The costumes fit at once, the scenery works, the orchestrations please and, most unusually, there is plenty of lighting equipment to play with. Even the cast is cool and doesn't try to rewrite the script. Such a fortunate show was the reborn "A Connecticut Yankee." After its first performance in New Haven, its Producer-Composer, Richard Rodgers, seriously considered sending a large part of its supporting staff back to New York, as excess baggage.

Unfortunately, the following week, the show went to Boston, where the critics usually have ideas that differ from those in New Haven. Sometimes one feels that they are not reporting on the same show that played New Haven. Those nasty Beantown executioners all agreed that it had been a big mistake to try to revive "A Connecticut Yankee" when the great 1927 original was still shining in the memories of many viewers.

After two discouraging weeks in Boston, realizing that "Yankee" was in no shape to tackle New York, Richard Rodgers tried to get more time to work on the show while it was still playing on the road. No Boston theatre was available, and the only bookings the Shuberts could offer were in Philadelphia or Pittsburgh. So after the second Saturday night performance in Boston, all concerned packed up and moved to Philly and the Forrest.

I remember talking with Larry Hart in that theatre's subterranean tunnel that connected the dressing rooms (in one building) with the stage and house (in the other building). As actors and dancers, stagehands and musicians brushed by us, I complimented Larry on the greatest lyric he had ever written: that incredible "To Keep My Love Alive." He was understandably proud of that masterpiece and its triple rhymes, thanking me for writing a most unobtrusive orchestration for it, supporting Vivienne Segal properly while avoiding music that might divert a listener from concentrating on those cunning words.

He said to me, "Let's go across the alley and grab a nice big drink. I'm dehydrated."

Surprised, I said, "I thought you were on the wagon, Larry, till the show is in New York."

He explained, "I *was* on the wagon, till every song was complete. Now I've finished every damn word, I haven't anything to do. My job is *finished,* understand? It's all over! Now it's time to celebrate! Come on! Let me buy you a drink!" (He waved in the general direction of the pub in the alley.)

I know, only too well, that I have an embarrassing lack of subtlety. There are times when some devilish gremlin pokes me with his trident, causing me "to spill the beans" instead of dissembling, as any sensible person would do.

Now I said, "Don't you know, Larry, that if I take one, only *one* alcoholic drink, I lose my ability to concentrate. I can't guzzle and work...and they still need me on this show. I promised Dick that I'll stay sober in this emergency. I did, I promised him."

"You promised that you'd try to keep me out of a saloon! That's what you promised! So you go right back to Dick and tell him that he can't fool me! He sent you to keep an eye on me! Hah-hah-hee-hee! Tell him that if he comes over to the gin mill across the way, I'll buy *him* a drink!" He stamped up the steps and out the stage door.

As he went out the door, I yelled after him, "HEY! LARRY! You forgot your raincoat!"

But he had disappeared, and it was still raining cats and dogs.

....

The last days of Lorenz (Larry) Hart can be divided into two clearly defined sections. In the first, or Philadelphian period, he wandered through the grogshops of that City of Brotherly Love, drunk, sick, and getting sicker. At night he would come to the show and stand in the back, making embarrassing, barely audible comments, on several occasions, forcibly removed by hired muscle-men. When the show closed in Philly, he was too sick to fight off his friends, including Dick, who had arranged to have him admitted to Doctors Hospital in Manhattan. There, on the evening of November 22, 1943, Larry went into a coma during a practice air-raid blackout. He was attended within by the best specialists and mourned without by Richard Rodgers, his wife Dorothy and a keening group of Larry's "drinking buddies." As the "All Clear" sounded and the lights came on, the great lyricist died. Mamoulian couldn't have staged the sequence any better.

....

"OKLAHOMA!" was a huge hit, requiring a good-sized business organization to handle its secondary income, such as performance fees from stock and amateur use, the sale of sheet music, royalties from

ASCAP, "house seats," and all the other "goodies" that rain upon the owners of a "smash." So Dick and Oscar formed an independent company to administer all the songs they expected to write in the future, plus the ones they had created for "OKLAHOMA!" There are conflicting stories that try to explain why they called the new company "Williamson Music, Inc." The first explanation claims that the partners bought an old, inactive music-publishing company outright. The second reason for that name is the surprising fact (?) that the fathers of Dick and Oscar were *both* named William! A likely story!

It is also possible to put both surmises together and come up with a third reason. It is also possible to disbelieve the whole bit. Anyway, they were organized to get the most attainable out of "OKLAHOMA!"

I had noticed...and it was almost impossible *not* to notice...that when Dick collaborated with a lyricist, the Rodgers name always came first: "Rodgers and Hart; Rodgers and Hammerstein." One day, when Dick was in a mellow mood, I asked him right out how that positioning came about.

He laughed and said, "Pure chance...the toss of a coin."

"With *both* Larry and Oscar?"

"That's right. I guess the Fates believe that music is more important than words!"

We were dangerously close to that old hackneyed question: "What comes first, the lyrics or the tune?" I remembered, years before, asking Sigmund Romberg that tiresome query, and he replied in typical Rombergian locution, "In de early nineteen hundreds, a bunch uv European musicians, including me, immigrated to New York. Ve didn't have much English, so ven ve tried to set music to English lyrics, ve had accents hitting in de wrong places. So ve had to svitch and just write good tunes, letting the Americans write de verds."

Porter, almost always, wrote the words first and then composed music to accompany them. By the time the lyric was finished, I think he knew what the music would *have* to be.

I wrote two complete, unlucky shows with Jack Lawrence, collaborating on both words and music. In both cases we wrote the words first, the music last, in total collaboration. So, you see, there are a number of ways to kill a cat or write the songs of a Broadway musical.

<u>Rommy Revenant</u> (Sigmund Romberg)

The years of the 1930s were relatively unfruitful for the composer Sigmund Romberg, who had dominated the musical stage in the 1920s, producing:

BOMBO: 219 performances,

THE STUDENT PRINCE: 608 performances,

LOUIE THE 14th: 319 perf.

THE DESERT SONG: 465 perf.

THE NEW MOON: 518 perf.

MY MARYLAND: 312 performances with a solid year in Philadelphia with a 2nd company. Suddenly, with the Crash and the following Depression, that all changed and Romberg was lucky to find promoters who would remain with him and his dated operettas during the thirties. Roughly, they were:

NINA ROSA: 137 performances,

EAST WIND: 23 perf.

MELODY: 79 perf.

MAYWINE: 213 perf.   (force-fed by ROMMY and the income from his Swift radio program.)

FORBIDDEN MELODY: 32 perf, (no relation to the above MELODY, but even more hopeless.)

I was with Rommy during most of that ghastly time and suffered with him. Then as the forties were upon us, he made a complete switch, forming his own thirty-five-piece concert orchestra, hiring an experienced agent to arrange long tours for it, and went into the sinfonietta business, traveling all over the United States and Canada, playing his "middle-brow" music, making friends and money, too.

The basic idea for "Up In Central Park," Rommy's last successful operetta, was born in the busy mind of its producer, Michael Todd who, upon seeing extensive demolition going on in the vicinity of Columbus Circle, was tempted to read a book about Boss Tweed and the beginnings of Central Park. Todd thought that the fight to keep the lush Park out of the grasping hands of the crooks could be exciting, with the beautiful green grass of the Park as a background.

Todd took his "idea" to Herbert and Dorothy Fields, the skillful writers of a number of musicals. They were immediately excited by the project and suggested Romberg as the right composer for it. Rommy had a high opinion of the Fields and as soon as he saw plans for the "period piece," he knew that it was for him. So his hardworking business manager, Harry Squires, had to cancel and try to reschedule almost a whole year's program of Romberg concerts!

That year of 1944–45 was a wild one for Don Walker. (1) I was working with Henry Clay (Buck) Warnick on a jazz version of H.M.S. Pinafore, (2) scoring selections from the latest musicals for Frank Black and Cities Service at NBC, and (3) getting Rommy ready for "Up In Central Park," which went into rehearsal in a former schoolhouse with many large blackboards, early in December, 1944.

At the time, there was an abnormal number of musicals preparing for Broadway. Mike Todd had no "stand-by" staff and had to depend upon whoever was available. All the usual choreographers were booked, so Mike signed Helen Tamiris, a highly respected modern dancer with no theatrical credits.

From the very start of rehearsals, Rommy treated Helen Tamiris as an alien force, bent upon destroying his songs. The lady had her own rehearsal pianist, a heavy woman who amused herself in rest periods by trying to demonstrate where some of Rommy's tunes might have come from. Even though she was clearly wrong, it was not a nice thing to do, for her tricks increased Rommy's blood pressure, already too high.

I remember one morning when Rommy came into rehearsal lugging a large package of manuscript pages, which he stored on the top of our upright piano. I snuck a look and found it a pile of ancient discards from forgotten shows, nothing of value. I wondered what he was going to do with that old dog-eared music.

Later in the morning, Tamiris brought all her dancers upstairs to participate in a full-stage scene. When they got to the spot where the fat lady accompanist started to interpolate some of her own inventions, there was a bloodcurdling scream from Rommy. He rushed to the piano and tore his package apart, ripping the old manuscripts, throwing the pieces in all directions, having a good old rampage. I think I saw little flames shooting out of his nostrils, but that's impossible...but was it? He was a fearsome sight, the rascal.

From that crisis on, the music department had no more trouble with the terpsichorean faction. Everyone cooperated, trying to keep Rommy healthy. Tamiris, with only one show, established herself as one of the leading choreographers on Broadway. (I think she got rid of that sassy piano player.) Her balletic treatment of skaters in the Park became a classic. "Up In Central Park" ran for 504 performances in New York City.

Rodgers and Hammerstein, Dick and Oscar

Near the end of the Philadelphia run of "Up In Central Park," I was attending a large brunch in Rommy's Bellevue-Stratford suite when a phone call came for me. (I had left my whereabouts at my hotel, the Sylvania.) The transferred call was from Selma Tamber, my whipcracker at Chappell & Company. She was excited.

"DON!" she cried. "What kind of shape are you in, down there?"

I said, rather smugly, "Pretty good, Selma. We're locking up the show tonight…no more changes and fixes."

"So you'll be coming back to New York?"

"Now wait a minute, Selma. Down here I'm only thirty-five miles from home, where there's two little kids and a beautiful wife who are beginning to forget they have a daddy."

"So go home! Give everyone a kiss for me. But be here in the office tomorrow morning at ten! Mr. Dreyfus has news for you…big news!" She slammed down the phone.

At five minutes to ten the following morning, having employed a most complicated method of transportation involving private auto, bus, commuter train, subway, and legs, I was seated on a bench, trying to get my breath, outside the office of Max Dreyfus, the high-muck-a-muck of Chappell & Co. Selma appeared and ushered me into the presence.

Lacking prior information, who could ever guess the extent of the power wielded by that mild-looking, everybody's-grandfather type. Now he said to me, "Don, the next two weeks could be the most important in your career. Russell Bennett was supposed to be the orchestrator of Rodgers and Hammerstein's new production, but now, after scoring two numbers, he is suddenly…out of the picture. Hans Spialek is busy with his own show…he may be able to score one number for you but that is all. What we need right now is someone to be responsible for the whole score of CAROUSEL, and the only one we have available right now is *you,* DON WALKER!"

I knew, through the musicians' grapevine, that CAROUSEL would carry an unprecedented number of players in the pit, somewhere in the vicinity of forty-five! I had no fear of not being able to handle such a large orchestra; my experience with Frank Black and Toscanini's NBC Symphony took good care of that. My worry came from the paucity of time, only two weeks, left to put all those notes on paper and then have them copied and played.

Suddenly confronted with the most difficult commission of my life, not sure it could be completed in the available time, worrying about Rodgers' reaction to some of my risky ideas, all those problems served to divert me from asking a certain question, not knowing the answer has bothered me all my life. Here's the puzzle: Why, oh, why? was Russell Bennett "not available" for CAROUSEL? Was he sick? Did he have a fight with Rodgers? Did he dislike CAROUSEL? Was there another show that was more important? That's almost unthinkable! So why? Oh, why? Oh, why?

In order to settle, once for all, who orchestrated "CAROUSEL," I furnish a blow-by-blow summary:

Carousel

Orchestrators

THE CAROUSEL WALTZ: Originally scored by Robert Russell Bennett, rescored by Don Walker at Rodgers' request.

JULIE JORDAN............................	Scored	by	Don Walker.
MISTER SNOW............................	"	"	" "
IF I LOVED YOU.........................	"	"	" "
JUNE IS BUSTIN' OUT...............	"	"	" "
BLOW HIGH, BLOW LOW.........	"	"	" "
A REAL NICE CLAMBAKE........	"	"	" "
SOLILOQUY..............................	"	"	" "
WHEN THE CHILDREN...........	Scored	by	Hans Spialek.
WHAT'S THE USE......................	Scored	by	Don Walker.
STONE CUTTERS......................	"	"	" "
BALLET.....................................	"	"	" "
YOU'LL NEVER WALK ALONE.	Scored	by	Stephen Jones.
FINALE ULTIMO........................	Scored	by	Don Walker.

THE ORIGINAL CAROUSEL ORCHESTRA:

WOODWIND:
Flute I (doubling Piccolo)
Flute II ("   "
Oboe (doubling English Horn)
Bassoon
B flat Clarinet I
B flat Clarinet II

STRINGS:
  6 Violin I
  4 Violin II
3 Viola
2 Cello
2 Bass   HARP.
etc.

BRASS:

Bb Trumpet I
Bb Trumpet II
Trombone I
Trombone II
Tuba
Horns I & II
Horn III

PERCUSSION:
Tympani, bells, cymbals, traps,

Rehearsal Piano.

COMMENT:

This was an extraordinarily large orchestra for a musical comedy to carry. Richard Rodgers always felt that it was light on strings. Some people are never satisfied even with 890 performances!